SHERMAN
The M4 Tank in World War II

CASEMATE | ILLUSTRATED | SPECIAL

C CASEMATE | ILLUSTRATED | SPECIAL

SHERMAN

The M4 Tank in World War II

MICHEL ESTÈVE

CISS0001

Published in the United States of America and Great Britain in 2020 by

CASEMATE PUBLISHERS

1950 Lawrence Road, Havertown, PA 19083, USA

and

The Old Music Hall, 106–108 Cowley Road, Oxford OX4 1JE, UK

This book is published in cooperation with, and under license from, Editions Heimdal.
Originally published in French as La Saga du Sherman © Editions Heimdal 2018

Hardback Edition: ISBN 978-1-61200-7397
Digital Edition: ISBN 978-1-61200-7403

A CIP record for this book is available from the British Library

Translated by Alan McKay
Additional text by Mike Guardia
Design by Myriam Bell, UK
Printed and bound by Megaprint, Turkey

For a complete list of Casemate titles, please contact:
CASEMATE PUBLISHERS (US)
Telephone (610) 853-9131
Fax (610) 853-9146
Email: casemate@casematepublishers.com
www.casematepublishers.com

CASEMATE PUBLISHERS (UK)
Telephone (01865) 241249
Email: casemate-uk@casematepublishers.co.uk
www.casematepublishers.co.uk

Unless otherwise indicated, all the photos are from the author's own collection.

Page 2: Some M4A2s from the Polish Armored Brigade rushing to Falaise. *(NARA)*

Title page: On the Island of Luçon, in the Philippines, this M4 is moving up a column of GIs, transporting a combat group. The whole crew is helmetless.

Opposite: Münsingen, West Germany, 1965. Digging in the anchor and deploying the boom for this M74 of the 2e Régiment de Cuirassiers.

Contents

Foreword....................................... 7

1. A Tank Named Sherman 8

2. Production............................. 16

3. The Chassis........................... 28

4. Turrets 50

5. Armament and Ammunition........... 62

6. The Sherman Crew........................... 74

7. Evolution of the Sherman............... 102

8. The Sherman Family 114

9. Logistics, Supply, and Backup........ 166

10. Numbering and Markings............ 178

11. Unit Composition and
    Organization 202

12. The Success of the Sherman......... 224

13. The Sherman Since 1945 230

Appendix 1
Military Operations—ETO 235

Glossary and Abbreviations 237

Sources and Bibliography................. 240

It was a metal bar with notches hinged at one end and fixed to the armor by a pin at the other. It could be opened up. It looked more or less like a comb. It wasn't always present but was installed on new

Bottom row, from left to right: M4 with armor made of concrete and sandbags.

Lots of sandbags piled up inside a metal armature, protecting this M4A3 E8 in Germany, 1945.

M M1A1 with M1A1 cannon whose armor consists of heavy wooden beams on its flanks.

Opposite, right: M4A3 E8 fitted with welded armor plates on the flanks and round the turret, armor that was inspired by the German Panzer IVs.

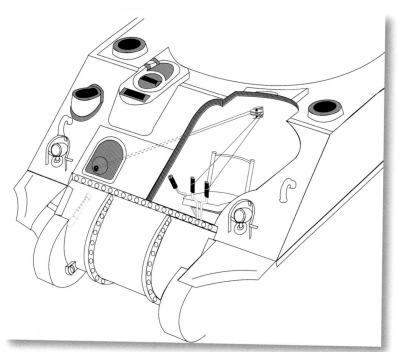

tanks traveling by sea or on some form of platform. It was there to prevent the tank from moving during transportation. Two cables were fixed to the steering levers in the driver's position; they were fed through the bow machine-gun housing and attached to the "comb." The two cables were then looped round one of the "teeth" of the "comb" and this was then folded down and held in place by a pin. The tank could no longer move and there was no need to hold it fast in the holds or to use embarkation chains.

The electric installation and auxiliary electricity generation

The batteries were located on the left-hand side of the hull, behind the driver's seat. On the first models, they were attached to the lower armor of the hull. On the following models, the batteries were fitted into a frame, itself mounted on the upper left-hand reinforcement. These reinforcements on either side of the tank were caused by the hull getting wider above the tracks. These were the sponsons.

Above: The Comb, a metal bar swiveling round on a pin and fixed to the armor by a bolt, was used to keep the tank "braked" when being transported.
Right: The different versions of the Comb.

Where the recharging circuit for the lead accumulators (the batteries) was concerned, this differed depending on the M4. For example, on the A3 version, the first models were equipped with two generators situated in the engine compartment on either side of the V8 Ford engine.

Later this set-up was replaced by a single generator fitted next to the propeller shaft. The transmission consisted of a bearing and a double groove pulley driven by the two generator belts. There were two variants of this last layout: a generator placed at the rear of the combat compartment, near the firewall, or a generator positioned in the front, on a level with the driver and bow gunner. A disposition of this type had the advantage of enabling the generator to be fixed or even changed without the engine compartment having to be opened or the engine taken out. Since these operations were "light," they were carried out at the unit echelon.

These generators could produce 50 amps with 30 volts. As for regulating the charging circuit, this was fitted with a three-stage system: a breaker/circuit breaker stage, an over-current stage, and finally a current regulation stage. These three stages were interactive and ensured the following functions:

The breaker/circuit breaker prevented the battery from losing its charge when the generator was stopped or did not feed the batteries. The generator output was

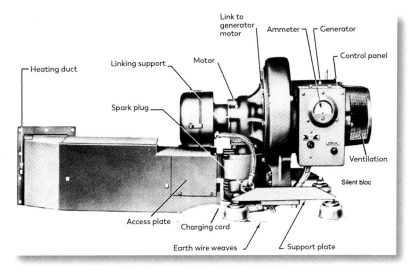

directly proportional to the speed of rotation, i.e. at low revs (below 800 rpm) the voltage was 0. This explains why on this type of armored vehicle the engines were kept running at 1,200 rpm when the tank was halted with its engine running.

A current regulator was there to maintain the current at 30v permanently.

The circuit breaker adjusted the amperage depending on what was needed for the current and battery charging. The road lights, the turret's electro-hydraulic

The M4A4 combat compartment

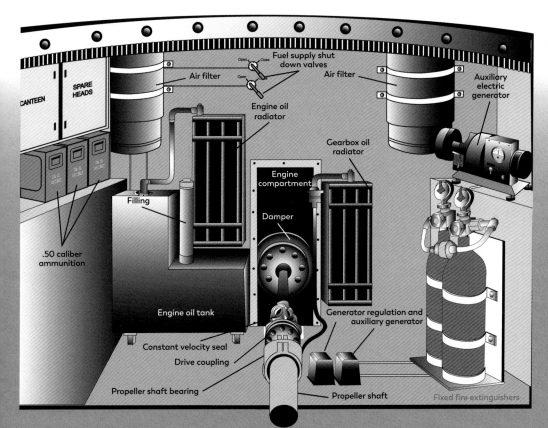

group, etc., made high energy demands and were greedy for amperage. In the case of tanks fitted with two generators, there were two regulating boxes.

With their engines stopped, the Shermans could still use everything. To be able to do this they were fitted with an auxiliary electric generator which took over the functions of the main generator but also, if needs be, recharged the tank's batteries. This system enabled the turret, the weapons, and the radio, but also the extraction ventilators and the electric firing systems, to function normally.

A Homelite HRU H 28 generator was mounted inside the left-hand sponson, on the firewall side (this position was changed depending on the M4 type). On the A4 tank, the auxiliary generator was on the hull floor, at the rear on the left.

The generator was driven by a little four-stroke single-cylinder air-cooled petrol engine—some tanks were equipped with a two-stroke engine—taking its fuel from the nearby tank using a pump through an inlet filter. On certain variants the generator had its own tank and filler port depending on the M4 type. Ignition was by means of a magneto.

The exhaust was attached to the left-hand pipe of the main engine. The engine and generator duo was attached to a bracket attached to four flexible mounts. The auxiliary generator was equipped with the same regulator as the main generator; its accessories comprised an ammeter and a ventilation casing; this generator produced 30 volts and 1,500 watts maximum power. It all weighed 60—70 kg, depending on the model of tank. This electricity generator equipped the M4, M4A1, M4A2, M4A3, and M4A4 Shermans.

Fire-fighting equipment

Being able to fight a fire in a tank was vital, given the quantities of ammunition, fuel, or napalm aboard. Shermans were equipped with hand extinguishers containing 2 kg of liquid to be used for any fire, but particularly for electric fires. One was located in the turret well, one near the bow gunner's position, and sometimes one near the driver's position.

A fixed anti-fire system comprising two (or one depending on the model) big bottles and installed at the rear of the combat compartment was added to the left-hand side of the installation. These containers were fitted with a distribution head from which copper pipes went through the firewall and then all around the engine. The pipe ends were fitted with diffuser cones. Two diffusers were place over the carburetors; two near the petrol pumps and two in the upper part near the intake.

Setting off the fire-fighting system was by means of sleeved cables, linked to two percussion heads on the bottles. There was also a handle in the driver's zone, between the driver and the bow gunner, and another in the turret well. A third one, depending on the model, was fitted on the rear deck, near the petrol filler port.

A 3rd Armored Division M4 Sherman on October 14, 1944 at Stolberg, Germany. The infantrymen probably belong to the 36th Infantry Division. (NARA)

Filters, radiator, and other items

Different Sherman types had different air and fuel intakes. For example, the M4A3 powered by the Ford V8 was fitted with two air filters and an oil bath located either in the engine or the combat compartment. Where the filters were next to the engine they were fitted with an additional duct linking the combat compartment.

In this case each duct was fitted with a handle. Push the handle and the filters took in air through the combat compartment; pull the handle and air was taken in by the engine compartment. For servicing, two inspection panels on either side of the firewall gave access to the air filters, if they were on the engine side. If the air filters were on the combat compartment side, the ducts and the inspection panels were not needed.

The M4A2s had six air filters on the right and left of the engine group. The M4A4s had air filters in the combat compartment—like the M4A3s—fixed to the firewall. The air filters in the M4s and M4A1s were fixed outside, under the rear panel.

General organization of the Sherman hull

1. Idler pulley
2. Track tightening system
3. Exhausts.
4. General Motors powerplant
5. Right sponson
6. Left sponson
7. Runner wheel
8. Running gear wheel
9. Bogey
10. Fuel tank
11. Propeller shaft
12. Fuel valves
13. Engine radiator
14. Transmission radiator
15. Fixed fire extinguisher
16. Auxiliary electric generator (AEG)
17. Battery casing
18. AEG regulator
19. .30 caliber ammunition stowage
20. Battery cut-out
21. Radio switch
22. 24-volt generator
23. Generator regulation
24. Generator drive pulley
25. Gearbox
26. Driver's seat
27. Driver's dashboard
28. Steering brake levers
29. Ventilator.
30. Steering brakes
31. Main differential
32. Propeller half-shaft
33. Sprocket reduction gear
34. Sprocket
35. Assistant-driver's seat
36. Gun ammunition rack
37. Manhole cover
38. Turret well
39. .50 caliber ammunition stowage
40. Fixed fire extinguishers control
41. Portable fire extinguisher

ORGANIZATION OF THE SHERMAN CHASSIS

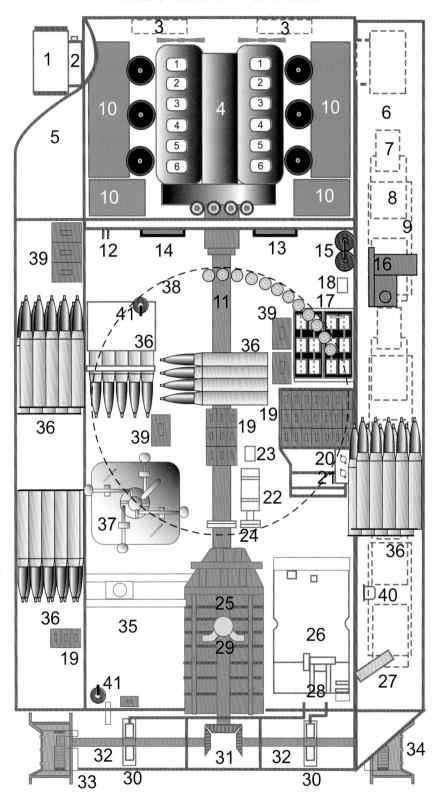

The fuel tanks

There were four of them, located in the engine compartment: two vertical ones against the firewall and two horizontal ones in the side sponsons, shaped like the rear armor.

On most M4 models, there was a fifth reservoir for the auxiliary electric generator. The filler ports and their inlet filters were on the rear deck of the tank and the drains were located under the tank for the vertical reservoirs, and below the sponson (above the track), for the horizontal tanks.

Two taps—or four—depending on the engine models, shut off the petrol supply. These cocks were on the firewall, on the right-hand side, and were accessible from the turret well.

Accelerators and carburation

Like most armored vehicles, the M4s were fitted with a hand and a foot accelerator. The hand accelerator control handle was located in front and to the right of the driver (like the A3), on the side of the gearbox. This handle could also block the engine at a given speed, like for warming-up, when a constant speed of between 1,000 and 1,200 rpm was required. Another time it was used was when the turret equipment was functioning when the tank was at a standstill and the auxiliary generator cut off. Because the generator didn't work below 800 rpm, the engine speed had to be maintained between 1,200 and 1,800 rpm.

The foot accelerator controlled the opening and closing of the butterflies on the V8 engine's two carburetors. A rod system mounted on bearings linked the pedal to the carburetors. These were placed between the two cylinder banks, under the air filter manifold. The carburetors were twin-bodied Stromberg NA-Y5Gs, each body being fitted with a recovery pump and a Degazer which cut the idling circuit when the engine was stopped. The carburetors were tuned differently, depending on the type of tank. Thus the TM9-750, the M4A3's technical manual, proposed different settings for an A3 Wet and 105 howitzer, or for a 75 Dry. In the first case, the idle setting was fixed at 800 rpm, with the clutch pedal engaged, whereas in the second case, the idling speed was set at 500 rpm.

Injection pump and feeder pump

The feeder pump was driven by the left camshaft. This pump fed fuel under pressure, between 2-3 kg/cm3. The injection pump made it possible to start the engine more easily in certain extreme weather conditions. This system had to be used carefully and

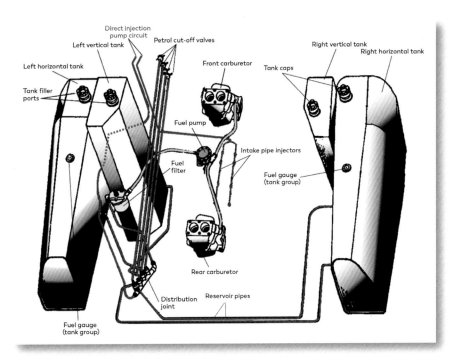

this was covered very clearly in the handbook. The principle was to inject fuel directly into the inlet pipes; it is obvious that the quantity injected had to be compatible with the startup phase, or the engine could be damaged. This pump control handle was either manual (a lever situated in front and to the right of the driver) or electric (a control button on the dashboard).

Fuel filtering

The fuel was filtered as it came out of the reservoirs by cartridge-type filters or by accumulating compressed filtration washers. The auxiliary generator feeder circuit was also filtered (depending on how it was configured and the model) by a filter cartridge in a glass container. Some circuits were fitted with two stopcocks: one on the outlet pipe from the tanks, the other before the fuel filter. One stopcock only was needed on the models having only one filter on the tank outlet.

The transmission sequence

Transmission started at the clutch and went on through to the sprocket reduction gear. It comprised a propeller shaft which sent the rotary motion of the engine to the gearbox. On the Sherman, the clutch was located behind the engine flywheel. This propeller shaft went through low down inside the tank, mounted on two bearing relays. On this shaft, there was a double groove pulley which drove the generator; depending on the model involved, this pulley could be situated on the firewall side, or immediately behind the driver. The generators on certain A3 and A2 models were in the engine compartment.

Drawing of the fuel circuit between the reservoirs and the engine of the M4A3

Opposite: M4A1 Sherman probably photographed in Italy during the winter of 1943-44. (Signal Corps)

1. Gear lever
2. Gearbox rear casing
3. Brake control shaft
4. Transmission armor
5. Output restrictor
6. Drive sprocket rim
7. Steering brake casing
8. Gearbox lower casing
9. Air valves
10. Filling pipe
11. Reverse control
12. Steering brake setting
13. Tachymeter socket
14. Drive shaft flange

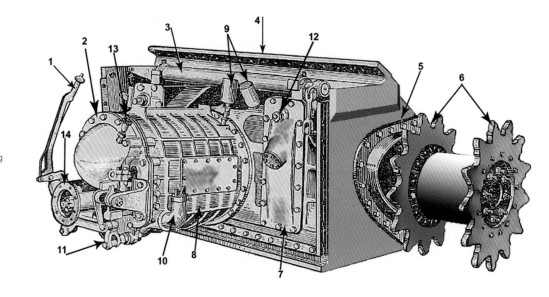

Steering and braking controls

1. Steering levers
2. Connecting rod
3. Adjusting clevis
4. Link arm G.
5. Control rod
6. Adjustment rod
7. Drive yoke
8. Control accelerator
9. Connecting rod
10. Accelerator pedal
11. Locking rack pinion
12. Clutch pedal
13. Lever locking pedal
14. Clutch control
15. Right-hand connecting rod
16. Return spring
17. Clutch control stick

(after TM 9-759)

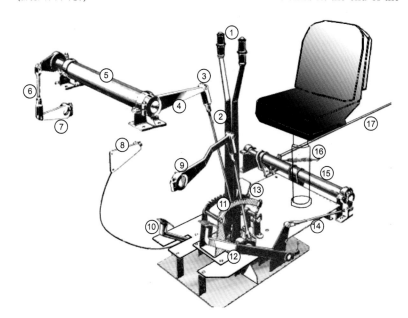

The propeller shaft entered the gearbox (five forward speeds and one reverse) and transmitted the motion to the primary shaft. The gearbox was fitted with a cooling system whose radiator was at the rear, on the firewall side. From the gearbox, the transmission went through 90° using the differential.

On either side was a transmission half-shaft which sent the movement from the differential to the sprockets. The differential is a system based on epicyclical gears enabling wheels (or sprockets) on the same axle to cover different distances at different speeds.

On the grooved parts of these half-shafts were fitted the steering brakes which were activated by levers in the driving compartment. Moving the two levers at the same time braked the tank. At the end of the

propeller shaft were the grooves which slotted into the reduction gear.

The reduction gear

The tank sprockets cannot be turned at the same speed as that of the gearbox. This would result in too great a circumferential speed, causing the parts to break, but also a lack of torque* when the tank started off. Using a single running gear pinion, the reduction gear reduces these speeds to more acceptable levels. At the end the sprocket is fitted to the reduction gear; it then engages the track, and the tank moves.

The transmission (big) end is located at the front of the tank, enclosed in the one- or three-piece armored transmission casing. In the case of the three-piece armored casing, the right-hand part was referenced E 4151 RH, the central part E 1232, and the left-hand part E 1231; there were two types of one-piece armor whose reference was E 4,186 for the "Early" models and E 8,543 for the "Late" or "Mary Ann" versions.

Steering and braking

One could say that in the case of the Sherman (as for many other tanks) braking meant turning, and that what might seem simple in theory turned out to be much less so in practice.

The two steering levers used by the driver acted on the transmission system. By pulling a system of rods, levers, and control bars, the driver acted on jaws which tightened around one or the other of the half-shafts.

These jaws looked like the ones used on drum brakes, but the surface touched was the inside surface—on a drum brake the braking surface is on the outside surface—and the half-shafts were fitted with

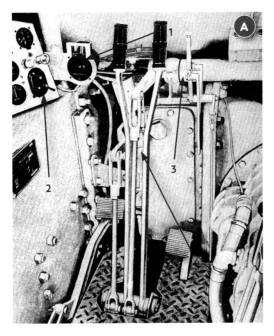

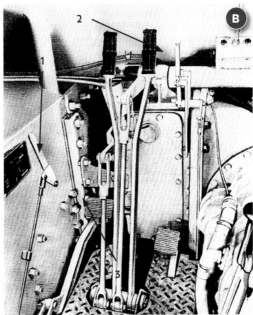

A. Driver's post in the "Early" M4
1. Compass.
2. Engine starter handle
3. Hand accelerator control
4. Steering levers

B. Driver's post for the M4A4
1. Choke control (cold start)
2. Hand accelerator control
3. Clutch pedals

C. Assistant driver's post
1. TL 122 mounting
2. .30 caliber machine gun ammunition box mounting
3. Differential breather

D. M4A2 driver's post
1. Siren contactor
2. Clutch commands
3. Parking brake lever (on the transmission)
4. Two hand accelerator levers
5. Clutch locks

flanges increasing the working surface, and hence the effectiveness of the braking.

This set-up of half-shaft flange and jaws was lubricated, making braking gradual and giving more flexibility round the bends. This lubrication had a price: the tank took longer to respond.

Because the half-shafts were part of the differential, the braking action on one side transferred the speed to the other half-shaft. Because of the increased speed, turning occurs. Therefore the higher the speed at the moment of the braking, the wider the radius of the turn.

To make things simpler: the tank would turn much better in first gear than in fifth, all the more so that as soon as the tank braked, engine speed tended to drop. It was therefore better for the driver, when he could foresee it, to change down before taking a bend, or to accelerate to keep up the speed and the torque.

Simultaneously moving both steering levers causes the tank to stop. This action was sufficient, although the efficiency of this system is not comparable to present braking systems.

At any rate, stopping the tank meant going down through the gears. As was emphasized at the beginning of the book: it was a question of actually piloting the tank rather than driving it.

The Running Gear

The running gear, VVSS, and HVSS

The "Early" M4s were equipped with the bogey running gear of the M3 tank. Its makeup was classic, namely:

- A sprocket fixed to the reduction gear and connected to the transmission (there were different types of sprocket wheels on the Shermans).
- Six running gear wheels mounted on three bogeys fitted with a return roller above them or offset to the rear, depending on the model of running gear.
- An idler wheel attached to its mechanism.
- Tracks made up of links articulating on connector rods.

The tracks were made up of different types of links. The first-generation tracks were (only) 42 cm wide and comprised 79 links of varying types. There was the T48

track with rubber links, the T 49 with links made up of three horizontal metal bars, the T51 with rubber links and chevrons, and finally the T 54 with steel chevron links.

All these different tracks were of the connector rod type (*see illustration of the tracks, below*).

The teeth of the sprocket wheel engaged the track in the space between the connectors and the guiding teeth, as part of the links, passed over and encased the running-gear wheels and return rollers.

Because the small track width greatly increased the ground pressure, several track widening systems were tried out. One of these was the Duckbills, little metal grousers fitted at the end of the connectors on the outside of the track. This set-up, improving "road holding" on soft terrain, was much too fragile and not used very much or even abandoned in the field. The vertical spring suspension type bogeys had two lateral arms enabling the running gear wheels to travel.

Developing the E9 was essential for this running gear because it enabled Duckbills to be fitted on both sides of the track, thereby reducing ground pressure.

These were crosspieces which were fitted between the hull side and the running gear attachments.

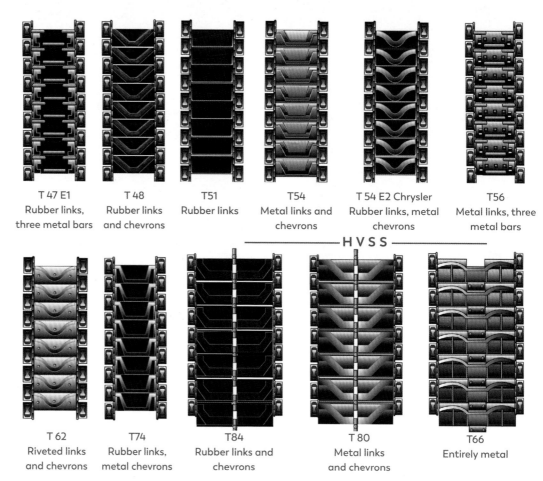

T 47 E1	T 48	T51	T54	T 54 E2 Chrysler	T56
Rubber links, three metal bars	Rubber links and chevrons	Rubber links	Metal links and chevrons	Rubber links, metal chevrons	Metal links, three metal bars

— H V S S —

T 62	T74	T84	T 80	T66
Riveted links and chevrons	Rubber links, metal chevrons	Rubber links and chevrons	Metal links and chevrons	Entirely metal

HVSS running gear, horizontal volute springs

On this running gear, the tracks were replaced by 58-cm wide T80s and T84s, with double links on the pins and the connectors. The guiding teeth slotted in between the two half-links. This assembly almost eliminated the risk of the tracks coming off; the running gear wheels and the return rollers above the bogeys were single and the wheels between the bogeys were double.

On this type of running gear, the volute springs were mounted horizontally and were supported by hydraulic horizontally installed shock absorbers. Another advantage of HVSS running gear was that it considerably reduced the ground pressure, thereby giving better performance on soft ground.

On subsequent tanks, torsion bar suspension and hydraulic shock absorbers replaced the bogeys, which was much more effective.

Method for undoing the track and special tooling

It was sometimes necessary to undo the track, either to remove a link because of track wear, to work on the return rollers, or to change an idler wheel or a sprocket wheel.

Cutting the track

It was also necessary to take apart the track when it came off. This work needed special tooling, which was naturally part of the on-board tools. The first part of

Grooves on the pulley shaft
Grooved plate
Locking clip
Tightening pulley flange
Split casing
Tightening bolt (left-hand thread)
Setting bolt
Case loosening bolts
Setting spanner

Drawing explaining the track tightening system.

1. Lengthened Duckbill
2. Type 1 Duckbill
3. Tank fitted with E9 modification
4. Tightening system
5. Type M3 bogey
6. Type M4 bogey
7. HVSS Bogey
8. Sprocket with a ring-like plug
9. Ford sprocket
10. Chrysler sprocket
11. Sprocket with molded rim

the operation was to loosen the track in question. On the Sherman this was done in three steps:

1. Separate the grooved shaft using the special spanner (41W-640-400).
2. Loosen the track using the cam situated on the tightening mechanism.
3. Put the apparatus holding the track in place and tighten them.

The connectors to be removed were then in the center of the apparatus. The bolts of the inside and outside connectors were loosened and taken out; then the holding hooks were loosened and the track was undone.

There were two types of devices for holding the track: one with chains and the other with worms. In both cases, they were used with a ratchet drive.

Making the track taut

To avoid the track coming off but also to get the most out of the transmission, the track had to be tightened to a particular setting, enabling it still to function easily. The tightness setting was obtained by measuring the gap between the track and a straight horizontal line; this gap was measured between two return rollers.

The other side of the coin was that by leaving the track slack, the tightening system was under less pressure, operational performance was better, and shock absorber and spring clearance was compensated.

Doing this meant that because the track was looser there was still a risk of the track coming off. To reduce this risk, the Americans added a compensating pulley on their torsion suspension bars. This extra pulley was mounted on the torsion bar and located at the rear of

the running gear, between the sprocket and the last running gear wheel.

How it worked

1st scenario—the tank is advancing in a straight line

There is no action on the differential; the tracks roll round the running gear, and the compensating pulleys keep the tracks taught by means of their torsion bar.

2nd scenario—the tank turns

Turning right: by the action of the differential, the speed of the left-hand track increases considerably; the slack of the track is projected towards the front, creating void between on the one hand the idler wheel, and on the other the section of track between the idler wheel and the first running gear wheel which then slackens off. There's a risk of the track coming off.

Through the action of the torsion bar, the compensating pulley pushes the track down, thus maintaining the right tension and limiting the risk of the track coming off.

The Rear Deck

The rear deck is the space between the rear lights of the tank and the turret bustle. As with the ammunition, the rear deck's configuration depended on the engine installed in the M4. The access panels to the engine and various filler ports were located on this deck.

It was also there that the pioneers' tools were stowed, and the drawing (*on the opposite page*) shows where they were depending on the type of M4.

On the rear deck there were the rear lights with their guards, and also the gills or air intakes to the engine compartment, the water and fuel filler ports, as well as the removable plates giving access to the engine for servicing, and for checking and topping up (oil), together with the pioneer's tools: spade, pick, sledgehammer, axe, crowbar, towing cable, crankshaft, and track tension spanner. On certain models, spare track links and the swab rod were fastened on the rear. On the "Late" A3 models, a folding rack was fixed on the rear deck.

This rack was for carrying equipment; the swab rod was under the folding part of the rack. This rear space was also used for carrying infantrymen and was very often used to fasten all that was not really regulation, but still ever so useful!

The different types of engines modified the shape of this rear deck, meaning you can tell one M4 type from another. For example, the rear deck of the A4 had a bulge because of the radiator and its filler port. Others didn't have the gills or air intakes, or ventilation for the petrol tanks. The M4A6 also had a bulge, whereas the A2s and A3s had ventilation grids.

THE REAR DECKS OF THE M4S

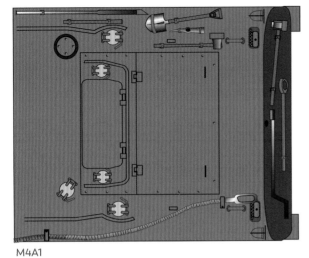

M4A1

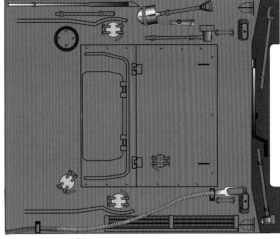

M4 and M4 105 Hw

M4A2

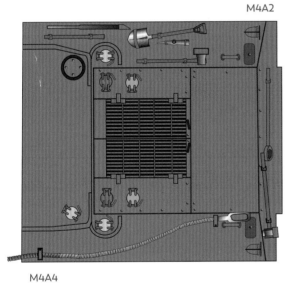

M4A4

M4A3

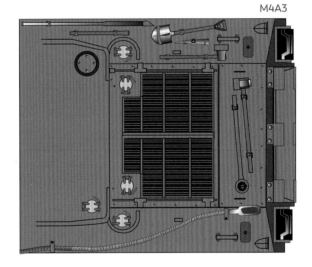

M4A6

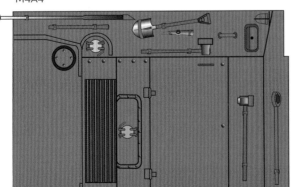

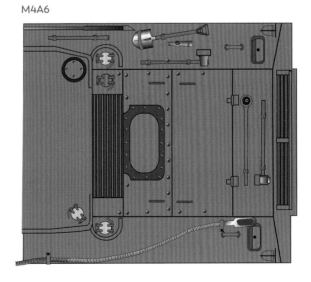

Powerplants

The engine compartment

The rear deck and its layout were different depending on the engine installed, and they enabled the Shermans to be distinguished. The M4s and the M4A1s were similar because they had the same Continental radial engine. Part of the rear deck armor was mounted on hinges, giving partial access to the engine. A "Late" model of the M4 was fitted with an extra filler port (oil), on the left of the rear deck. On these models, the track tightening spanner and the sledgehammer were fixed to the same rear panel. The other M4s and M4A1s carried their track tightening spanner, sledgehammer, and crankshaft on the rear end.

On all the M4 models, the pioneer tools were fastened above the right sponson: spade, pick head, axe, pick handle, and crowbar. The towing cable and sometimes, in the case of the M4 105, the swab rods, were fastened on the left sponson. The crowbar on some A1 models was fixed on the left-hand side.

On the M4A2s, a two-part armored grid opening sideways gave access to certain parts of the engine. The rear part comprised an armored plate held in place by bolts. These plates were removed when the engine was taken out (GM 60-71 twinning). Because it was this engine, there were two oil filler ports on the rear deck, two water filler ports, and two fuel filler ports, and a filler port for the auxiliary generator fuel.

The M4A3 was different because of its Ford V8 powerplant. The armored grids protecting the ventilation took up the whole width of the rear deck. The two-part grids were hinged and mounted on two torsion bars, making handling easier. There were two torsion bar models: short and long. This assembly was completed by the rear armor: a bolted-on plate that had to be withdrawn when the engine was taken out. The sledgehammer and the track tightening spanner were fastened to the rear section of the rear deck because of the folding rack fixed to the rear end. The water filler port was located towards the front center of the rear deck.

The four fuel tank filler ports were spread out on the side and the auxiliary generator filler port was in its usual place (left), with the fixed fire extinguisher trigger handles.

The M4A4's 30-cylinder Multibanks engine meant lengthening the chassis, and a hinged bulge had to be set up on the rear deck so that the engine compartment could house the cooling radiator and its filler port.

The armored floor was specially fitted out to take the ventilation casing.

Right up against the turret was an armored grid for cooling and circulating air. Like on the other models, there was an armored plate on the deck which had to be taken off before removing the engine. The sledgehammer was fixed at the back of the rear deck and the track tightening spanner was fastened to the rear end. There was a fuel filler port to the right and left. The filler port for the auxiliary generator was in its usual place.

The M4A6, which also had the M4A4's lengthened chassis, adopted the same layout, though the cooling bulge was bigger because of the Caterpillar engine. On these models the top plate of armor had two hinges. The two fuel filler ports were at the front of the deck and the oil filler port was in line with them. The auxiliary generator filler port was in its usual place.

So what? Start it with the crankshaft!

As you can see in the photographs, some Shermans were equipped with a (large) crankshaft. These were the R-975 radial-engined models. It was fixed to the rear of the tank, not far from the engine doors. This might lead you to think that it was used for starting the engine. This reasoning could be taken as perfectly acceptable—for anyone who isn't in the know. Those of us who do have some notions of mechanics—or those who have already started a vehicle using a crankshaft—know that to do so is verging on the irresponsible. "Turning over" a large capacity nine-cylinder radial engine fast enough to get it to start is an experience that can end in disaster … above all for those handling the crankshaft.

The crankshaft in question was used for something quite different.

In the case of a radial engine with integral dry sump pressure lubrication, at the moment the engine stops, the pressure drops in the greasing circuit. Because of the cylinders' radial layout, the oil drops into the fifth cylinder's piston skirt, through the oil expander ring, infiltrating the combustion chamber. Where the fifth cylinder's two valves are shut and the big end is at the beginning of the "compression" stage of the cycle, hydrostatic blocking will occur if the engine is turned over because the liquids are not compressible. And that is in the best of cases.

Starting American tanks was slightly different. Their engines were fitted with a booster (a system to intensify the ignition) which when it was set off made starting the engine easier. In case the fifth cylinder was hydrostatically blocked and at the beginning of the compression phase, the sixth cylinder would be at the ignition/explosion stage. The booster doing what was

Hey, Sarge, it won't start! Well, you dummy, use the crankshaft!

expected of it, the engine would start and it was then the big end and crankshaft which absorbed—badly—the shock, leading to engine deterioration.

Before starting after a prolonged engine standstill, the bow gunner inserted the crankshaft into the special hole; he then turned it 50 times—a complete engine cycle. If there was hydrostatic blocking (it was easy to spot), the sparkplugs from the two bottom cylinders were removed, the oil was drained, and the sparkplugs put back.

After which the driver started the engine normally.

Now that we've mastered the starting phase, let's have a look at the story of the M4 powerplants. It is interesting to note that with each type of engine there were corresponding models of access openings, cooling grilles, air intakes, etc.

The Wright Continental R 975-C2 or C4

The Continental Wright R 975-C2 or C4 15.9 liter, 460 bhp petrol engine. Fuel capacity: 662 liters. Engine weight: 850 kg.

This was an originally an aircraft engine and was installed in the M3s. This nine-cylinder radial engine was simply built and therefore reliable and quite satisfactory. It was exactly what was needed for an army which didn't have an engine powerplant for its tanks.

The engine did have some shortcomings, and first and foremost among them were its mass and size because it had a radial engine. Indeed, although this type of engine was *ad hoc* for an aircraft, where fuselages were getting bigger and engines could adapt easily to the aircraft's aerodynamics, it was quite a different kettle of fish for a tank.

In the case of the Sherman, the hull had to be heightened, giving the tank its "long legged" appearance. Besides, the proportions of a medium tank did not allow for the turret to be lowered or the hull to be widened so as to trim down the silhouette. It wasn't until the M24 and M18 "Hellcat" appeared that the American tank was built with proportions prefiguring those of modern tanks.

The Continental R-975 was the Sherman's powerplant for a long time. Due to the engine being shut up inside its compartment, an extra cooling system had to be added; it comprised a big fan located at the rear, on the prop shaft side, and a radiator. The generator was also housed on the transmission side, just under the prop shaft linked to the gearbox.

At the time nobody was particularly worried about petrol consumption, so note the size of the (single) carburetor on this Continental engine. It was twin-bodied and the size of the floats gives an idea of the fuel quantities pumped in when the driver put his foot down hard on the accelerator.

The service and repair handbook for the Continental engine was the TM9-175D, published by the War Department in August 1942. This manual, like all American technical documentation fascicules, was so precise that it brought keeping these tanks in good condition within the reach of any mechanic. All the operations were listed and detailed; the ordinary and the special tools were well specified and none of all the various settings were left out.

At the top of the list, there was a troubleshooting method for a variety of breakdowns and incidents that might have to be dealt with, from the engine not starting to air filters via high oil temperatures, or a drop in power or cold weather problems. Take, for instance, a lack of compression on a nine-cylinder Continental radial engine.

The procedure stipulated:
- "Check each cylinder's compression by removing the rear spark plug (two plugs per cylinder) and inserting the compression gauge.
- Note the information for each cylinder; it has to be between 105 and 110 psi.

Cutaway drawing of the Continental R 975-C1 (*after TM9-1751*)

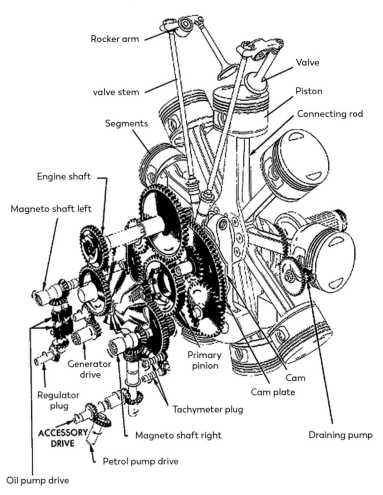

Rocker arm
Valve
valve stem
Piston
Connecting rod
Segments
Engine shaft
Magneto shaft left
Generator drive
Primary pinion
Cam
Regulator plug
Cam plate
Tachymeter plug
ACCESSORY DRIVE
Magneto shaft right
Draining pump
Petrol pump drive
Oil pump drive

The Ford GAA V8 engine
A. Oil filter
B. Filler port
C. Fixation
D. Drive
E. Exhaust duct
F. Exhaust outlet
G. Carburetor duct
H. Water duct
J. Rocker arm cover
K. Manifold
L. Cylinder head
M. Fixation
N. Starter
P. Engine block
Q. Oil sump
(RA PD 27 200)

- If a cylinder has no compression, check the valves are in a good state, check they work and are properly set.
- Remove all cylinders with more than 10 psi difference compared with the norm and check:
  - the state and the wear of the segments;
  - the state and the elasticity of the valve springs;
  - for sticking valves, absence of breaks, or burns;
  - for badly fitting or leaking spark plugs;
  - for cracks on the sleeve heads or the pistons;
  - the state and wear of the valve seats."

The different sub-assemblies making up the tank were clearly indicated by drawings, e.g. the position and the layout of the four fuel tanks, the feeder and communication pipes, the various filler ports, the stopcocks and the manual injection pump, the filters, and the mechanical pump.

The carburetor was a Stromberg NA-R9D, whose dimensions give a good idea of the tank's very "honorable" consumption. It was fitted with the usual circuits like starting, idling, and normal running, and what was more, it included an idling circuit cut out to stop the engine.

This device consisted of a needle mounted on a spring activated by a solenoid controlled by the driver on the dashboard: this was the "Degazer."

The ignition system of the Wright Continental consisted of two magnetos, an ignition intensifier called the "Booster" (acting on the right-hand magneto), spark plugs, and armored cabling. The magnetos were VAG 9 DFAs equipped with an ignition advance/retard mechanism as well as an anti-interference device for the radio equipment.

The right-hand magneto lit the front row of spark plugs, and the left-hand the rear row. How to set the magneto and the relevant markings were well explained in the handbook.

The 2,600 rpm 550 bhp V8 GAA Ford engine

Water-cooled petrol engine. Fuel capacity: 636 liters. Engine weight: 1,200 kg.

The Americans have never been short of engines, and Ford had hidden away somewhere an engine which was something like what a powerplant for a tank should be: the GAA V8. It was installed in the M74 and then powered the 45-ton M47 for many years.

The origins of this engine

Just before World War II, Ford finished off preparing an engine at the same time as Rolls Royce/Allison did theirs. This was an aluminum block, double overhead camshaft, four-valve cylindered, 60° V 12 engine. It was built to equip fighter aircraft and the engine was therefore built to aeronautic standards: lightness, high performance, and reliability. Everything had double cabling or double conduits.

This engine was not built for the naval air arm as the US Navy decided to hang on to radial engines for its planes. The shortage of tank engines was beginning to be felt, so the US Army got in touch with Ford. Thus the Detroit firm decided to take four cylinders off its V 12 so as to get it inside the Sherman.

And so the GAA V8 Ford was made: a V engine which, unlike the others, was set at 60° not 90° (like the T 34's), reducing its volume. It was 90 cm wide.

It was a water-cooled, four-stroke, double overhead camshaft petrol engine. The ignition system comprised two Bosch MJF4A magnetos and armored ignition ramps. The cylinders fired in the following order (R for Right, L for Left): 1R, 2L, 3R, 1L, 4R, 3L, 2R, and 4L, or 1-6, 3-5, 4-7, 8-2.

Two side ventilators driven by two double fan belts cooled the engine. These belt pulleys were located on the casings and were linked to the engines by drive shafts. The radiator, which was as wide as the engine compartment, was located behind the two ventilators. The two engine banks were fed by two Bendix-Stromberg NA-Y5G carburetors. The moving parts were lubricated under pressure, the oil being filtered by a Cuno self-cleaning filter.

Unlike other engines used on the M4s, this one powered two generators in the engine compartment. They were synchronized by two regulation boxes. In the case of the M4A3, there were three regulation boxes, including the one for the generator. The M4A3 75Ws and 105 howitzers were equipped with a single generator, driven by the prop shaft and located behind the driver. On this model, the air filters were in the combat compartment.

The Chrysler Multibanks engine

Chrysler Multibanks* AC 57 petrol engine, 470 bhp at 2,700 rpm. Fuel capacity: 606 liters. Engine weight: 2,884 kg.

Chrysler was well-known worldwide, but for a European "Multibanks" was a bit more vague. This was surprising because the engine was a little technological marvel.

If you were a builder like Chrysler, you'd design and create an ensemble made up of five six-cylinder inline engines with a common transmission. The result was 30 cylinders and 21,000 cc! The starting point for this ensemble was the six-cylinder inline 4.12-liter engine. A small cylinder head modification brought the compression ratio to 6.2:1 and the original carburetor was replaced by a Dodge, a multi-position carburetor used in aircraft engines. These carburetors were later replaced.

The five engines were put together to form a semi-circle; the five engine flywheels engaged on a central pinion, itself interdependent of the beginning of the transmission and the clutch. The result was as follows: one vertical bank, two 45° banks and two 90° (horizontal) banks. After all, the final assembly

was compact enough to fit into the tank engine compartment. Installing the Multibanks meant lengthening the chassis. The engine prototype suffered from big carburation difficulties due to the length of the admission ducts making feeding and synchronizing the carburetors difficult.

They were therefore repositioned so they would be on the same level, making maintenance easier, too. Besides, the fact that the carburetors were aligned simplified the control linkage and air filter problems. The ignition fittings for the 30 cylinders were the same type. The igniter heads were originally fitted vertically halfway up the engine; they were repositioned further forwards and mounted at the end of the camshaft; each bank kept its igniter. At the same time, the original chain distribution system was replaced by a pinion driven one.

Installing a Chrysler Multibanks AC 57 engine. (NARA)

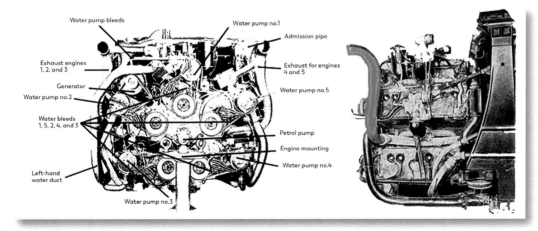

Water pump bleeds
Water pump no.1
Admission pipe
Exhaust engines 1, 2, and 3
Exhaust for engines 4 and 5
Generator
Water pump no.5
Water pump no.2
Water bleeds 1, 5, 2, 4, and 3
Petrol pump
Engine mounting
Left-hand water duct
Water pump no.4
Water pump no.3

Cutaway drawing of the Chrysler Multibanks AC 57 engine

The cooling system was seriously rethought. Five pumps, five pulleys, and five belts were indeed all very well if the engine was outside. With the engine shut up inside its compartment, the installation became more than uncertain. The designers therefore changed these five pumps into a single one driven by a secondary shaft, itself driven by the central pinion of the five engine flywheels.

In the case of an engine with five water pumps, the right-hand manifold fed engines 4 and 5, and the left-hand engines 1, 2, and 3. Because of the engine layout there were three different types of water pumps. The pump parts were interchangeable but not the pump bodies. Engine 1 was vertical and central and had a special pump; engines 2 and 3 had another model and the same thing applied to engines 4 and 5. The petrol pump was driven by the camshaft on engine no.4 and on the last production M4A4s, the generator was placed in the combat compartment, driven by the prop shaft with pulleys and belts. To lubricate this "factory," an integral dry sump pressure lubrication system was fitted.

Each bank—or engine—had its own carburetor: this was a down-draft carburetor and the five carburetors were commanded by a system of rods linked to the accelerator controls. The same applied to the chokes. Likewise for the ignition, each bank having its own igniter, distributor head, and ignition coil.

These changes were important because magnetos didn't produce the ignition on this engine. The initial models used a single generator, driven by engine no.2.

There was only one starter and it was positioned between engines 1 and 2. The engine banks were numbered looking at the group of engines from the distribution side, and counter-clockwise, which gave:

- Engine no.1 at the top
- Engine no.2 on the left of engine 1
- Engine no.3 bottom left
- Engine no.4 bottom right

- Engine no.5 on the right of engine 1

The exhaust from engines 1, 2, and 3 was collected in the manifold pipe on the left, that from banks 4 and 5 in the pipe on the right.

This jewel of mechanics equipped the M3A4s and M4A4s; it was the heaviest Sherman powerplant.

Conforming to TM 9-754, the crew carried out servicing but also certain settings and repairs. The handbook described the methods for servicing and setting or exchanging the contact plate of the igniter very precisely, how to set it in case the igniter needed changing.

The General Motors GM 6-71

The General Motors GM 6-71 diesel engine, rated at 410 bhp at 2,900 rpm. Fuel capacity: 560 liters. Engine weight: 1,030 kg.

Mount two bus engines side by side and you get a very acceptable 12-cylinder engine. This powerplant was installed in the M3A3s, M3A5s, and M4A2s. This was a diesel engine group covered by the Technical Manual 9-1750G published by the Ordnance Corps. They had a serial number on the engine block and the numbers started at 6046-1. The term "engine group" designated two six-cylinder inline engines and consisted of a Type 671 LA 24M and a Type 671 LC 24M.

The letters LA meant the right-hand engine and the LC the left. The latter engine was on the left-hand side of the tank looking forwards. The two engines were connected by a transfer box situated at the rear. The serial number was engraved on the casing of the transfer box. Each engine had its own lubricating and cooling systems, and a generator mounted at the end of the camshaft. Cylinder no.1 was situated on the ventilator side.

The 6046 engine was a two-stroke diesel internal combustion engine with side distribution. As a result, it was fitted with a pump to send the hot air into the cylinders under pressure. This evacuated the combustion gases first and then filled the combustion chambers with fresh air.

The next steps were common to all diesel engines: injection, compression, and ignition; the last stroke expelled the exhaust gases, injecting reheated fresh air. On this type of engine, admission and exhaust were part of the compression and engine stroke, hence the name "two stroke."

The fuel pump had to feed the diesel to the injectors at a constant pressure. On each cylinder three rocker arms commanded an exhaust valve, an admission valve, and the injector movement.

This engine was fitted with a carbon/manganese steel alloy crankshaft. A regulator commanded the pump in order to maintain the mini-maxi flow in

The General Motors GM 6-71 diesel engine

Cooling pipe
Cooling system bleeder
Thermostat
Air filter
Secondary air filter
Emergency halt solenoid
Oil radiator
Emptying cooling system
Clutch casing
Starter
Clutch check opening

Exhaust manifold
Upper liaison module
Tachymeter plug
Fuel feed
Generator
Clutch stop greasing
Clutch control greasing
Engine shaft
Transfer box Filling
Draining

Left-hand engine
Right-hand engine
RA PD 36018

relation to the engine speed. Engine lubrication was by means of an integral dry sump pressure system and comprised three pumps: a pressure pump and two lift recovery (or dry out) pumps. These pumps enabled the engine to work without danger at less than 35°. The oil was filtered by two filters set out in series and a regulator kept the pressure at a constant level. The oil was also maintained at the right temperature by a calorstat-equipped "water" exchanger enabling the temperature to rise more quickly during the warming-up period.

A regulator valve at the inlet limited the pressure inside the exchanger. The air filters were inside the engine compartment, on either side of the engines. There were three on each side.

The clutch was positioned where movement came out of the transfer box, between the engine and the transmission, drive for the latter being situated between the two clutches. These were single disk types with a fork and clutch stop. The engine group was started by driving the right-hand engine.

The tank could move using a single engine and in this case the top speed was 38 kmph.

The Caterpillar RD 1820 and D22A radials

The Caterpillar RD 1820 and D22A radial engines, 500 bhp at 3,000 rpm. Multi fuel. Fuel capacity: 552 liters. Engine weight: 1,950 kg.

These engines were installed on the A6 models.

RD 1820 Cyclone 9: this engine was a development of the Wright P2, itself dating back to 1925. The RD 1820 entered production in 1931 and was produced until the 1950s. This engine was made under license by Lycoming, Pratt and Witney Canada, but also by Studebaker Corporation during World War II.

The USSR bought a license and Shvetsov OKB built this engine under the designation M-25. This engine was also built by Hispano-Suiza (Spain) under the appellation V9.

The cylinders fired in the following order 1-3-5-7-9-2-4-6-8. It was fitted with two 24v starters, air-cooling, and air-heating for low-temperature starts.

The RD1820 equipped the most famous aircraft: the Douglas DC3, a few DC 5s, the B-17 Flying Fortresses, and for the Russians, the Polikarpov I-16 and the Piasecki H21 helicopter.

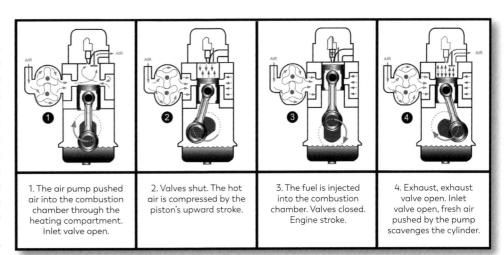

1. The air pump pushed air into the combustion chamber through the heating compartment. Inlet valve open.

2. Valves shut. The hot air is compressed by the piston's upward stroke.

3. The fuel is injected into the combustion chamber. Valves closed. Engine stroke.

4. Exhaust, exhaust valve open. Inlet valve open, fresh air pushed by the pump scavenges the cylinder.

Under the designation D200, this engine equipped other AVs, like the M6 Heavy Tank. In this case, it was the nine-cylinder petrol engine, rated at 900 bhp at 2,300 rpm, idling speed basically. It was Caterpillar Inc. that converted it into a diesel engine.

Concerning powerplants

From all that has been said here about Sherman powerplants, we can see that American engineers knew how to use engines from a civilian range of products and adapt them to drive their armored vehicles.

We must add Cadillac to the builders mentioned above. This American designer, specializing more in large road limousines, was put to work to power some M3s and M5s, then the M24 Chaffee Light Tank, with its V8 engines.

As for the Ford V8 GAA, it went on to equip the M26 Pershing Heavy Tanks. Concerning the weight/power ratio: the standard used later, i.e. 20 bhp/ton, was not in use in 1941, which explains why the ratios were sometimes low (15 bhp/ton) on certain Sherman models.

How the General Motors four-stroke Grey Marine 6046 engine works.

Cutaway drawing of the Caterpillar RD 1820

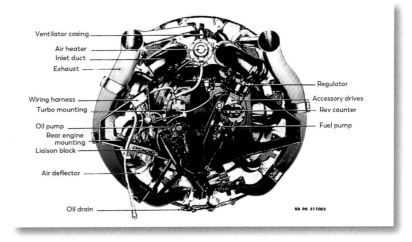

Ventilator casing
Air heater
Inlet duct
Exhaust
Regulator
Accessory drives
Rev counter
Wiring harness
Turbo mounting
Fuel pump
Oil pump
Rear engine mounting
Liaison block
Air deflector
Oil drain

RA PD 311003

4 Turrets

The Shermans could be equipped with five different types of turrets.

- The D 50878 and D 78461 turrets, intended for the 75-mm cannon, then for the 105-mm howitzer.
- The T23 turret, for the 76-mm cannon.
- The Jumbo turret.
- The Firefly turret, for the British 17-pounder.

The Sherman turrets could be fitted with electric, hydro-electric, or exclusively manual swivel commands.

The turrets could be divided into two great families: "high bustle"* or "low bustle" (these names were not official). There were three types of hatches: the "Split Hatch," the "Vision Cupola," and the "Oval Hatch." There was one with a single opening but two "Split Hatch" flaps (there were two different types of hatches with different openings) or one with a cupola—the "Vision Cupola" —on the right, and a hatch on the left. There were two models of radio operator's hatch: either a semi-oval hatch, smaller than the tank commander's "Oval Hatch," or the tank commander's old split hatch opening outwards and sideways with an episcope on one of the flaps. In this case, it was current practice for the AA machine gun to be mounted on the radio operator's side, in line with the junction of the two flaps of the hatch. The cartridge case evacuation slot was called the "Pistol Port."

Why "Pistol Port" when it should be "Spent Shell Case Disposal Port"? Originally the turrets were fitted with a loophole-style opening, enabling the cannoneer to shoot with his pistol or .45 caliber Thomson SMG* machine gun. Then the designers said to themselves: "Why not widen the opening to get rid of the empty cartridge cases?" The idea was validated but the original name stuck.

A project for a T26 turret with a 90-mm cannon saw the light of day in 1944, but was abandoned because of the—too many—changes that needed to be made to the tank. This turret was the one that later equipped the M26 Pershing.

The Firefly's turret was special. The M10 and M36 TDs' turrets were specific and will be dealt with later, as will their hulls. As we will see in the chapter on the M4 used by other countries, a lot of versions were made, there were opportunities to be creative, and none of this simplifies classification.

The standard turret for the Sherman was the D 50878, designed around the 75-mm cannon. This turret

was later modified to take the 105-mm howitzer or the British 17-pounder gun. The T23 turret was designed to take the 76-mm cannon and the turret of the M4 Jumbo was a T23 with extra armor around the turret.

Originally the T23 was a prototype tank that was turned down. However, its turret turned out to be an excellent solution for enabling the Sherman to be equipped with a new cannon. This is why the 76-mm turret is called the T23.

The standard Sherman D 50878 turret was equipped with the 75-mm M3L40 cannon with 90 shells in and around it. The first examples were armed with a M2 75-mm cannon requiring a counterweight to be fitted—on the muzzle—for it to remain compatible with the armament's gyroscopic stabilization.

The need for this counterweight was eliminated when the M3 cannon was mounted. The first gun carriage, the M34, was quickly replaced by an M34A1, which was wider and used direct sights and its predecessor's periscope. The cannon mantle incorporated the machine-gun mantle, which previously had been separate. The Anti-Aircraft (AA) armament comprised a heavy .50 caliber (12.7-mm) machine gun, the Browning M2 HB, with 300 rounds. Close quarters defense was provided by a .30 caliber 06 Browning M 1919 A4 or A5 machine gun mounted coaxially with the cannon and a second fixed M1919 A4 machine gun, in the bow gun position. Some M4A3s were equipped with a heavy .50 caliber (12.7-mm) machine gun on the rear of the turret and a flexible .30-06 caliber Browning M 1919 A4 machine gun mounted in front of the tank commander's hatch.

The 105-mm howitzer turret existed in two versions: one with tank commander's split hatch, the other with the tank commander's cupola with six episcopes. The cannoneer's hatch could likewise be oval (small opening) or round with the same diameter as the tank commander's.

The Sherman's turret was based on the T6 model. This turret, mounted on an M4 hull with side doors, was equipped with an oscillating periscope for firing, and the M3 tank cupola incorporating machine gun, cartridge case openings, and vision slots on the right-hand and left-hand turret side. The gun mantle was simplified and did not have any lifting rings; neither did the turret. On the definitive models, the rings were installed. The M3's cupola was replaced by a tank commander's split hatch with an episcope swiveling through 360°.

The AA machine gun mounting and the gun lock clip support were located on this hatch. The pistol port, for evacuating spent cartridge cases, was on the left-hand side only; the vision slot was suppressed. The turret was designated D 50878 and called "Low Bustle."

Another turret type, the D 78461, was called "High Bustle." The different shape of these two models is shown on the M4 plate (Page 47). These turrets were equipped with a 75 M1 cannon, mounted on either the M34 or M34 A1 gun carriage. The M34 carriage had a small protective shield fitted with two cheeks which incorporated only the cannon. The two lifting rings for the cannon were located on either side of the shield. There were three lifting rings on the turret: one at the front in line with the cannon and two at the rear. On the "Early" models, these two rear rings were welded on the high part of the turret at the rear.

On the "Late" models, the M34 A1 carriage was installed with a new, wider shield. The protective cheeks disappeared and the shield incorporated the coaxial machine gun on the left and new telescopic sights on the right. The two flaps on the tank commander's split-hatch were fitted with lock bolts to hold them open. These modifications were carried out by the FDI (Field and Depot Issues) with the help of "kits" supplied on delivery. The "Late" models were also fitted with a searchlight on the bracket fixed near the turret ventilator protection.

For the D50878 turret equipping the tanks with the 75-mm cannon, the position of the turret swivel mechanism meant the designers had to "nibble" into the thickness of the lateral armor in order to house the new mechanism.

A new assembly of extra armor plates to reinforce this weak point had to be studied and built. The MWO G104-W 57 gave instructions on how to mount the

THE M4 TURRETS

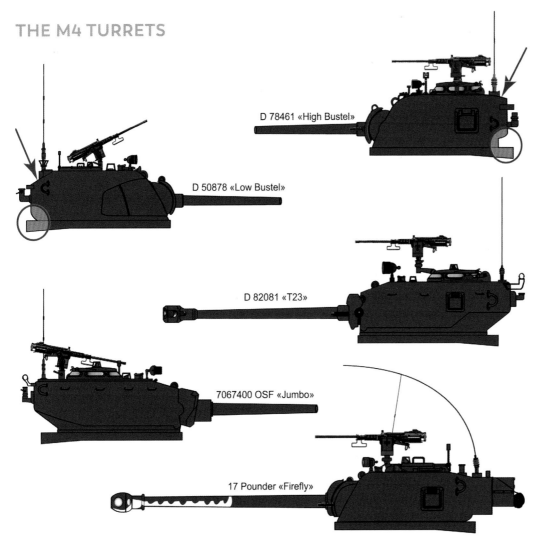

D 78461 «High Bustel»

D 50878 «Low Bustel»

D 82081 «T23»

7067400 OSF «Jumbo»

17 Pounder «Firefly»

additional turret armor, on the right-hand side. This armor comprised two 3-inch (76.2-mm) armored plates slightly curved to follow the shape of the turret, and welded to the front and sides of the turret.

Depending on the tank, this extra armor was not welded to the lower part when the shrapnel screen of the turret's weak point covered this armor. In the case of smaller plates, the lower part of the armor was welded. The M34 carriage was also modified. Indeed it quickly became obvious that telescopic sights had to replace the periscope sight.

The M34 A1 gun carriage had resolved the problem, but in the meantime several thousand Shermans had been equipped with M34s. One modification, applied

THE "EARLY" AND "MID" TURRETS WITH 75-MM CANNON

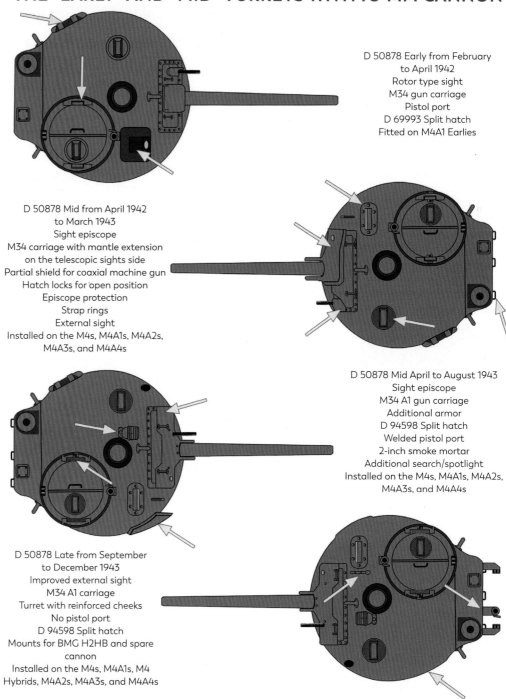

D 50878 Early from February
to April 1942
Rotor type sight
M34 gun carriage
Pistol port
D 69993 Split hatch
Fitted on M4A1 Earlies

D 50878 Mid from April 1942
to March 1943
Sight episcope
M34 carriage with mantle extension
on the telescopic sights side
Partial shield for coaxial machine gun
Hatch locks for open position
Episcope protection
Strap rings
External sight
Installed on the M4s, M4A1s, M4A2s,
M4A3s, and M4A4s

D 50878 Mid April to August 1943
Sight episcope
M34 A1 gun carriage
Additional armor
D 94598 Split hatch
Welded pistol port
2-inch smoke mortar
Additional search/spotlight
Installed on the M4s, M4A1s, M4A2s,
M4A3s, and M4A4s

D 50878 Late from September
to December 1943
Improved external sight
M34 A1 carriage
Turret with reinforced cheeks
No pistol port
D 94598 Split hatch
Mounts for BMG H2HB and spare
cannon
Installed on the M4s, M4A1s, M4
Hybrids, M4A2s, M4A3s, and M4A4s

mainly on tanks outside the USA, concerned the following: adding a curved half shield to the right-hand part of the carriage, including the firing sights aperture (ref. no.D 52869); on the carriage plate, adding a semi-circular side (ref. no.D 52873) which followed the shape of the curved half shield; and adding a maximum sight stop on the M34 carriage plate.

The right-hand lifting ring was removed.

Glacis armor

Sometimes tanks were delivered with kits which were not always assembled, either from lack of time or of means. The tanks intended for instruction and training centers were not equipped with additional armor plates, which were likewise not always fitted on the M4A2s and M4A4 intended for Lend-Lease, these additional armor plates usually being delivered as separate kits.

In April 1943, the Ordnance Corps decided to suppress the empty shell case aperture: it was considered to be a weak point on the turret. At the time, they were welded over (*see the turret equipment plate*).

The D 50878 turrets were therefore redesigned without the empty case aperture. Another modification on this new model was the right-hand side of the turret at the spot where the reduced thickness had been given additional plates. The new turret design provided an extra thickness of cast armor just in front of this thinner right-hand part. This bulge was visible on the lower part of the turret. On certain French turrets, the additional turret armor was mounted even though the turrets delivered included the new extra thickness.

In July 1943, the Ordnance Corps decided to bring back the shell case apertures and, at the request of the units using them, equipped the D 50878 with an oval cannoneer hatch (from November 1943 onwards).

The D 78461 "High Bustle" turret

On these turrets, the rear section was raised to enable the large type of driver's and bow gunner's hatches to open. The six-episcope cupola for the tank commander was fitted to the D 50878 and D 78461 turrets. On the latter, a bulge on the right-hand side of the turret enabled the cupola to be repositioned outwards.

The "Late" 105-mm turrets were equipped with a second smoke extractor mounted on the rear of the turret. This meant a new mounting for the .50 caliber AA machine gun. (*see armament plate*).

The T23 turret

This turret came from the T23 tank prototype. The tank was abandoned but the turret turned out to be interesting, and adaptable to the Sherman hull. It was given the reference no.D 80081 at the beginning and the initial models were delivered without the turret

ventilation because the T23 prototype had a different ventilation system. The ventilator was added to the Sherman turrets later; the evacuation hatch was located on the turret bustle with the extra mounting for the AA machine gun welded to its guard.

Another peculiarity on the "Early" 76 model was the two flaps, the two halves of the tank commander's hatch which opened at right angles, which made operating the 12.7-mm machine gun a bit tricky. There was a modification—which could be carried out in the field—which enabled the shutters to open to 135°.

The M4A1 was the first model to be equipped with this turret; it equipped the 2d and 3d US Armored Divisions in 1944 for the Battle of Normandy. These tanks were armed with the 76-mm M1 A1 cannon.

The end of the barrel of the following 76-mm cannon was threaded to take a muzzle brake. In the meantime, a protective cover was screwed onto the cannon using the muzzle brake thread. These cannon were designated M1A1C.

You can see an example of the M4A1 at the entrance to the Quartier Delestraint at Mourmelon

This shot of an M4A1 penetrating the Santiago Fort in Manila during the reconquest of the Philippines gives us a marvelous view of the characteristic rear of its turret. (*Signal Corps, NARA*)

A Sherman M4A3 76 W or M4A2 76 W from the 2e Compagnie of the 501e Régiment de Chars de Combat, 2e DB, Paris, August 1944. (*Private collection*)

in northeastern France. There was another important change on the T23 turret: the cannoneer's split hatch was replaced by an oval hatch. As the earlier hatch carried the 12.7-mm machine gun, the mounting was repositioned between the two hatches, towards the rear of the turret. This turret was no.70 54366.

The crews often changed the position of the machine-gun mounting to suit them. On the 76-mm turrets, the shield had a canvas protective cover clipped on between the turret frame and the shield. This modification was made in 1944.

Some turrets were very particular, like the T23 equipped with a ring on the left-hand side, in front of the cannoneer's hatch. It was an anchoring point for a lifting device (like a hoist) which would have enabled the crew to change the engine or handle heavy items of equipment without needing to bring in a breakdown truck.

The Sherman turret was foundry-cast. It was almost round, except for the bulge towards the rear (a compartment housing the radio equipment). It was fitted with an electro-hydraulic group which enabled it to swivel through 360° in both directions. Elevation pointing was done manually. Inside the turret most of the available space was taken up by the cannon, its cradle, the firing brake jacks, and the kickback.

A small amount of ammunition—the emergency shells—was ready for the loader on a rack in the turret basket. Apart from the crew seats, there were also interphone radio casings, the hand-grenade racks, the turret motor, episcopes, the telescopic sights, an azimuth indicator (for blind firing), ammunition for the coaxial machine gun, a portable fire extinguisher, the slip ring (the system under the turret basket which supplied electricity no matter what position the turret was in), the crew's individual weapons, the ventilator extractor, spare episcopes, binoculars, a smoke-grenade launcher, and a Thomson .45 caliber submachine gun with 600 rounds in 20 magazines.

Depending on the type of M4, towards the rear of the turret, on the firewall, were the fuel stopcocks, the emergency stop box, and a heater for warming up—just a little—the combat compartment, the engine, and transmission oil radiators. Add to all this everything each crew member could bring, regulation or not, and you get an inkling of the "living space" inside the turret.

The equipment was just as complete on the outside. Aside the lifting rings for taking the turret off, there was the ventilator protection and the spent case ejection aperture. Also on the outside were the ball-mounted spotlight, the cannon and coaxial machine gun mantle, and the ring mounted 12.7-mm AA machine gun either in front of the tank commander's hatch, between the tank commander's and the cannoneer's hatches, or ball-mounted at the rear of the turret.

Some photos show turrets equipped with a 12.7-mm machine gun at the front and a .30 caliber machine gun at the rear, but this practice was rare. The service issue tables show only two .30 caliber machine guns: one mounted coaxially and the other for the bow gunner. So, were these special fittings? As far as the machine guns in service with the M4 were concerned, the following possibilities have been noted. The models dating from the start of production were equipped with twin .30 caliber fixed machine guns mounted on the glacis plate and fired by the driver. Later, a .30 caliber machine gun was fitted to the bow gunner's position, making three .30 caliber machine guns, plus the coaxial .30 machine gun.

On the M4A3 "Jumbo," the turret was fitted with an AA machine gun bracket on the turret bustle and a mounting for a .50 caliber machine gun between the tank commander's and the cannoneer's hatch. The gun's road cradle was this time in front of the turret, in the center. On this A3, the spare machine-gun barrel was attached on its clip mounting on the rear deck, near the rear panel. The turret ventilator was incorporated into the .50 caliber machine-gun bustle support. There was an alternative layout: equipping the turret with a swiveling tank commander's split hatch, and the .50 caliber machine-gun mounting was installed on the front of the hatch (the revolving part) and the cannon lock bolt directly opposite on the hatch. A second mounting was installed between the tank commander's and the cannoneer's hatches, with the barrel lock bolt on the front part of the turret. The third mounting for the .50 caliber machine gun was on the turret bustle.

The turret with the 105-mm cannon

A mounting for the .50 caliber machine gun was set between the tank commander's and the cannoneer's hatches, with a road lock bolt towards the front of the turret. A second mounting was on the turret bustle, above the additional ventilator.

The turret with the six-episcope cupola

A .50 cal. Machine-gun mounting was installed next to the cupola, with a barrel road lock bolt directly opposite. There was an extra bracket on the turret bustle.

The turret with two large hatches

The .50 caliber machine gun was fixed on the cannoneer's (circular) hatch, with a canon lock on the ring directly opposite at 180°. There was another mounting on the turret bustle.

THE "LATE" AND "JUMBO" TURRETS WITH 75-MM CANNON

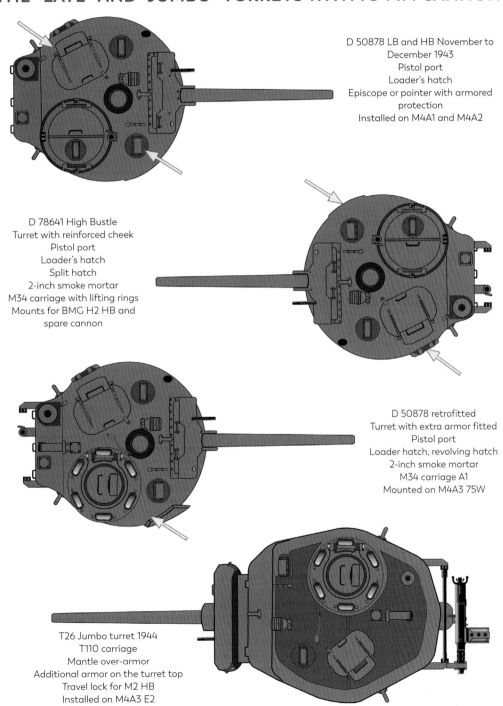

D 50878 LB and HB November to
December 1943
Pistol port
Loader's hatch
Episcope or pointer with armored
protection
Installed on M4A1 and M4A2

D 78641 High Bustle
Turret with reinforced cheek
Pistol port
Loader's hatch
Split hatch
2-inch smoke mortar
M34 carriage with lifting rings
Mounts for BMG H2 HB and
spare cannon

D 50878 retrofitted
Turret with extra armor fitted
Pistol port
Loader hatch, revolving hatch
2-inch smoke mortar
M34 carriage A1
Mounted on M4A3 75W

T26 Jumbo turret 1944
T110 carriage
Mantle over-armor
Additional armor on the turret top
Travel lock for M2 HB
Installed on M4A3 E2

Special case

Some M4A3 E8s were equipped with a .30 caliber machine gun in front of the tank commander's hatch and a .50 caliber machine gun in front of the cannoneer's hatch (*see .50 and A3 versions plate*).

Apart from the "Jumbo" model, the spare barrel for the M4's .50 caliber machine gun was attached to the turret bustle, with two clips and a strap*. Also on the turret were the machine-gun barrel locking system(s), the sighting equipment enabling the tank commander

THE TURRETS WITH 76-MM, 105-MM HOWITZER, AND 17-POUNDER

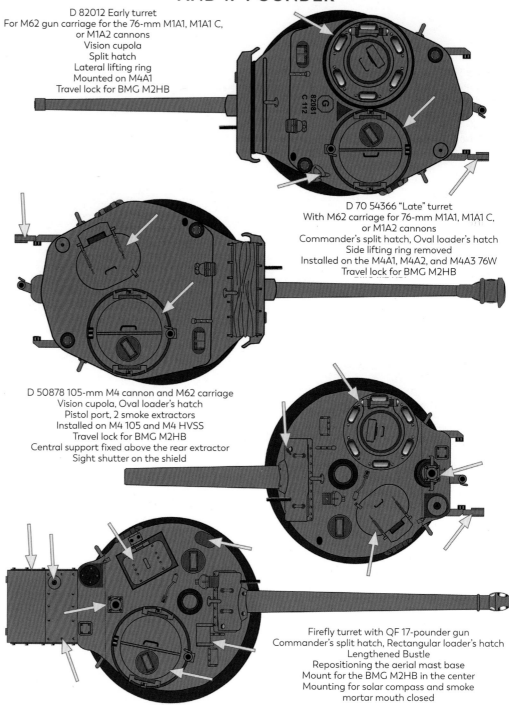

D 82012 Early turret
For M62 gun carriage for the 76-mm M1A1, M1A1 C, or M1A2 cannons
Vision cupola
Split hatch
Lateral lifting ring
Mounted on M4A1
Travel lock for BMG M2HB

D 70 54366 "Late" turret
With M62 carriage for 76-mm M1A1, M1A1 C, or M1A2 cannons
Commander's split hatch, Oval loader's hatch
Side lifting ring removed
Installed on the M4A1, M4A2, and M4A3 76W
Travel lock for BMG M2HB

D 50878 105-mm M4 cannon and M62 carriage
Vision cupola, Oval loader's hatch
Pistol port, 2 smoke extractors
Installed on M4 105 and M4 HVSS
Travel lock for BMG M2HB
Central support fixed above the rear extractor
Sight shutter on the shield

Firefly turret with QF 17-pounder gun
Commander's split hatch, Rectangular loader's hatch
Lengthened Bustle
Repositioning the aerial mast base
Mount for the BMG M2HB in the center
Mounting for solar compass and smoke mortar mouth closed

for setting the sights and increasing the rate of fire, the radio antenna mast base at rear left, and spread out round the turret were rings for attaching various accessories. The mouth of the smoke-grenade launcher was on the left towards the front for those turrets equipped with them.

Turret armor

On the M4s and M4A1s, the turret had 51-mm armor on the sides, back and front. The upper surface of the turret was 24-mm thick.

On the M4A3s and M4A4s, the armor was 51-mm thick on the turret sides and 76-mm thick on the front and rear; the cannon shield was 89-mm thick. The extra armor on the left-hand side of the A3s was 25-mm thick.

The M4A3 E8 76W's armor was 64-mm thick around the turret, 89-mm on the shield, and 25.4-mm (1-inch) on the turret top.

The turret layout

The gunner's post

The turret's Logansport electro-hydraulic group was the most common to be found on M4s, but there were two other models: one similar to the Logansport and the other an electric one produced by Westinghouse which used an extra generator to supply its motor. It was driven by the propeller shaft at the bottom of the hull.

The hydraulic group turned the turret and the swivel speed was proportional to the distance the control handle was moved. The electric motor which put the hydraulic system under pressure was located at the bottom of the mechanism on a level with the floor of the turret, and right next to the two electrical contacts: with the foot for firing the cannon and the machine gun, and the mechanical pedal (cable) for firing if the electrical system was out of order.

Some "Late" models had a tank commander's turret swivel control.

Stabilizing the barrel

This system, although not very much used, was nonetheless satisfactory. It is obvious that by today's stabilization standards, it didn't have the same degree of effectiveness, but it did enable the guns to be fired on the move, on the condition that they be properly served and well calibrated. It worked well if the driver and the gunner were well coordinated. Nonetheless, if all this was transposed to a combat situation, it might explain why the men were reluctant to use stabilization.

How it worked

The gyro-stabilizing system kept the barrel in a given position, the target being the reference here; the action

Missing caption

only applied to the elevation. An actuator linked the gun carriage to the turret block frame; the link was controlled by a command box situated under the cannon. The pressure on the actuator was maintained by means of a hydraulic circuit. The stabilization system obtained its hydraulic power from the turret. This power maintained a constant pressure in the actuator chambers; the pressure varied because of the movement caused by the barrel moving up and down. The surge return circuit allowed the (incompressible) oil to absorb these variations. It was this balance inside the actuator chambers that created the stabilization.

How did stabilization work? It was gyroscopic. A gyroscope is an instrument comprising four main parts: a flywheel turning at great speed; the flywheel axis; and two roll bars mounted like a universal joint. These allowed the axis to remain fixed in relation to the Earth's rotational axis, and as a result obtain an unvarying directional axis.

In this case, the gyroscope would constantly correct the actuator's variations by bringing it back to the reference sighting. When the gunner started the stabilization, he had to de-clutch the elevation command, trigger the hydraulics, and start the gyroscopic command motor (high-speed rotation). The gunner took a sighting and this became the gyroscope's reference, keeping the barrel along the given axis by means of the actuator.

The set-up was never used very much (and therefore quickly abandoned) but the crew did use the rings to hang their gear on. This lifting system on the "Early" M4A3 76s T23s was installed by Chrysler, supplied with turrets by American Steel foundry and Continental Steel.

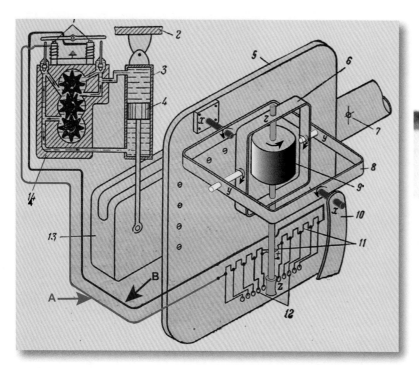

1. Pump solenoid-operated control valve
2. Turret frame
3. Support actuator
4. Piston
5. Side support
6. Inner support frame
7. Cannon case link axis
8. Outer support frame
9. Gyroscope wheel
10. Exterior roll bar support
11. Resistors
12. Contacts
13. Cannon cradle
14. Hydraulic pump
15. Wheel control axle

As long as the gunner did not touch the elevation control, the gun remained pointing at the same target. As you can imagine, such an installation needed to be set for it to work properly. Apart from the force of the movements borne by the cannon, the system had to be calibrated too. To do this the gunner had two main settings:

• The setting for the rigidity of the gyroscope casing which reacted to the movement of the engine. Turning the controls altered the settings and this would be translated by large variations for the cannon. In this case, the control was turned the other way until the vibrations disappeared.

When the gyro-stabilization was activated, the pump put the hydraulic circuit under pressure which balanced the piston (4) in the actuator chamber (3). At the same time, the electric circuit fed the motor of the gyroscope wheel, which was set in fast motion by the axis (15). This is the dimension Z. The wheel maintains its rotational axis by means of the frames (6 and 8). These are dimensions X and Y. The settings coming from the stabilization controls (sensitivity and recoil) transit through circuits A and B and act on the

THE PRINCIPLE OF STABILIZATION

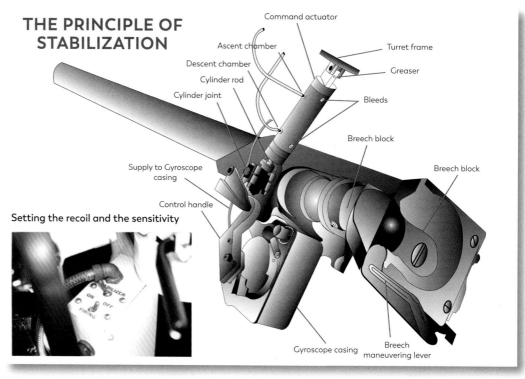

Command actuator
Ascent chamber
Descent chamber
Cylinder rod
Cylinder joint
Turret frame
Greaser
Bleeds
Breech block
Supply to Gyroscope casing
Breech block
Control handle
Gyroscope casing
Breech maneuvering lever

Setting the recoil and the sensitivity

control valve (1) to keep the piston (4) (fixed to the cannon cradle) in position.

- Regulating the recoil rheostat. At the moment the shot was fired, the cannon drew back, recoiling on its cradle, with the breech tending to plunge downwards. The rheostat regulated the cannon, keeping it horizontal during the recoil phase.

If the breech tended to drop, the control was turned to the right; the control was turned to the left if it was the opposite.

Bore sighting (as described by a Sherman turret gunner during the 1940s):

"On the right-hand side of the turret, at the gunner's post, I had very precise telescopic sights. To set them, you took a church steeple as a target at about 2,000 or 3,000 meters. You pulled back the gun's firing hammer and this gave you an opening of about 4mm. You set up two hairs crosswise over the mouth of the gun, held in place by grease. Taking a pair of binoculars and setting them, you tried to see the hair cross and the church steeple, if it was chosen as the target.

"By playing with the turret and the cannon elevation controls but without allowing anything to vibrate at all, the telescopic sights were loosened and with the help of the elevation handle, the cross on the sights was brought back—elevation 0—on the church steeple."

This was the so-called "campaign" procedure. When conditions allowed, bore sighting, a relatively meticulous operation, was carried out using sights calibrated on, and specific to, the tank involved.

During this operation, using the sights made the cannon, the coaxial machine gun, the telescopic sights, and, if installed, the telemetry, converge.

The Firefly turret

The British engineers did have a few little problems to solve before installing their QF 17-pounder cannon in the Sherman turret.

Originally the 17-pounder gun was an anti-tank gun on wheels. No problems of mass or size but to get it into the turret, the following had to be taken into account:

- the length of the barrel;
- the diameter of the firing brake actuators and recuperator;
- the length of these two actuators;
- the direction in which the breech block opened (originally horizontally);
- the barrel recoil when fired. The 17-pounder gun recoiled over 40 inches;
- balance of the gun in relation to the carriage.

To house all that in an M4 turret, the British had to reduce the length and diameter of the actuators, reduce the gun recoil, and pivot the gun itself through 90°, so as to load from the left, remove the voluminous SCR

508 radio sets from the turret bustle, and lengthen the turret with an armored chest holding the radio.

Typical of British tank organization, they added a chest to this new turret bustle. But not all the difficulties were solved. Indeed there was a problem with the cannon cradle. It had been reduced in size to get in through the mantle opening and it was now too light for the barrel length and unbalanced the gun. A new cradle thus had to be created, wider at the bottom; likewise the firing brake and recuperator actuators had been placed on either side of the barrel to make use of the greater width of the turret.

But that was still not the end of the problems!

In the M4 turret, the cannoneer got out by the split hatch like the gunner. When the 17-pounder was

THE M4A3 TURRETS

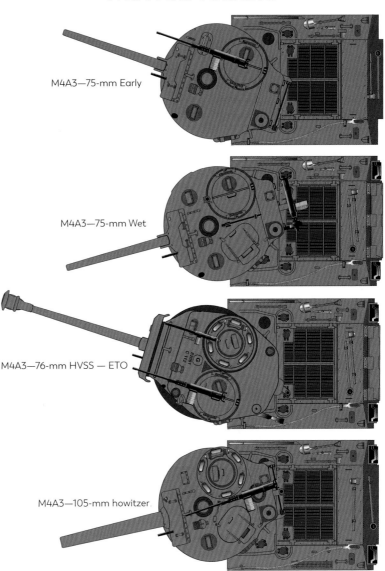

M4A3—75-mm Early

M4A3—75-mm Wet

M4A3—76-mm HVSS — ETO

M4A3—105-mm howitzer

1. View of the gunner's post. You can see the gun recoil protection, the forehead-rest of the telescopic sights, the elevation and bearing commands, and the azimuth indicator.
2. T Turret ETO improvement. Note the rudimentary mounting for the .30 caliber machine gun.
3. Handling the smoke mortar; in the foreground the gun's recoil guard.
4. Telescopic sight for the gunner.
5. The two models of tank commander's hatch: Split Hatch and Revolving Hatch. Note on the Revolving Hatch the presence of an azimuth indicator and a pointer.
6. The slip ring fixed under the turret and its principal components.
7. Welded over pistol port; all the hinged part has been suppressed.
8. Organization of a turret. The Track Grousers were removable additions to the tracks to improve "road holding" on soft ground.

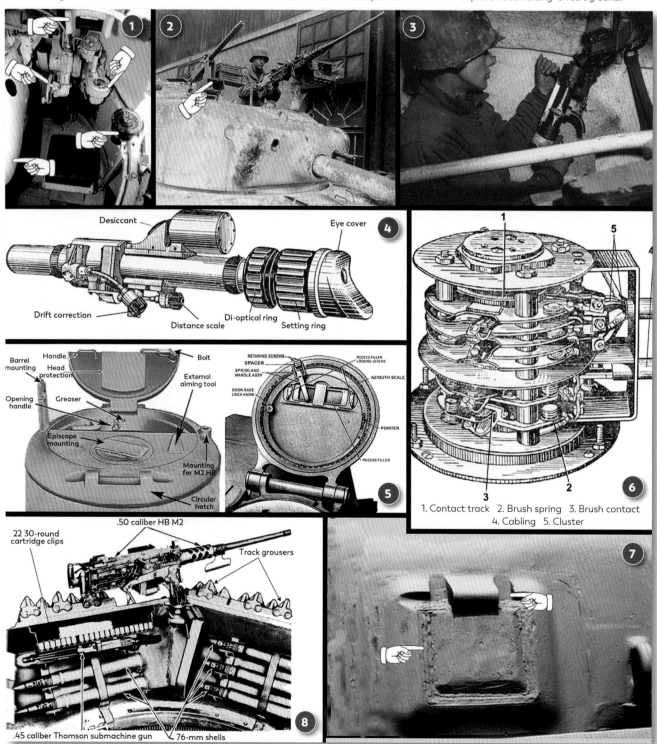

Desiccant

Eye cover

Drift correction

Distance scale

Di-optical ring

Setting ring

Handle

Bolt

Barrel mounting

Head protection

External aiming tool

Opening handle

Greaser

Episcope mounting

Mounting for M2 HB

Circular hatch

RETAINING SCREWS

SPACER

RECESS FILLER LOCKING LEVERS

SPRING AND HANDLE ASSY

AZIMUTH SCALE

DOOR RACE LOCK KNOB

POINTER

RECESS FILLER

1. Contact track 2. Brush spring 3. Brush contact
4. Cabling 5. Cluster

.50 caliber HB M2

22 30-round cartridge clips

Track grousers

.45 caliber Thomson submachine gun

76-mm shells

60

installed, the hatch was almost impossible to use. W.G. Kilbourn (the mastermind behind the modifications) made a separate opening on the cannoneer's side to enable him to get to his post more easily and more quickly. This cannoneer's hatch was rectangular and large.

The last modification on the turret concerned the disposition and the stowage of the emergency ammunition, since the 17-pounder shells were much longer than the original 75-mm ones. One might question the difference between 75-mm and 76.2-mm cannon. The performance lay not in the difference of millimeters but in barrel length and threads, and also the type of ammunition used. In the case of the 17-pounder, the initial velocity of its shells was very much greater than the 75-mm ammunition; a greater power of penetration due to the type of charge used gave this gun a combat elevation of 1,000 m, unlike the 75-mm's 850 m. This ammunition could therefore pierce 130-mm-thick armor under an angle of 30° at that distance.

Details of the Firefly turret are given in the section on the OP Command M4 tank, since the model was based on the turret modified by the British. In the case of OP Command tanks, the 17-pounder was replaced by a dummy wooden barrel. The Firefly conversions were carried out exclusively by the British up until December 1944 and mainly in the workshops of the Woolwich, Hayes, and Nottingham arsenals.

The Fireflies were a privileged target for enemy tanks because of the danger they represented, and very quickly the British thought up two ways of camouflaging the barrel (see the plate in the Firefly Chapter).

Solution 1

As the British cannon was about twice as long as the original 75-mm one, a false muzzle brake was fitted midway along the barrel, painted olive drab like the rest of the tank and the first part of the barrel up to the false muzzle brake; beyond it, the lower part of the barrel was painted white, including the real muzzle brake.

Solution 2

When the tank was used on the road, the turret was turned around to six o'clock, with the 17-pounder therefore facing backwards. On the additional radio chest at the back of the turret, the crew fixed a dummy 75-mm cannon and mantle, which gave the impression that the tank had a 75-mm cannon (facing forwards). The real 17-pounder was camouflaged with netting or branches.

This second solution was not used very much because it took too long to install the dummy gun at the front and then to set up the 17-pounder again later.

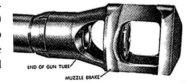

END OF GUN TUBE
MUZZLE BRAKE

Figure 2

RA PD 104379

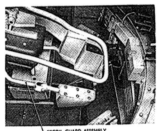

RECOIL GUARD ASSEMBLY

Figure 3

RA PD 104380

Supply of parts required:
(1) Source of supply: KIT, MWO-ORD C64-W1 (breechguard) Stock No. G104-5700274, from Anniston Ordnance Depot, Anniston, Alabama, by direct requisition on that establishment. The 76-mm muzzle brake M2, 7225946, and the 76-mm threaded gun tube D69297 should be requisitioned separately through regular supply channels.
(2) Date available: Now.
NOTE: Modification parts must be requisitioned on the basis of actual present requirements. Surplus stocks of modification kits created by departure of organizations whose equipment was to have been modified, or by other causes, are to be returned immediately to the issuing depot.

Weight and cubage:
(1) KIT, MWO-ORD C64-W1 (breechguard):
(a) Weight: 350 pounds.
(b) Cubage: 8 cubic feet.
(2) BRAKE, muzzle, M2 (76-mm):
(a) Weight: 87.5 pounds.
(b) Cubage: 1.5 cubic feet.
(3) TUBE, gun (threaded, 76-mm):
(a) Weight: 1,450 pounds.
(b) Cubage: 31 cubic feet.

Special tools, jigs and fixtures: None.

Special instructions:
Applied by: Ordnance mechanic.
Time required: From 2 to 10 man-hours, depending upon whether or not it is necessary to change the gun tube.

c. Procedure of operation:
(1) In order to accomplish this modification it is necessary that the tank be equipped with the THREADED gun tube. Most tanks are so equipped; however, if not, it will be necessary to remove the gun mount from the tank and change the gun tube. The gun mount is removed from the tank as follows. Remove:
(a) Top, bottom, and side splash plates on the front (outside) of the turret, surrounding mount opening.
(b) Elevation quadrant M9.
(c) Recoil guard.
(d) Co-axial machine gun cradle intact.
(e) Bracket holding gyro control box.
(f) Top and bottom pivot pins holding gyro piston cylinder (do not disconnect hydraulic lines).
(g) 76-mm firing solenoid assembly and electrical harness without disconnecting.
(h) Micro-switch and wiring intact from cam ejector bracket.
(i) Firing mechanism bracket.
(j) Telescope headrest.
(k) Direct sight telescope mount.

The "Jumbo" turret

The "Jumbo" version was not a medium tank but an assault tank. It therefore used explosive ammunition. This was why the tank kept its M3 75-mm cannon. Since it was required to face up to Tigers or Jagdpanthers, its specifications were increased, in particular its armor protection. The front glacis had extra armor added and the M4A3 E2 75 "Jumbo" had 152-mm armor around the turret and 25-mm on the top. The gun shield armor was 178-mm thick. The last models of Jumbos were equipped with 76-mm cannon.

The M4 Jumbos had neither road lights nor blackout lights.

One of the first T23 turrets mounted on an M4A1 76 W tank. (NARA)

5 Armament and Ammunition

1. The 90-mm cannon were used in the ETO at the end of 1944 on the M 26 Pershing and the TD M36s.

2. All the American documents of the period only mention the 1919 A4 model machine guns and we have not found a photo showing a 1919 A5. Likewise for the issue of ammunition: some talk about the Thompson collective comprising 20 30-round magazines, whereas there were 23 positions for stowing magazines. Ammunition packaging also varied. Thus for the 12.7-mm machine guns, some photos show boxes of 110-round belts and 105-round belts. Standard issue for the Sherman was 600 rounds of 12.7-mm, corresponding to six boxes, so 660 or 630 cartridges. Another document fixed the issue at six boxes of 50 cartridges. In this case, the crew had to put together two belts to reach 100 rounds, which corresponded to the contents of the M1 box to be mounted on the D 69820. Not very easy to see your way around all that.

Military vehicles and armor were equipped with varying types of armament depending on their use or mission. There were:

- Large-caliber weapons: cannon, heavy machine guns, mortars, smoke grenade launchers, and individual rocket launchers.[1]
- Small-caliber armament like the light machine guns, sub-machine guns, and handguns.[2]
- Specific armament like multiple rocket launchers, howitzers, 20- or 30-mm AA cannon, and flamethrowers.

As it was the Medium Tank M4 Sherman in service in the ETO (not including the Tank Destroyers and self-propelled guns), the cannon was a 75-mm, a 76-mm or a 105-mm caliber gun (of different models) capable of firing several types of ammunition. Some British, Polish, or Canadian M4s were equipped with the 17-pounder anti-tank gun, the Americans receiving several examples which they didn't consider particularly useful, since they were quite satisfied with their own 76-mm.

The arms in service aboard a Sherman and used in the ETO were designated:

BMG* US M2 HB*.50 cal. Browning Flexible also called *"Ma deuce"* or *"Fifty."*

SMG M1A1 .45 cal. ACP. Thompson submachine gun.

SMG M3 .45 cal. ACP *"Guide Lamp"* called *"Grease gun"* or *"Greaser."*

US 1911 A1 .45 cal. ACP Colt automatic pistol.

BMG US 1919 A4 Fixed, .30 cal.-06 Browning Coaxial or *Ball mount*.

BMG U.S 1919 A5 Fixed, .30 cal.-06 Browning. Machine gun. Post-1945 on French tanks.

BMG US 1919 A4, .30 cal.-06 Browning Flexible. Machine gun.

BMG US 1919 A6, .30 cal.-06 Browning. Light machine gun version.

AT M20 (Bazooka). Anti-tank weapon after World War II used by the French in the Recovery Units.

80-mm Mortar installed on the TRV and ARV

2-inch Smoke Mortar M3 fixed in turret.

75 M Cannon on M 34, M34 A1, or T110 gun carriages.

76 M A1, M1 A1 C, or M1 A2 Cannon on M 62 gun carriage.

105 M4 Cannon on M 52 gun carriage

To be more straightforward, we shall use the expressions ".50 cal." for the US M2 HB .50 cal., and ".30 cal." for the US 1919 A4 .30 cal. The 2-inch smoke mortar will be the smoke-grenade launcher.

The heavy machine gun in service in 1943 was the M2HB caliber .50 (50/100-inch or 12.7-mm). It was mounted on the M4 turret as an AA defense gun. In general, there were three positions, situated one on the circular part of the tank commander's hatch, one between the tank commander's and the cannoneer's hatches, and one towards the turret bustle, in the center. In this particular case, the M2HB machine gun could therefore be served from the rear deck too.

On certain Sherman models, there was another position called "Travel," which was a bracket on the turret bustle. This mounting was used when the tank moved around outside the combat zone and enabled the machine gun to be fixed on the turret with its ammunition box and its belt inserted ready for use, the barrel being held in place by a barrel clamp fixed to the turret roof.

All the machine guns in service on the M4s were equipped with a spare barrel, fixed on its support and attached at the rear of the turret. When not in use, the .50 cal. was held in the standby position by a barrel clamp attached to the turret roof on a swivel mounting.

The tank's equipment also included an M3 tripod so that the .50 cal. could be used on the ground. A bag of items including several spare components together with the cleaning and maintenance equipment was standard

The .50 cal. BMG M2 HB was mounted for AA use on the D 80030 mounting

The Colt .45 ACP 1911 was carried in a holster

The SMG Thompson .45 cal. was mounted above the SCR 508 with 30 20-round magazines

Spare barrel for the BMG M2HB

The SMG M3 Grease gun .45 cal. of the gunner and the loader was attached to the rear of the turret basket

Spare barrel for the BMG .30 cal.

The BMG 1919 A4 .30 cal. was mounted on the Ball Mount at the assistant driver's post

The M2 Smoke Mortar was mounted on the left of the loader, under the turret

U.S BMG 1919 A4

U.S BMG 1919 A5

The BMG 1919 A4 or A5 was mounted on the coaxial support on the left of the cannon

The SMG M3 .45 cal. Grease gun for the driver and the assistant driver were fixed on the sides of the gearbox

issue. When on the turret, the .50 cal. was mounted on a support consisting of the D 80030 cradle pintle and ammo box holder, specially developed for use on a tank. This assembly was easily recognizable by the big handle on the right-hand side for adjusting its balance spring.

The D 90077 ammunition box tray was added to the D 80030 assembly; it was a mounting intended to take the AMM .50 cal. M2 box. Sometimes, in particular on the "Early" turret versions, the D 80030 was equipped with a D 40731 Ammunition Box.

This box was attached to the mounting by two bolts and was filled with 50-round cartridge belts manually; this corroborates that the issue was for six 50-round boxes. These box-mounting assemblies were used on the M4 Medium Tank, the M36 Gun Motor Carriage 90-mm, the M24 Light Tank, and M26 Pershing.

This machine gun equipped other vehicles like Jeeps, Scout Cars, and Half-Tracks, in which case the mountings and the cradles were different depending on

the vehicle. When installed on a GMC CCKW 352/353, a Dodge Weapon Carrier, and AM M8s or M 20s, the M2 HBs were mounted on M32 or M36 circular carriages.

There were three main versions of the .30 cal. 06 light machine gun: the A4, A5, and A6.

The .30 cal. A4 was called "Fixed" or "Flexible": "Fixed" when it was installed on a vehicle, in which case the mountings varied depending on the vehicles' use and could be on the side, on a central column, or on a ring; "Flexible" when the machine gun was used with the Tripod US M2.

Only the M4A3s with Upgrade ETO had a .30 cal. A4 installed on the turret, in front of the tank commander's hatch. This time the 12.7-mm was installed in front of the cannoneer's hatch on the split hatch mounting, or between the two hatches.

On the M4s, a .30 cal. was installed at the assistant driver's post. This machine gun was installed on a ball mounting so it could be fired in any direction. The

Previous page: The turret of this M4 (M4A1) has been fitted with a British-designed split hatch. The circular addition reducing its diameter can be seen clearly. The two half-hatches are fitted with padding on the inside, as the British crews did not wear protective helmets. On the right of the turret is the solar compass support, used extensively in Libya. The outside focusing system for the telescopic sights was the "Late" type.

1 Spent cartridge bag
2 Sheath containing cleaning materials
3 Sheath for the spare .30 cal. barrel
4 Canvas belt for .30 cal. cartridges
5 Box of 30-06 ammunition
6 Comb wrench for the .50 cal.
7 Extractor for broken sheath (.50 cal.)
8 Headspace adjustment gauges
9 Glove for changing the .50 cal. barrel
10 Box of ammunition belts for the .50 cal.
11 Accessories for the .30 cal. A6, submachine gun version
12 Specific mounting for the .50 cal. for the 105-mm howitzer
13 .50 cal. on its travel lock with its protective sheath
14 RIA .30 cal. E1
15 RIA .50 cal. A5

Note the difference between the two arming levers

mounting was fitted with a system to hook it to the machine gun, allowing the belt to be inserted. There was also a bag for recovering the spent cases. The spare .30 cal. machine-gun barrel was clipped (in its canvas sheath) on the transom on the right of the assistant driver, above the three boxes of 250 cartridges strapped to the right sponson.

This weapon was used for fighting on the ground, and in this case it was mounted on the M2 tripod (crew drill FM for Medium Tank M4 series).

The .30 cal. A5 was derived from the A4 version and had a specific arming lever, longer and guided, permitting the cannoneer to rearm after loading another belt.

Mounting the machine gun coaxially next to the cannon didn't leave much room for handling the arming lever in normal conditions. This machine gun was fitted, however, with a foot-activated electric trigger in the gunner's post (*see plate above*).

The .30 cal. A6 machine gun was the light version: it replaced the famous BAR (Browning Automatic Rifle)

which was also meant to be mounted on vehicles, the Jeep in particular. It had a special fixture adaptable to column or offset mountings.

This A6 version could be equipped with a shoulder butt that was screwed onto the pistol handle. The same trigger was used. There was also a bipod that fitted on the front of the barrel, so it could be fired on the ground. A flame shield completed the assembly (*see the armament accessories plate*).

The M4s were issued with a .45 cal. Thompson ACP, or an 11.43-mm caliber. The use of this weapon was twofold: defending the tank at close quarters or fighting on the ground. It had 20 or 22 30-round magazines.

The .45 cal. M3 submachine gun was produced by Guide Lamp. It was better known as the Grease gun or Greaser. It was an 11.43-mm caliber, like the Thompson M1A1, and equipped the later American armored vehicles. It was standard issue for the driver, assistant driver, gunner, and cannoneer.

In the turret and at the driver's posts clasps were fitted to hold the weapon with its magazine (folder) in place when the tank was moving. The Colt 1911 A1 .45 ACP was the tank commander's weapon. It was an 11.43-mm caliber, with a seven-shot clip, plus a reserve of three clips.

Collective weapons were operated by more than one of the crewmen. The individual weapons were for each man's personal use and varied according to the man's job. The .45 cal. Thompson was put in a rack fixed above the tank's radio operator.

The crews did receive the ammunition needed for these arms but they also received their own combat issue of ammunition carried on their belts or over their shoulders. The ammunition was received in different types of packaging depending on the circumstances or on what was needed. It was up to the crew to reload the magazines or repack the boxes of cartridge belts.

Stowing the shells in the MA A4 (CN 75)

In "combat dress," the tank carried 96 75-mm shells stowed as follows:

8 rounds in a rack on the left sponson in front of the toolbox.

15 rounds in a rack on the right-hand sponson in front of the AA machine-gun ammunition caisson.

17 rounds in a rack on the right-hand sponson on the assistant driver's right.

30 rounds in the rack on the floor of the hull behind the manhole hatch.

8 rounds on the turret basket floor (under the cannon).

18 rounds in the magazines around the turret basket (emergency stock).

In the case of the M4 and the M4A1, there were eight rounds for emergencies. The M4A1 76 W had six. The M4A4 had 12 emergency rounds, of which eight were in a box under the cannon. In the case of the "Late" models, the A2 76W had six emergency shots. The M4A3 75 had eight, whereas the A3 75W had four. The M4A3 76 lined up with six emergency rounds and the 105-mm didn't have any emergency rounds at all.

The smoke grenades were stocked on the turret floor near the cannoneer's left foot; the number varied depending on the model of M4.

The different Sherman shells

The ammunition differed depending on the type of cannon (*see the tables "different M4 Medium Tank ammunition," pp. 66 and 69*).

From August 1944 onwards, the 76-mm cannon ammunition had a tungsten core inside an aluminum nose cone–the M93 HVAP. The 75-mm cannon equipped the A1s, A2s, A3s, and A4s. The 105-mm howitzer cannon only equipped the M4s and M4A3s.

The ammunition for the different Sherman guns was made mainly in the USA, but also in Britain for its Firefly or CN 75 versions. The British shells were totally different; originally the 17-pounder cannon was confined for anti-tank ammunition, as can be seen on the drawings on the following pages. All shells were identified by a color code as well as the writing on the shell cases or nose cones. This saved people from

Near Vicht in Germany on 17 November 1944, a Sherman from an unknown unit is used as a campaign artillery piece. The tank was nicknamed "Ink Spots." (NARA)

Holland, September 1944. Two Sherman M4A1 crew members—probably the gunner and the loader—are cleaning the 75-mm barrel of their tank using a standard issue ramrod. (NARA)

having to look for the right ammunition at the moment of firing, bearing in mind that the speed of reaction was a decisive factor during a tank battle.

The smoke, shrapnel, flare, or canister shells were generally placed in the rack under the cannon. The armor-piercing shells were on the emergency rack and the explosive shells on the rear right-hand rack.

The types of ammunition marked "Hypervelocity" were high muzzle velocity shells; those marked "Reduced" with a black stripe had a reduced propulsion charge; those marked "Normal" with a black stripe had a classic propulsion charge; and those with two black stripes around the word "Super" had a bigger propulsion charge.

The Americans generally used blue to identify training ammunition, whereas the British used yellow.

Ammunition carried in the M10 Ammo Trailers was transported in shell (nose cone and base) supports with three compartments without a crate and with padding. A metal caisson with compartments in which the shell rockets were stocked was fixed on the M10 trailer shafts. "Equipped" shells could not be transported in a trailer because of the very high risk of an uncontrolled explosion. These trailers could carry 117 x 75-mm, 44 x 405-mm, and 16 x 155-mm shells. A second hook was fitted to the rear so a second trailer could be hitched up.

The CN 76s and 17-pounders used the shells with highest muzzle velocities. They reached 1,200 m per second (for the British APDS).

Ammunition markings included inscriptions on the base of the shell and they stipulated:
- the lot number and the initials of the technician who made the charge;
- the shell case caliber and model;
- the shell case lot number and the technician;
- the production year;
- the weapon type and model firing the ammunition.

Packing and marking (containers)

The tank shells were packed by twos, in reinforced, hooped wooden crates with two rope handles at the ends. The shells were packed "assembled and complete."

On the crate, apart from the information applying to the ammunition it contained, were the shipment details like weight, volume, and AIC symbols (Ammunition Identification Code). All American ammunition crates were marked with a four-flame grenade.

How the shells worked

The Shermans fired different types of ammunition ignited by nose cone rockets. The drawings on page 65 show how they worked; this was in four phases.

Phase 1: Safety

The rocket is screwed to the shell nosecone, and the protection cover to the rocket. The arming levers are held in the "up" position by a compression spring. The locking segments are held "down" by the arming levers and the firing pin is locked in the standby position by its spring. The detonator is maintained in an retracted position by the locking cam.

Phase 2: the shot is fired

The protective fairing is of course removed. The inertia compresses the slide of the firing pin spring (by means of the arming lever), and this action frees the locking segments. The firing pin is held in place by its spring.

Phase 3: Trajectory

The locking segments withdraw totally. The slide spring sends the arming lever back to the "up" position (spring thrust). The trigger lock withdraws and frees the trigger, which places the detonator in a central position.

Phase 4 Impact

The protective fairing of the detonator is crushed on impact, compressing the firing pin retainer spring which itself hits the detonator, activating the charge in the container.

The gunner and the cannoneer of this M4A3 E8 76 are comparing the High Velocity Armor-Piercing (left) and the Armor-Piercing TNT (right) shells. (NARA)

Ammunition packing

The .30 and .50 caliber ammunition was packed differently.

The .30 cal. ammunition was packed in "light" wooden boxes (reinforced plywood) with hoops, secured with wire coils. Each box contained 1,100 rounds in four metal M1A1 containers. Each container comprised a belt with 275 rounds.

The .50 cal. ammunition was most often packed in a metal box of 105 rounds (Linked Belt); these boxes were fitted to the machine-gun mountings and had a runner to make feeding the belt into the receiver/lifter of the breech mechanism easier. The .50 cal. ammunition was delivered in "light" wooden boxes, each case containing two metal boxes or 210 cartridges.

Loose ammunition. All ammunition could be (but rarely was) delivered unpacked, the crews then having to make up the magazines and the belts themselves. The .30 cal. ammunition could be delivered in cases of 1,500 cartridges in six 250-round belts; these belts were then put into A1M1 metal boxes.

The .50 cartridges could be issued loose in M10 60-round light metal boxes. The .50 ammunition was then packed in cardboard sheathes, each containing five cartridges.

Aboard the Sherman, there were two machine guns, including the AA machine gun mounted on the turret, which was a Browning HB M2 .50 cal. The ammunition for the .50 cal. could also be delivered loose, in cartridges fitted with a ring for hooking onto, and making up, the belt. The extra M2 boxes (105 cartridges each) were attached to the inside of the tank in the following places:

On an M4A4: 315 cartridges in three metal 105 round boxes, all in the right-hand sponson, in front

Anatomy of a shell

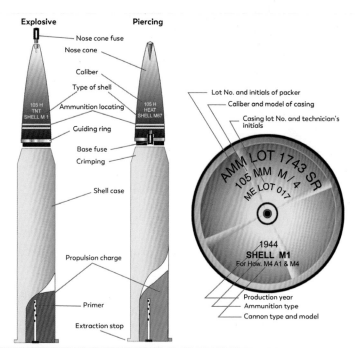

Explosive

- Nose cone fuse
- Nose cone
- Caliber
- Type of shell
- Ammunition locating
- Guiding ring
- Base fuse
- Crimping
- Shell case
- Propulsion charge
- Primer
- Extraction stop

105 H TNT SHELL M 1

Piercing

105 H HEAT SHELL M67

- Lot No. and initials of packer
- Caliber and model of casing
- Casing lot No. and technician's initials

AMM LOT 1743 SR
105 MM M/4
ME LOT 017

1944
SHELL M1
For How. M4 A1 & M4

- Production year
- Ammunition type
- Cannon type and model

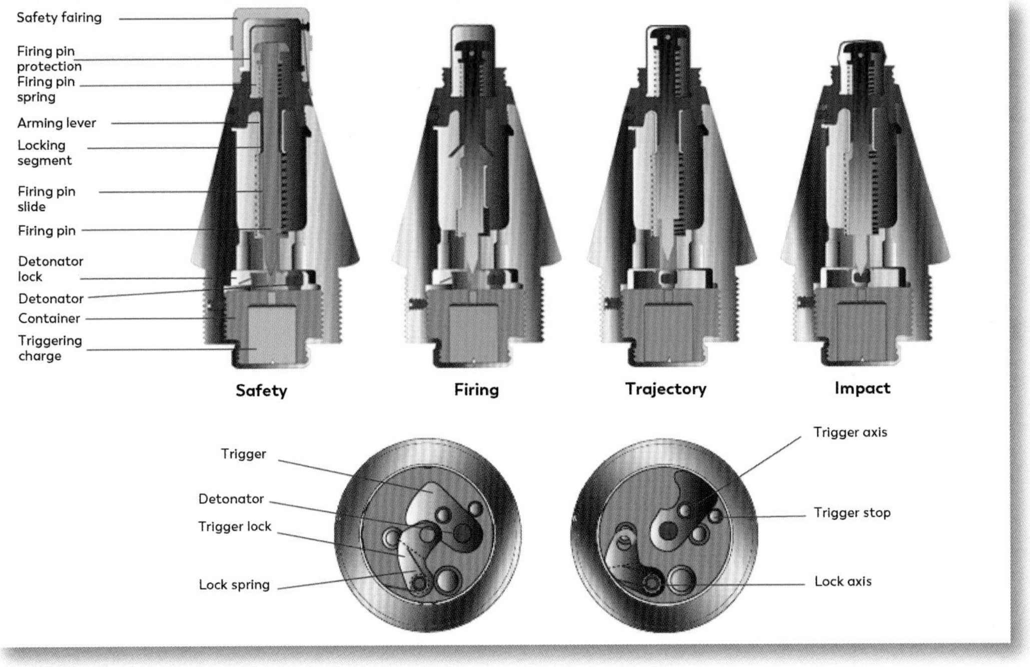
Safety fairing
Firing pin protection
Firing pin spring
Arming lever
Locking segment
Firing pin slide
Firing pin
Detonator lock
Detonator
Container
Triggering charge
Safety
Firing
Trajectory
Impact
Trigger
Detonator
Trigger lock
Lock spring
Trigger axis
Trigger stop
Lock axis

The four phases of an operational nose cone fuse

of the firewall; 315 cartridges in three boxes spread in three metal 105-round boxes, each strapped to the floor of the turret basket. Total 630 cartridges.

The .30 cal. M1919 A4 machine gun was installed to the left-hand side of the M34 or M34 A1 carriage. This was the coaxial gun, so-called because it moved at the same time as the canon.

A bracket fixed on the left under the smoke-bomb launcher held a box containing the cartridges belts. In the case of the M4A4, the box mounting was under the machine guns with a spent cartridge case bag.

.30 caliber ammunition: The boxes were dispersed as follows (applying to both Browning M 1919A4s):

- 5,500 rounds in 22 250-round disposable packing cases, stowed in a rack on the hull floor, in front of the battery case.
- 1,750 cartridges packed in seven 250-round disposable boxes, each stowed in a rack on the turret floor under the cannon.
- 250 rounds in the belt rack of the coaxial machine gun.
- 250 rounds in the rack in the assistant driver's post.

.45 caliber ammunition: 600 cartridges in 20 30-round magazines, the Thompson SMG's rack above the radio chassis.

Grenades: Four fragmentation grenades, two offensive grenades, and two smoke grenades in a case under the gunner's seat.

Two smoke grenades and two incendiary grenades in a case on the left side of the turret.

Signal rocket stowed in a case above the battery coffer:

- Three Type-M17 parachute flares
- Three Type-M18 white flares
- Three Type-M19 green flares
- Three Type-M21 amber flares

The differences between the M34 and M43 A1 gun carriages

On the M34 A1 gun carriage, the M55 or M70F telescopic sight was incorporated into the cannon mantle, which was not the case with the M34. A breech counterweight was added to compensate for the weight of the new barrel shield. A protective seal was also added to the telescopic sight.

Markings, techniques and marks on the wooden 76-mm shell box.

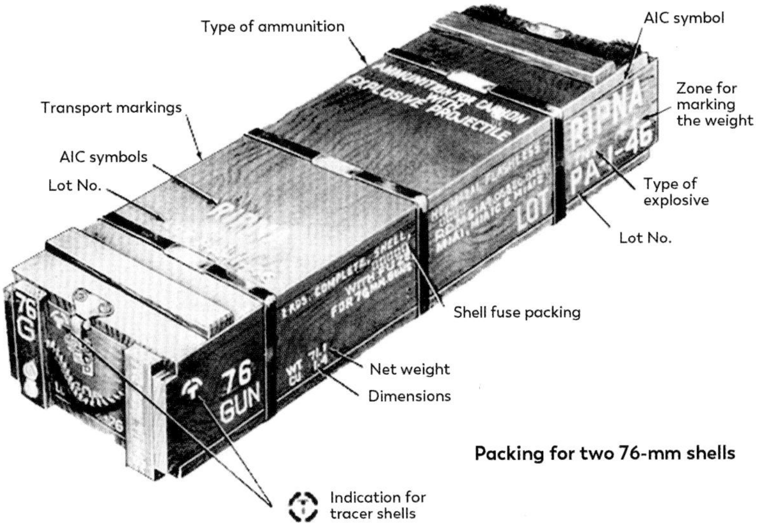
Type of ammunition
AIC symbol
Zone for marking the weight
Transport markings
AIC symbols
Lot No.
Type of explosive
Lot No.
Shell fuse packing
Net weight
Dimensions
Indication for tracer shells
76 GUN
RIPNA
PA-46

Packing for two 76-mm shells

Warhead rocket trunk
Handbrake
Blackout switch
Drawbar eye
Tow hitch
Handbrake
Stand
Taillight cable
RA PD 85019

Above: The different types of containers for shells.

Above, left: The M10 Ammunition Trailer

In a tank, the cannon ammunition was stowed away according to how it was used and to the firing sequences. In general, and for as long as possible, a stock of shells was held in the turret (in the emergency rack) for situations needing a quick reaction.

The ammunition stowed in the racks in the sponsons or on the turret floor was passed to the cannoneer by the driver or assistant driver, depending on the type of ammunition used: armor-piercing, explosive, incendiary, smoke, or exercise shells.

With the M4A2 or A3 75-mm cannon, the ammunition was taken from and used in the following order:

1. The turret racks.
2. The racks on the front left sponson.
3. The racks under the turret floor.
4. The racks on the rear left sponson.

The emergency shell racks and the shells stowed in the left-hand sponson were kept for rapid loading since they were easy to get at for the cannoneer, and as soon as possible the racks situated in the right-hand sponson and under the turret were used to refill them.

With the 76-mm cannon M4, the 76-mm shells were much longer than the 75-mm ones and the stowage areas needed modifying; there were three areas. Two diagonal stowage racks were located on the left-hand side of the transmission tunnel, one in front, the other at the rear. These were zones 1 and 2, situated in fact under the cannoneer's feet. The third rack, horizontally, was situated on the right of the transmission tunnel, behind the assistant driver. The supply zones were used in order, 1, 2, and 3. Zone 3 was used to fill up zones 1 and 2 as soon as the combat situation permitted. As with the 75-mm, using the emergency rack was reserved for quick loading.

The smoke-grenade launcher, M3 Mortar, was on the cannoneer's left.

Ammunition stowage: wet and dry

In all the M4 tanks, the shells were stowed "conditioned"—i.e. fuse, nose cone, cartridge, and primer already assembled, ready to fire—into the racks and containers. At the time, shells were fitted with central percussion and putting them into racks or containers meant the primer had to be protected,

PRINCIPAL AMMUNITION USED BY THE M4 MEDIUM TANK			
Cannon model	Ammunition Type	Ammunition weight	Muzzle velocity in m/sec.
75 M2 L31	AP	7,5 kg	563
	APC M61	7,5 kg	583
	APCBC	7,2 kg	584
75 M3 L40	APC	7,5 kg	615
	APC M61	7,5 kg	613
	AP		696
76 M1, M1A1, M1 A1C, M1 A2	APCT M62		787
	HVAP	7,8 kg	10,30
76 m1a1, m1 aé l55	APCBC	8 kg	787
	HVAP	7,8 kg	1030
105 M4	HE	18 kg	469
2 inches Mortar	M89	3,3 kg	260

ABBREVIATIONS USED FOR MARKING DIFFERENT AMMUNITION	
AT	Anti-Tank
BD	Base Detonating
BE	Base Ejection
HE	High Explosive
HEAT	High Explosive Anti tank
HV	High Velocity
HVAP	High Velocity Armor Percing
PD	Point Detonating
SQ	Super-Quick
AP	Armour Plercing
APC	Armour Piercing Capped
APCBC	Armour Piercing Ballistic Capped
APDS	Armour Piercing Sicarding Sabot

either with a cap or by removing it. The drawing at the top of page 65 gives the typical composition of a shell in service at the time.

The **nose cone fuse** was armed either when the shot was fired (inertia) or when it hit the target (kinetic). It was this fuse that triggered the charge (penetration for armor-piercing, fragmentation for explosives, phosphorus for incendiary shells, clouds of dark smoke for the smoke bomb).

The **nose cone** contained the destructive substances. The **shell case** was usually made of brass and contained the **primer** (activated by the firing pin) which ignited the propulsion charge.

The different methods of stowing cannon ammunition changed the way this ammunition was stocked.

Usually on the Sherman, the ammunition was split up between the left- and right-hand side sponsons, under the turret floor, and the emergency rack. The

CN 75

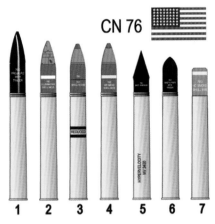

1 = High Explosive
2 = Armour Piercing Tracer
3 = Armour Piercing Explosive Fuse
4 = High Explosive M48
5 = Phosphorus smoke grenade
6 = Armor Piercing M72
7 = Smoke grenade

CN 76

1 = Armour Piercing TNT
2 = Eclairant
3 = High Explosive
4 = Phosphorus smoke device
5 = High velocity Armour Piercing
6 = Armor Piercing Tracer
7 = Smoke grenade

CN 105

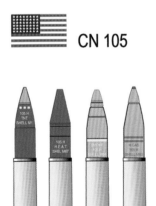

1 = HE M1 High Explosive
2 = H.E.A.T M67 High ExPlosive Anti Tank
3 = Smoke HC WP Fumigène White Phosphorus
4 = M60 Persistant Gas H

17 POUNDER

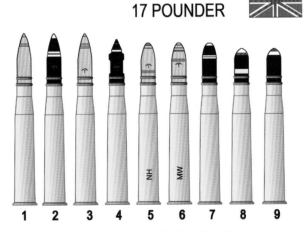

1= HE-T-HC High Explosive With Tracer
2 =Solid Armour Piercing Shot
3 HE-Hc- Super MK1
4= Armour Piercing Discarding Sabot
5= HE-T-MK 1 High Explosive With Tracer
6= HE-T-MK2 High Explosive With Tracer
7= Armour Piercing Capped Ballistic Capped
8= Armour Piercing Practice
9= Armour Piercing Capped

The sign ⇑ indicates a shell fitted with tracer.

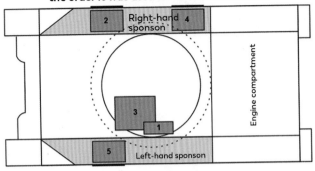

Stowing ammunition and the order it was used for the 75-mm cannon

2 Right-hand sponson 4
3
1
5 Left-hand sponson
Engine compartment

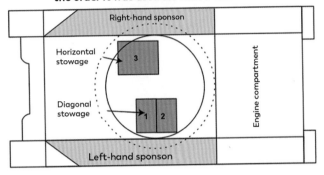

Stowing ammunition and the order it was used for the 76-mm cannon

Right-hand sponson
Horizontal stowage 3
Diagonal stowage 1 2
Left-hand sponson
Engine compartment

Ammunition distribution on the Shermans armed with a 75-mm or a 76-mm cannon.

stowage plan for the 75-mm and 76-mm cannon on page 68 gives the location of the shells for the CN 76 and the CN 75, and also shows the order in which the ammunition was used in both cases.

Note that the ammunition was transferred to the turret and the cannoneer's post by the gunner, the assistant driver, or the cannoneer himself in certain cases. In the case of "dry" stowage, the shells were placed in cavities arranged in a case, itself fixed to the stowage position.

These cavities protected the nose cone fuse from any "untimely arming" of the fuse in question. Likewise, the cavities protected the cartridge primer against any accidental percussion. The racks and the mountings gave access to the ammunition whilst holding it firmly during the tank's cross-country movements.

For the "wet" stowage, the racks comprised watertight cavities which were enveloped in a liquid solution which protected the shells in case the tank was hit. In that case, there was a fire but the ammunition also exploded. The liquid solution prevented the fire from spreading and the shells from exploding inside the tank.

In the case of a shell rack exploding, the shells exploded either by impact or in "sympathy" with the other ammunition in the tank. The "wet" mode took up more space so less ammunition was carried.

A Sherman Firefly crew from C Squadron, 1st Northamptonshire Yeomanry of the 33rd Armoured Brigade loading its heavy 17-pound shells into the racks installed in the machine-gunner's post. These racks could only be reached from the outside. (IWM B8793)

Type of Tank	Turret	Canon	Carriage	Shells	Bearing	Sight	AA Issue	Co-Axial and Hull Issue	Stabilisation	Smoke
TURRETS, ARMAMENT AND AMMUNITION FOR THE M4 TANK										
M4	T23	75 mm M3	97 of which 8ER	Manual and hydraulic	Manual from +25 to-10	.50cal. M2HB MG 300 rounds	2 x .30cal. M1919 A4 4750 rounds	Gyroscope	2" Mortar, M3 with 12 rounds -35°	
M4-105	T26	105 mm M4	M52	66 rounds	Manual	Manual from +25 to-10	.50cal. M2HB MG 600 rounds	2 x .30cal. M1919 A4 4000 rounds	No	2" Mortar, M3 with 12 rounds -35°
M4-105 HVSS	T26	105 mm M4	M52	66 rounds	Manual	Manual from +25 to-10	.50cal. M2HB MG 600 rounds	2 x .30cal. M1919 A4 4000 rounds	No	2" Mortar, M3 with 12 rounds -35°
M4 A1 Early	T23	75 mm M3	90 of which 8ER	Manual and hydraulic	Manual from +25 to-10	.50cal. M2HB MG 300 rounds	2 x .30cal. M1919 A4 4750 rounds	Gyroscope	No	
M4 A1 76 W	T26	76 mm M1A1 M1A1C-M1A2	M-62	71 of which 6ER	Manual and hydraulic	Manual from +25 to-12	.50cal. M2HB MG 600 rounds	2 x .30cal. M1919 A4 MG 6250 rounds	Gyroscope	2" Mortar, M3 with 12 rounds -35°
M4 A1 76 W HVSS	T26	76 mm M1A1 M1A1C-M1A2	M-62	71 of which 6ER	Manual and hydraulic	Manual from +25 to-12	.50cal. M2HB MG 600 rounds	2 x .30cal. M1919 A4 MG 6250 rounds	Gyroscope	2" Mortar, M3 with 12 rounds -35°
M4 A2	T23	75 mm M3	M34 A1	97 of which 8ER	Manual and hydraulic	Manual from +25 to-10	.50cal. M2HB MG 300 rounds	2 x .30cal. M1919 A4 MG 4750 rounds	Gyroscope	No
M4 A2 76 W	T26	76 mm M1A1 M1A1C-M1A2	M62	71 of which 6ER	Manual and hydraulic	Manual from +25 to-12	.50cal. M2HB MG 600 rounds	2 x .30cal. M1919 A4 MG 6250 rounds	Gyroscope	No
M4 A2 76 W HVSS	T26	76 mm M1A1 M1A1C-M1A2	M62	71 of which 6ER	Manual and hydraulic	Manual from +25 to-12	.50cal. M2HB MG 600 rounds	2 x .30cal. M1919 A4 MG 6250 rounds	Gyroscope	No
M4 A3	T23	75 mm M3	M34 A1	97 of which 8ER	Manual and hydraulic	Manual from +25 to-10	.50cal. M2HB MG 300 rounds	2 x .30cal. M1919 A4 MG 4750 rounds	Gyroscope	No
M4 A3 75 W	T23	75 mm M3	M34 A1	104 of which 4ER	Manual and hydraulic	Manual from +25 to-10	.50cal. M2HB MG 300 rounds	2 x .30cal. M1919 A4 MG 4750 rounds	Gyroscope	2" Mortar, M3 with 12 rounds -35°
M4 A3 76 W	T26	76 mm M1A1 M1A1C-M1A2	M62	71 of which 6ER	Manual and hydraulic	Manual from +25 to-12	.50cal. M2HB MG 600 rounds	2 x .30cal. M1919 A4 MG 6250 rounds	Gyroscope	2" Mortar, M3 with 12 rounds -35°
M4 A3 76 W HVSS	T26	76 mm M1A1 M1A1C-M1A2	M62	71 of which 6ER	Manual and hydraulic	Manual from +25 to-12	.50cal. M2HB MG 600 rounds	2 x .30cal. M1919 A4 MG 6250 rounds	Gyroscope In Sight	2" Mortar, M3 with 12 rounds -35°
M4 A3 105	T26	105 mm M4	M52	66 rounds	Manual	Manual from +25 to-10	.50cal. M2HB MG 600 rounds	2 x .30cal. M1919 A4 MG 4000 rounds	No	2" Mortar, M3 with 12 rounds -35°
M4 A3 105 HVSS	T26	105 mm M4	M52	66 rounds	Manual	Manual from +25 to-10	.50cal. M2HB MG 600 rounds	2 x .30cal. M1919 A4 MG 4000 rounds	No	2" Mortar, M3 with 12 rounds -35°
M4 A3 E2 Jumbo	T26	75 mm M3	T110	104 of which 4ER	Manual and hydraulic	Manual from +25 to-10	.50cal. M2HB MG 300 rounds	2 x .30cal. M1919 A4 MG 4750 rounds	Gyroscope en Site	2" Mortar, M3 with 12 rounds -35°
M4A4	T23	75 mm M3	M34 A1	96 of which 16ER	Manual and hydraulic	Manual from +25 to-10	.50cal. M2HB MG 300 rounds	2 x .30cal. M1919 A4 MG 7750 rounds	Gyroscope	No
M4 A4T	T23	75 mm M3	M34 A1	96 of which 18ER	Manual and hydraulic	Manual from +25 to-10	.50cal. M2HB MG 300 rounds	2 x .30cal. M1919 A4 MG 7750 rounds	Gyroscope	No
M A6	T26	75 mm M3	97 of which 8ER	Manual and hydraulic	Manual from +25 to-10	.50cal. M2HB MG 300 rounds	2 x .30cal. M1919 A4 MG 4750 rounds	gyroscope	2" Mortar, M3 with 12 rounds -35°	

The models M4 A3 75W and M4 A3 E2 Jumbo were those that carried the largest number of shells and the smallest in the emergency rack. Because of their function, the 105 versions had no emergency rounds.

ER = Emergency Round

6   The Sherman Crew

The crew consisted of five men with the following tasks.

In the turret

On the left-hand side there was the radio-operator/loader (or **cannoneer**), and as the name suggests, his job was to supply ammunition for the cannon and the coaxial machine gun, to get rid of the spent cartridges as and when needed, and to set off the smoke-grenade launcher. To these tasks was added the use of the radio set or sets depending on whether it was a normal tank or a command tank. In the first-generation turrets, the cannoneer got to his post by going through the tank commander's hatch. He had a fixed periscope at his disposal. He got in first. The cannoneer took part in everything to do with maintaining the turret, and in particular the coaxial machine gun. He had a box of grenades and the ammunition for the coaxial machine gun at his disposal.

In the sponson towards the rear, he could get to the auxiliary electric generator and the shell bin at the front. On certain M4 models, the battery rack was also in this sponson, whereas on other models the batteries were still fixed on the same side, but on the bottom of the hull. The floor of the turret basket under his feet had a hatch giving access to the stowage space for the shells. Finally, behind him on the right he had the emergency shells. On the left-hand side of the turret, above the spent case ejection slot was the smoke-grenade mortar.

On the right-hand side of the cannon was the **gunner**. His seat was placed at the bottom of the turret well and he had the pointing (elevation/bearing) and firing controls near him. The firing controls were by the gunner's left foot; they were electric; he opened fire with the cannon or the coaxial machine gun as the situation dictated. The coaxial machine gun could also be fired from the hydraulic turret controls. He got into the turret second by using the commander's hatch too.

When not fighting or moving around, the gunner did his part keeping the turret in good condition, performing tasks like checking the hydraulics and the condition of the targeting and firing systems, and greasing the M34 gun carriage.

The post of the **tank commander** was still on the same side, but slightly above the gunner. He had several periscopes for all-round vision (or one swiveling periscope mounted on the half-hatch), the

turret controls, a firing system, and an interphone and radio for communications. He could also use the AA machine gun.

Looking after and checking the cannon was everybody's job.

Inside the hull

The **driver** sat on the left-hand side on an adjustable seat, enabling him to drive with closed hatches using the driving periscope or the vision slots.

The starting, driving, and steering systems were set out all around the seat. The driver's hatch closed using a pivoting shutter on a hinge with two springs. The shutter had a system to lock it "open." Apart from driving the tank, the driver was tasked with looking after the engine and the hull. He was helped in this by the bow gunner. These tasks comprised checking all levels and refills for the engine, gearbox, and reduction gear, air filters, and radiators (on an M4A4 the cooling circuit contained 129 liters of water or anti-freeze, and the engine 30 liters of oil, with different viscosities depending on the ambient temperatures), not to mention the running gear and the outside accessories.

Behind the bow gunner's seat,[1] at the bottom of the hull was the (escape) manhole cover.

The **bow gunner/assistant driver** was on the front right-hand side and his hatch and seat were identical to the driver's. He had acquired the certificates enabling him to replace the driver if needs be and he was tasked with the tank's close defense since he had a machine gun mounted on the tank's bows. He and the driver were also tasked with checking the hull and its maintenance.

In the American Army, the crews were designated differently. They were the tank commander, the gunner, the bow gunner, and the radio-operator/loader was known as the cannoneer. These crewmembers climbed in, in a precise order.

Once at their posts, they each went through a checklist to verify everything: the presence and working order of the weapons, the radio installation, the hydraulic system, ammunition, unlocking various things, fastening accessories, etc.

The crew members knew the roles and tasks of all the other crew members; they had to. Remember that the crew was a cohesive unit, used to Spartan conditions but, above all, the tank men reacted to different situations in ways which had been tested many times

---

1. This set-up was used a lot by the Marines in Korea; they used it to recover the wounded who were under enemy fire.

and were proven. This way of life created links between the crew members because they all knew each other.

In the 1940s, in order to reach a very high level of preparation, the crews were put through drills. During these drill sessions, the movements were repeated a hundred times and perfected. Driving, observation defilade, firing defilade, firing guns, or anti-aircraft watch; nothing was left to chance. And when the mission was over, the tank had to be serviced, the fuel topped up, ammunition restocked, getting ready for the next mission. These drills were subsequently given the name of "crew school."

In order to make all these preparations, the crews did have documentation at their disposal; with a typically military concern for detail and efficiency, these documents told them all they needed to know, how to do it, and when to do it. For the Sherman tanks these documents were of course drawn up in English and the M4A3 crews consulted the "FM 17-67 Crew drill and service" published by the War Department.

The crew of an M4A3 (76) of the 31st Tank Battalion of the 7th US Armored Division. The bow gunner must be feeling the cold as he is wearing a padded jacket and a "beanie." *(Signal Corps)*

The initials FM stood for Field Manual. This document was usually accompanied by a TM (Technical Manual).

For the M4A4s served by French crews, there was a version translated into French; this was the "TM96754 FR" (FR for French) published by the Ministry of War in 1943. Whereas the Field Manual told them how to embark and how to evacuate through the manhole, how to prepare the tank, and the firing sequences, the TM described the procedures dealing with servicing, repairs, and checking all the technical parts of the vehicle. Thus from the radio antenna right down to the tracks, or from the front to the exhaust, everything was checked, set, and lubricated.

It was unimaginable to train a crew without using these manuals. Take for example getting the tank ready for a combat mission. All the various types of ammunition—right down to the hand grenades—and weapons had to have their precise place so that, even in the dark, the crew could find them, use them, or even dismantle and reassemble them. The same thing applied to binoculars, individual weapons, spare periscopes, or individual rations. The pool tools, or the pioneers' gear, were set out on the rear deck, whereas the tools for general repairs were stowed in the appropriate boxes.

Spare parts, like the extra track links, were fastened to the superstructure along with all sorts of protection that the crew chose to put there. The same applied to any extra ammunition which the crew took aboard. The on-board documentation also included a logbook, which recorded all the tank's movements (dates, mileage, and routes) but also all the different tasks that had been carried out—periodic maintenance and settings. The gun also had a logbook to be kept up to date, in which the types of shells fired and the various operations carried out were noted.

Crew tasks

Keeping military vehicles in top condition was the role of different echelons. The first level was for the crew, the direct users. These operations were divided into three categories:

1. Checks
2. Maintenance
3. Small repairs

The checks were a list of operations to be carried out before the tank left, when it halted, and at the end of the mission. Before setting off, it was a matter of making sure the various tank components were "operational," i.e. ready for combat.

The checks

Each crew member had to carry out a set of checks round the outside of the tank, such as making sure there were no leaks, that the running gear was in order, and that the various items of equipment and external weapons were there and properly fastened to the superstructure.

On the inside they had to check that the cannon ammunition, the machine guns, the individual weapons, different categories of hand grenades, optical equipment, and radio sets were all present and stowed properly.

Maintenance

This was a series of operations needing partial dismantling, which could be done by the crew who had the necessary tools aboard, and included checking levels, dismantling and servicing the filters, and lubricating all the moving parts following the lubrication order with the on-board documents.

Small repairs

These included changing the spark plugs (on the petrol engines), the bulbs and fuses, setting the firing mechanisms on the automatic weapons, checking track parts or running gear wheels, replacing defective optical instruments, or replacing radio accessories by using those stowed in the "radio quiver"*.

The higher echelons were responsible for the more important operations and repairs needing specific tools the tank did not carry. Note that on military vehicles the on-board tools comprised all the pioneers' gear (consisting of a towing hook, shackles and coupling plates, towing cable, axe, spade, pick, sledgehammer, and crowbar), together with the engine crankshaft, the track tightening spanner, a camouflaging net, and a tarpaulin.

Still with the aim of having as high an operational readiness as possible, these maintenance operations were to be done at regular intervals. The checklists gave details of what servicing was to be carried out after every 25, 50, or 100 hours of operations, remembering that the 100-hour services were time-consuming and complex, needing the engine or even sometimes the turret to be removed.

These operations were noted in the tank's log book.

Servicing to be carried out

For the checks and equipment, each Sherman crew member had a list of operations to do so that nothing was missed out when the tank was got ready for operations. These tasks were shared out among the crew as follows:

The **driver** made sure he had a portable fire extinguisher, a torch, a set of three pennants, a pair of

goggles with three spare Plexiglas lenses (plain, yellow, and dark green), a pair of gloves, a tool bag containing a hammer, a pair of universal pliers, cutting pliers, two screwdrivers, monkey wrench, adjustable spanner, and a set of socket wrenches with accessories, his radio equipment comprising a T 30-Q laryngophone, a CD 507 cable, a CD 318 cable, a SW 41 transmitting cable, M38 tank headphones, and two HS 14 earphones. All crew members had these. The tank commander also had a T-17 microphone, a BC 60 amplifier, and a set of HS 18 earphones.

A Sherman M4A2 seen from above. A second hatch for the purveyor appeared on the turret in 1943. (*Tank Museum 2717/B2*)

Cape Gloucester, New Britain, 1943: the driver of a US Marines Corps M4A1. Note his tankman's helmet, the oldest model. *(US Signal Corps)*

Opposite, top: The driver's access hatch, seen from the inside. *(TM 9-748, 162-163)*

Opposite, bottom: The No.22 Manipulator had several functions:

The switch on the top was for cutting, starting, or testing the magnetos. The bottom left-hand switch controlled the boosters (ignition intensifiers) and the right-hand switch the starter. So, to start the engine, the driver:

1. Activated the starter switch making sure that the engine ran normally.
2. Put the magneto switch on "Both."
3. Pushed both bottom switches simultaneously inwards to "On" (combined action on the boosters and the starters). The engine starts. The L and R positions are for testing the ignition ramps. *(Drawing by the author)*

The **assistant driver** checked that all the following were present: the tarpaulin, the pioneers' gear, a portable extinguisher, the crankshaft, the track tightening spanner, a set of fastening straps, the first aid kit (bandages), the .30 cal. machine-gun tripod and its cover, the billet nose cone cover on the bow machine gun, the .30 cal. machine gun, the spare barrel for the bow machine gun and its sheath, a pourer spout for the jerrycan, a 10-liter water bag, and his radio equipment.

The **cannoneer** checked that the following were all present: interphone and radio systems, mobile extinguisher, six M6 periscopes, six boxes of .30 cal. ammunition belts, three boxes of .50 cal. cartridge belts, a 20-liter jerrycan, a cover for the coaxial machine gun, a cover for the AA machine gun, the AA machine-gun mounting, the .50 cal. Browning machine gun, the servicing bags for the .50 cal. Browning and .30 cal. coaxial machine guns, the radio quiver containing among other things spare antenna wires, the cables, and his radio equipment.

The **gunner** checked that the following were all present: his M4 periscope and its spare, a bag of specific tools, a canvas breech cover, the muzzle cover, the rods of the ramrod, the pads for the cannon, oil burette, a TL 122 Lamp, a T17 microphone, and his radio equipment.

The SCR 508, 528, and 538 type radios were dealt with in the TM 11600.

The crew's viewpoint

There are two things which men always argue about: theory and practice. Producing the Sherman was no exception to this rule, be it for using the equipment daily or in combat. What was written in the manuals, be it technical or didactic, was not therefore always applied, or not well, or only partly.

This was due to several factors:

1. The experience gained by the crews

The manuals stipulated that, for example, checks were to be done at very precise time intervals. Each crew member had therefore to do his checks before, at a halt, and after the mission. Although these checks—even though there were a lot of them—were easily done in peacetime or during training, when in combat or moving through an insecure zone it was all quite different. It was logical, therefore, for one or several checks to be "missed out," meaning the tank was not out of action.

With time these omissions turned into "experience" and practice took over from theory, the crew changing into an experienced and conscious user and their experience replacing the manual. Naturally, military rigor at the time would not tolerate these "adaptations" but, having insisted on applying the texts strictly, everybody accepted theses practical "changes."

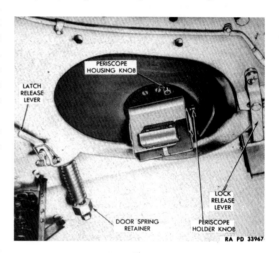

2. Modifications made to the equipment

It is only when something is put to use that you see how good it is. Before series production started, the prototypes were put through their paces, on the test benches or over wide-ranging types of terrain. Even so, all these tests could not replace using the tank in combat conditions, in varying weather conditions, over different types of terrain, and with beginners' lack of experience. In brief, for as long as the user hadn't broken the tank, got it bogged down, or missed his target, the machine was not at its best, performance-wise. Moreover, it was at moments like these that the crew's experience mentioned above came into play, and this experience was taken into account with the modification projects which saw the light of day. Thus, using HVSS running gear solved the ground pressure problem but also made driving comfort and tank behavior better when on the move. The same thing applied to ammunition stowage, or the type used.

The accessory fixtures or positions also changed, for example, for the jerrycan holder, the outside telephone, powerplants, armored chests, and first aid kits.

3. The real performances of the machines

The type of engine the various Sherman models used changed but did not necessarily evolve. The 30-cylinder Multibanks was less powerful than the Ford V8. The A4s intended for the Allies always had a 75-mm cannon, whereas the British equipped theirs with the 17-pounder cannon. The Americans spurned the Duplex Drives and the Russians preferred the M4A2 to all the other models.

4. The—rare—omissions in documentation

The American documentation was complete, detailed, and well-structured. There were, however, some gaps in the documents relating to specific materiel. This was the case for the Dozer versions whose models were equipped with a Bulldozer blade or one made by Caterpillar.

The same applied to the flamethrower version.

5. The means (financial or logistical) used

War effort cost money. In spite of all the imperatives, the purse strings had at times to be held firmly. The result of these economies could be seen mainly in how the sub-contractors were selected, especially those producing components. Where logistics were concerned, the US Army had a huge organization, but at any particular moment the supply chain could break down, with dire and often dramatic consequences on men and equipment.

6. The circumstances in which the units were engaged

It is obvious that a crew driving out of an LCT under fire with the risk of getting bogged down in the sand or sinking reacted differently from the one taking part in the fighting in the Ardennes with very low temperatures and almost zero visibility. Likewise for the vehicles which found it more difficult to move forward in water or on soft ground, or in 50-cm of snow at -20°C.

Fitting out the crew positions

The driver and the bow gunner had different dashboards. Several tank versions meant different dashboards versions. The illustrations on the following pages give an idea of the different models that were fitted.

The M4 dashboard

With the A1s, it was the simplest dashboard and although it dated from before 1941—it was already fitted in the M3—it was not pared down and had all it needed for driving a tank and for controlling the engine. Button No.20, called "degasers," was used to stop the engine. This was a command that cut the idling circuit on the carburetor using a solenoid. Indeed, if the engine was stopped by switching off the magnetos, the crankshaft continued to turn, causing the cylinders to also move, taking in fuel, which caused a problem the next time the engine was started with a risk of flame out or buckling connecting rods.

The driver's post seen from front left. *(Private collection, DR)*

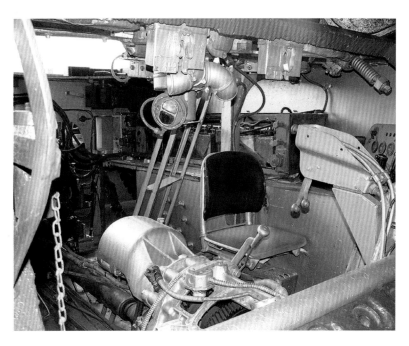

THE DRIVER'S DASHBOARD

M4

M4 A1 LATE

M4 A2 & TD M10

M4
1   24 V plug for accessories (windshield, portable light)
2   Light switch
3   Battery contact
4   Degaser fuse
5   Lighting fuse
6   Accessory fuse
7   Main lighting fuse
8   Siren fuse
9   Warning light
10   Lighting switch
11   Fuel tank selector
12   Tank gauges
13   Cooling liquid temperature
14   Transmission high temperature warning light
15   Engine oil temperature
16   Ammeter
17   Dashboard light
18   High water temperature and low oil pressure warning lights
19   Rev counter
20   Degaser command
21   Tachymeter
22   Magneto and starter commands

M4A1 Late
1   Blackout command
2   Accessories plug
3   BO drive fuse
4   Roof light fuse
5   Magneto fuse command
6   Engine pressure and temperature fuse
7   Transmission temperature fuse
8   Carburetor gauge fuse
9   Voltmeter fuse
10   Injection pump command
11   Magneto switch
12   Degasers
13   Main lighting command
14   Voltmeter
15   Ammeter
16   Lighting selector
17   Clock
18   Tachymeter
19   Dashboard lighting
20   Tank selector
21   Fuel gauge
22   Transmission temperature

23   Engine temperature
24   Engine oil pressure
25   Low engine oil pressure warning light
26   RAZ km counter
27   Rev counter
NB   The clock wasn't always there. It was then replaced by a metal insert.

M4A2 & TD M10
1   Accessory plug
2   Left-hand starter command
3   Emergency stop
4 & 5 Injection circuits contactors
6   Right-hand starter command
7   Emergency stop
8   Accessory plug
9-15 Fuses
16   Right bank injection warning light
17   Left bank injection warning light
18   Right bank injection command
19   Left bank injection command
20   Lighting command
21   Road lighting command
22   Blackout command
23   Clock
24   Right-hand engine rev counter
25   Ammeter
26   Voltmeter
27   Left-hand engine rev counter
28   Fuel tank selector
29   Dashboard lighting
30   Fuel gauge
31   Left-hand engine temperature gauge
32   Left-hand engine oil pressure manometer
33   Low oil pressure warning light
34   Tachymeter
35   Low oil pressure warning light
36   Right-hand engine oil pressure manometer
37   Right-hand engine temperature thermometer
38   Transmission oil temperature thermometer
39   Kilometrage reset

M4 A3 75W

M4 A3 75W AND 76

M4 A4

M4A3 75

A 24-volt plug
B Starter
C Manual injection pump
D Lighting blackout command
E Road lighting command
F Magneto selector
G Degasers command
H Right-hand accessories fuse
J Left-hand accessories fuse
K Blackout fuse
L Siren fuse
M Degasers fuse
N Instrument fuse
O Clock
P TB lighting rheostat
Q Ammeter
R Voltmeter
S Transmission oil temperature
T Rev counter
U Engine oil pressure
V Low engine oil pressure gauge
W Engine oil gauge
X Tachymeter
Y Engine oil temperature
Z Fuel tank selector
AA Fuel gauge
BB TB Lightning

M4A3 75 WS and 76

1 Right-hand accessories circuit fuse
2 Siren fuse
3 Left-hand accessories circuit fuse
4 Blackout fuse
5 Degasers fuse
6 TB instruments fuse
7 Fire detection circuit fuse
8 24v plug
9 Magneto selector
10 Road lighting contactor
11 Starter

12 Blackout lighting contactor
13 Degasers command
14 Fire warning light
15 Fire circuit test circuit warning light
16 Fire circuit test circuit contactor
17 Rev counter
18 Voltmeter
19 Ammeter
20 Clock
21 TB lighting rheostat
22 TB lighting
23 Transmission oil temperature
24 Engine oil level
25 Engine oil pressure
26 Low oil pressure warning light
27 Tachymeter

M4A4

1-6 Fuses
7 Road lighting contactor
8 Blackout lighting contactor
9 High exhaust temperature
10 Fuel tank selector
11 Starter
12 Low engine oil pressure
13 24v plug
14 High temperature cooling
15 Clock
16 Selector
17 Ignition contactor
18 Oil pressure manometer
21 Selector
22 TB lighting
23 Fuel gauge
24 Tachymeter
25 Ammeter
26 Voltmeter
27 Rev counter
28 Temperature
29 Daily RAZ counter

Besides, everybody knew that cutting off the ignition and starting it again caused a nice deflagration, especially for those who were not far from the exhaust pipes.

Over the degasers control was a plate explaining how to stop the engine: return to idling speed, maintain the speed at 1,100 revs, press on the button, and return to idling speed at the same time. Having the engine running at 1,100 rpm, was to keep the generator outputting during the engine cut-out procedure, bearing in mind that, in the best of cases, a generator starts producing at 900 rpm, unlike the alternators which produced at idling speed (500 rpm).

M4A1 dashboard

On the A1 the dashboard was rethought. The starting manipulator and the degaser control were still there, because the tank still used the Continental engine. On the other hand, keeping an eye on the engine group and choosing the fuel tank when filling were improved.

Transmission temperature could be watched. Dashboard lighting was improved and fitted with a rheostat. There was also a clock (well, yes, it was an American tank!), but this was not installed systematically.

M4A2 dashboard

This was totally different from the A1's because it had a diesel engine. Moreover, the powerplant consisted of two coupled engines so the instruments were doubled up: temperature, pressure, rev counter, emergency stops, starters, and preheat circuit.

M4A3 and A3 "Late" dashboard

This dashboard was for watching over and controlling the Ford V8, so there was a new ignition contactor with a modified booster function; the degasers reappeared and the Utility Outlet plug was doubled.

M4A4 dashboard

In this case there were the five banks of the Chrysler engine that had to be watched. On top of the usual pressure and temperature instruments, a group of five captors took the temperature at each exhaust outlet and a high temperature light set off an alarm on the dashboard.

The Driver's Post

How the driver's and bow gunner's posts were fitted and laid out depended on the Sherman model.

Commands and checks

On the driver's side of course were the driving and other controls.

Driving elements

In front of the driver were the two steering and braking levers, the driving "head down" (or "closed hatch")

This artillery observer is scrutinizing the Ardennes forest from the tank commander's turret hatch of an M4A3. (*Signal Corps*)

periscope, the hand accelerator, and the manual injection control. In the case of the M4A2, this was where the two manual accelerator levers and their locking control were situated. In the lower part were located the clutch pedal, the small light/headlights reverser, and on certain models the siren control pedal, and the steering lever blocking pedal[2] in "braked" position. The M4 model had a "starter"* command on the left side of the driver's post.

On the right-hand side were the gear lever, the PM M3 Grease gun mounting, the rack for the four spare periscopes, and six periscope heads; above the rack was the folding windshield (to protect the driver if he had to drive with his head outside during violent storms, fog, snow, etc.). This windshield comprised a glazed armature fitted with a windscreen wiper and de-icing. A waterproof canvas gusset made up the ensemble. This gusset folded down behind the pilot's nape, thus shutting off the hatch opening which was locked in the open position. The windscreen wiper motor was powered from the dashboard using the Utility Outlet plug for just that purpose. There was also a connections box between the interphone and the radio set. The ventilation control was located between the driver and codriver seats.

The radio connection boxes were identical for all the posts: a connection for the micro and radio helmet, a voltage light, a volume control, and a two-position manipulator (a radio position and an interphone position). The tank commander's box had an extra position (radio/interphone), enabling him to go onto both networks at the same time.

On the driver's right was also the gearbox with its gauge, filler and drain plug, the rev counter, and tachometer plugs.

On the left, towards the front were the dashboard, a navigation compass, and a gyroscopic compass (so it could function in a metallic environment). The mounting and the lamp were plugged into the dashboard utility outlet; the 24V box comprised a battery circuit breaker, a radio circuit breaker, an outside plug socket (used to recharge the batteries or even start the engine if the batteries were low), and the generator regulating box. In the driver's and bow gunner's areas there were also various greasing and lubrication points.

Working conditions

The driver had a bit more space because of his function in the tank. The driving controls and instruments were spread out for ease of use and comfort. His seat was wider than the others, and was fitted with an adjustable back. This seat was adjustable upwards and sideways, so the tank could be driven in the heads down (hatch closed) position. On the right, the gearbox lever was equipped with a safety pawl which enabled the driver to put the tank deliberately into reverse gear only.

When the seat was in the lower position, activating the lever was also less easy (the handle was at shoulder height). When the driver moved the tank with the hatches down he could see through the driving periscope, and although this could be adjusted both in bearing and elevation, he had to handle it with his left hand in certain situations (bends, steep climbs, descents); driving was not made any easier since, unlike with a steering wheel, the right hand had to deal with both steering levers at the same time and if he had to change gears, we get an idea of the agility needed to drive the tank.

From the next generation onwards, the tanks were equipped with a three-periscope system in the driver's post, recalling the three windows of the driving cupola.

In the driver's immediate vicinity was the propeller shaft (it went through the whole combat compartment), which made a deafening noise, particularly in the low gears. Adding to that were all the other noises generated by the tank and heard by all the crew. The main sources of unbearable noise were the clacking of the tracks and the clicking of the running gear, the whistling of the ventilators evacuating the smoke from all the shooting, the noise from the hydraulic generator for the turret, and the noise from the engine.

All the crew members wore radio equipment and sometimes received their communications on the interphone or radio amid a lot of interference, with the transmitter's background noise (especially when the squelch was badly set), whistling from the frequencies, etc.

The Bow Gunner's Post

In certain cases, the bow gunner was called the driver/radio; this was in a tank fitted with an SCR 506 (or another) radio system mounted in the right-hand sponson near the bow gunner. The A4 .30 cal. machine gun was mounted on a ball mount (type D 51070). This machine gun was in front of the bow gunner's seat and was fitted with a spent cartridge recovery

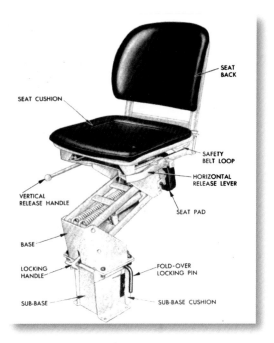

The bow gunner's seat (TM 9-748, 162-163)

2. Depending on the model of M4, the blocking pedal was replaced by a lever which blocked the transmission at the entry to the gearbox. It was the case on the M4A3 where the lever was in the lower part, to the right of the driver. In the case of the M4A2, the linkage system for the clutch pedal commanded both clutch forks at the same time.

case. The spare barrel of the .30 cal. machine gun, in its canvas sheath, was fastened on the bow gunner's right, against the side of the sponson. The bow gunner's position also included a portable fire extinguisher, .30 cal. ammunition, a shell rack in the sponson, and at the rear, stowage space for fastening down boxes of individual rations and a spare hatch periscope.

The M3 Grease gun was fastened like the driver's, above the transmission, to the left of the bow gunner. Still on the left, attached in the upper part was the radio/interphone connection box, a roof light, and a mounting with clasps holding a Type TL 122 torch.

In the upper part, between the driver and the bow gunner (depending on the Sherman model), were the fixed fire extinguisher controls. Behind the bow gunner's head, high up, was the hatch lock handle; for the driver, his handle was in the same place. Behind the bow gunner's seat, on the floor of the hull, was the manhole (escape) plate*. In the tank there were places

marked "Canteen" where the soldiers hooked up the individual flasks usually hanging from their belts.

Working conditions

The bow gunner's seat was like the driver's and his post was similar to the driver's. Having gained the same certificates as the driver, he could, if needs be, replace him if the situation allowed or required. He could also use the extra radio set when the tank had one. The bow gunner helped transfer shells on the rack on his right (in the sponson). He also served the bow machine gun, looked after loading it, and changed the barrel when necessary. The machine-gun barrels were changed after a certain number of shots had been fired continuously, whether it was the .30 or .50 caliber gun.

The bow gunner was also tasked with setting up the portable fire extinguisher near him. He also helped to keep the tank in working condition and do the necessary repairs with the driver. With the tank moving

This tank commander, sitting on the turret of his tank, an M4A1, is cleaning the barrel of his Thompson submachine gun, very quickly replaced by the M3 A1 Grease gun which took up much less room inside a tank. (*US Signal Corps*)

around with the hatches shut, he did the observing and guided the driver on his right. On the M34 and M4A1 models, the bow gunners turned their seats around backwards to get to the shells more quickly and easily, and hand them through the turret basket. Other bow gunners chose to remove the seat back, making it easier to move from serving the front machine gun to loading the shells.

The turret crew consisted of three men and each had very precise tasks to perform. They all had different equipment, although some installations were doubled up, like, for instance, the emergency stop system, the radios, the turret command, and many others.

The Tank Commander's Post

The tank commander had an emergency system for stopping the engine on the firewall, accessible from the turret. This system directly controlled the circuit-breakers for the idler (on the A3). He also had a control for the turret hydraulics (according to the type of M4). The vision equipment varied according to the type of turret: on a turret equipped with a single two-flap hatch, the tank commander had a 360°-swiveling periscope. The tank commander's cupola, equipped with six fixed periscopes giving a panoramic view, replaced this hatch on later models. The central part included the hatch itself, on which a swiveling periscope was mounted.

In his post, the tank commander used either the radio or the interphone network, a connecting box

enabling him to select the type of network he wanted to use. There were some hooks near this box on which to hang the head equipment (headphones, microphone, and cords) when not in use. He also had the air-to-ground panels under the radio chassis in their stowage sheath.

On the right-hand side of the turret, on a level with the turret drive was an azimuth indicator. This could be used by the gunner, who could use the cannon as an artillery piece. A tank cannon fired different types of ammunition. The armor-piercing shells (the majority)

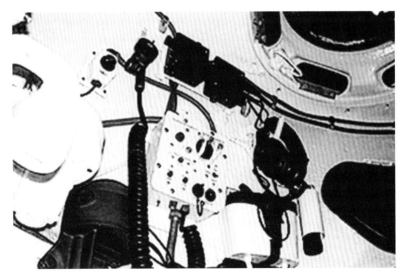

The gunner's post, on the right of the cannon. (*Private collection*)

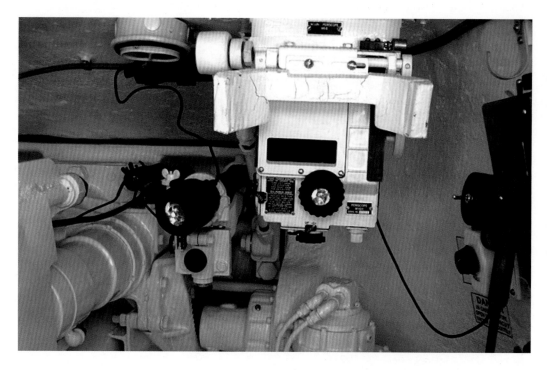

were used in direct fire, i.e. the gunner could see his target, and the target was called "direct." In certain cases like concealed firing or mortar-type (indirect) fire, the crew could not see the target, but did know where it was. This was the case when shooting over a hill or at something several kilometers away, without seeing it. This was where the azimuth indicator in conjunction with a firing table (functioning as artillery) came into play. The two levels, M1 and M9, equipping the tank determined the angle of fire (elevation), whereas the azimuth was visible on the indicator which the gunner had put on zero during the location firing.

A pair of binoculars hung from a bracket on the right-hand side of the turret. Under the seat, a portable fire extinguisher was fixed in a fitting to the turret floor.

The tank commander could also reach the AA machine-gun ammunition and in certain cases the 75-mm ammunition in the rear rack in the right-hand sponson. A chest next to the radio sets contained a periscope and three spare periscope heads. The gunner's and the cannoneer's weapons were near the turret bustle, under the radio sets. The fuel stopcocks were on the right near the air filter on the firewall. The tank commander was also in charge of the radio network.

Depending on the type of M4, the cannoneer's and gunner's Grease guns were fixed to the side, under the radio chassis. A spare spotlight was fixed behind the tank commander on his left, whereas the mounting for the TL 122 torch was on his right. There were two radio/interphone cases on the right and towards the

front: the tank commander's and the gunner's. Nearby were two hooks for hanging the T17 microphone and the headphones when they were not in use. Behind the tank commander, near the radio sets, was a bin containing a spare periscope.

Working conditions

The tank commander managed the tactical situation within the platoon*; he could also be the platoon commander, or a unit's CO. For this he used the radio and interphone networks as well as the maps where these were available. He started firing operations, observed the results with his binoculars, and changed the sighting if necessary. He watched through his cupola periscopes. The tank commander set the line of advance the tank or the formation (platoon, company, or squadron) had to take.

As for firing, he had aiming and observation equipment, leveling (M1 and M9) and firing tables (depending on whether he was firing a CN 105 or a CN 75), the latter often being homemade.

The tank commander was "shut up" in a rather restricted space compared with the cannoneer, and when he was sitting, his feet were on a level with the gunner's shoulders. His seat was the same as the cannoneer's; moreover, he had to get up and stand on his seat for the "head outside" position. In this position, the tank commander served the AA machine gun. In certain cases—mainly with the M4A3s—this machine gun could be used either by the tank commander or the cannoneer.

WHERE THE AMMUNITION WAS STOWED IN THE M4A4 CN 75 TM 9-754 FR

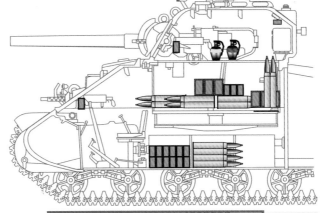

Stowing the ammunition in the hull of the Sherman tank.

75-mm shells

Emergency stock

12.7-mm cartridges

7.62-mm cartridges

11.43-mm cartridges

Fragmentation grenades

Offensive grenades

Smoke grenades

Incendiary grenades

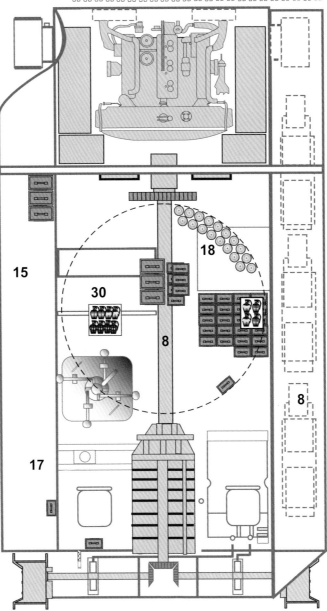

The Gunner's Post

The gunner's position was the lowest in the turret. His seat was in front of the tank commander's feet, stuck between the cannon on the left and the turret commands on the right. A fixed periscope, telescopic sights with headrest, the hydraulic control panel for the turret, and the mechanical command for firing were all in front of him.

On his right were the hydraulic turret command handle, the turret lock, the manual swivel controls, and a radio/interphone connector box. At his feet was the turret hydraulic group with the gyroscopic stabilization system pump for the cannon, an oil tank with a gauge glass, and an electric casing containing a circuit breaker for the turret electricity supply, two thermal fuses, canon fire warning light and the gun stabilization start switch.

On his left was the elevation pointing wheel. On the turret floor, near his left foot, was a box containing the two electric triggers for the cannon and the coaxial machine gun.

Further below, on the right, were the hydraulic generator and the oil sump. The gunner had access to the ammunition on the front right-hand side. A box containing hand grenades was under his seat. On the gunner's right, in the sponson, was a place for stowing rations and a rack for the stove.

In front and on the right-hand side was the turret electricity box with switches for the hydraulics, firing, and gun stabilization and switches for setting the gyroscopic stabilization. On the left-hand side was the elevation pointing wheel. The bearing pointing was on the right, as were the hydraulic commands, the azimuth indicator, and the turret lock.

An interior roof light completed the equipment for the gunner's post. Between the hydraulic group and the azimuth indicator there was a set of three pennants (red, green, and yellow), stowed in their sheath.

Working conditions

The gunner was the least well-off in terms of space. At his post at the bottom of the turret, he had a seat with a back—the only concession to comfort. Under his seat was a container with grenades; in front of him was the telescopic sights with its headrest.

When the tank was moving around, he could only see through his periscope and, depending on the terrain, could barely make out the land from the sky, a far from pleasant situation.

The gunner was responsible for anything to do with the firing sequences. This included: finding the target designated by the tank commander, pointing (later he would be able to use telemetry beforehand), and triggering the shots. The gunner fired using the hydraulic trigger or the trigger pedal. He also opened fire with the coaxial machine gun. He was also tasked when needed with using the azimuth indicator.

To turn the turret, he used the pointing elevation wheel (elevation by manual controls) and the hydraulic commands for the bearing (the turret swiveled). During the firing sequences, he resupplied the ammunition and made up the stocks.

The Cannoneer's Post (the radio-operator/loader)

As his name suggests, he was tasked with operating the radio sets and loading the cannon. The ammunition used first was that stowed on the floor of the turret, right next to the gun. The quantity of ammunition varied, depending on the type of gun used.

The shells were usually located in the rear right-hand part of the turret basket. After firing, the cannoneer got rid of the spent shell cases through a hatch.

This opening was situated on the left-hand side of the turret, half way up the outside right-hand panel. It was opened by using a locking lever from the inside. Again on the left was a box containing the radio-interphone, a hook for radio accessories and a bracket for the TL 122 torch. The cannoneer could access the stock of smoke grenades at the front, next to the periscope. On his right, the loader pulled the lever to open the cannon breech.

In front of him on the turret ceiling were the fixed periscope, a roof light, and on the right, the jack and the stabilization mechanism for the barrel. Fixed to the left-hand side of the turret, at head height, was a container holding hand grenades.

Hinged panels on the turret floor below the cannoneer's post lifted to reveal the racks of cannon ammunition at the bottom of the hull. Facing the cannoneer was the coaxial machine gun and under it the bracket for the box of .30 cal. cartridge belts. Through the floor panels, the cannoneer could also reach the signal flares above the battery rack.

Under the turret floor there was also the slip joint, a system designed so that electricity could be transmitted to the various turret circuits, no matter what position the turret was in. This was a casing containing different circular tracks along which brushes conveyed the electric current (see turret equipment).

Working conditions

Like all the other crewmen, the cannoneer did his jobs within a limited area and had to handle the ammunition before and after the firing. For this his small seat—a 40-cm diameter jump seat—could be folded up. When he was standing, he had to open the cannon breech, bring the opening lever to its initial position, grab a shell in the emergency rack, and engage it firmly home in the firing chamber—taking his fingers out quickly because once the shell case was lodged in the firing chamber, it activated the breech locks and the breech locked in the closed position. The gun was then ready to fire, and the cannoneer cried "Loaded."

His job also included supplying the co-axial machine gun, for this he had boxes of .30 cal. belts packed and set out either in the turret or under the turret floor. It was always the loader who fired the smoke mortar, when ordered by the tank commander.

Two images of the cannoneer at work. On the left in the top photo is his little seat. (*Private collection*)

His job also included implementing the radio equipment (SCR 508/528), frequency changes, and changing accessories or head equipment. When the shooting was over or when the tactical situation allowed, the cannoneer got rid of the spent cases, either through the pistol port or the main hatch. He was also tasked with using the auxiliary electricity generator. Like all the other crewmen, he had a well-defined sector to watch out for, in his case, between 9 and 12 o'clock.

Preparing The M4 Tank

Preparing the tank involved a set of procedures to make the tank operational, i.e. ready for combat. To do this the tank had to carry all the materiel to ensure the following:

- the tank's mobility,
- its servicing and any emergency repairs,
- its firing capability with all weapons,
- its functioning logistics,
- its means of communication,
- and that the crew had all the equipment it needed.

In peacetime, armored vehicles could easily be used partly prepared. In this case, the tanks were fitted with the minimum needed for moving on- or off-road. Preparing the vehicle completely was a long operation in which the whole crew took part.

A tankman's helmet. It was inspired mainly by the helmets used by the American Football players of the time. Initially it was unadorned, then equipped like in the photo below, with headphones and microphone, shown to the right. *(Private collection)*

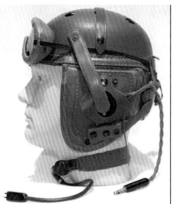

Preparing The Turret

Equipping the turret so it could carry out a mission properly ensured that everything installed— collective and individual arms and their ammunition, radio communications, optical apparatus, observation and sighting equipment, signaling apparatus, spares, and everything else needed by the turret crew—was ready for use.

Turret armament

Collective and individual weapons and their ammunition.

Communications equipment

Radios, pennants, and air-ground panels.

On-Board Radio Communication

Communications on board the Sherman were generally by the SCR (Signal Corporation Radio). Depending on the tactical situation, an ANVRC 3 (Army Navy Vehicular Radio Com.) or an ANPRC 10 (Army Navy Portable Radio Com.) was sometimes added to this equipment. The SCR 508 was a radio set comprising a BC 604 transmitter and two BC 603 receivers mounted on an FT 237 chassis. This configuration was reserved for the corps commanders' or company commanders' tanks.

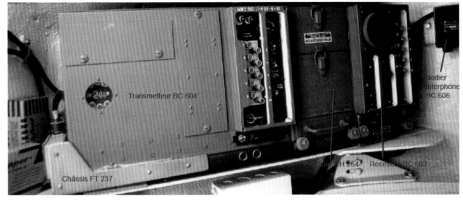

The SCR 528 was a set like the 508 but with a single BC 603 receiver. The SCR 538 comprised a BC Interphone amplifier, all mounted on an FT 237 chassis.

This equipment was used when the transmitter was not needed. The accompanying vehicles (jeeps or half-tracks) were equipped with SSCR 510 or another set, depending on whether they belonged to the infantry, artillery, or the engineers.

Individual equipment varied depending on the period and the units; only the radio helmet was common to all units. This helmet, the M38, made by Sears Saddlery Company, comprised two R14 earphones. To communicate, the other crewmen were equipped either with a throat microphone or a "mustachophone."

Helmet and microphone were linked to the SW 141 transmitting pedal, which enabled the crew to transmit using the radio network or interphone. The radio accessory quivers included spare antenna wires, bracing cables with snap clasps, and head equipment for the crew: earphones, microphone or throat microphone, and transmitting pedal. Some Sherman models were equipped with an outside telephone placed at the rear of the tank (right-hand side, photo opposite).

This set-up enabled the accompanying infantry to be in touch with the tank commander in his turret. The radio antenna was fixed the outside of the turret; it was attached to its mast base with a spring, a type AB 15/GR. This antenna was made up of three wires, MS 116, 117, and 118.

Radio networks: how they worked and were used

The M4 medium tank was designed to accompany infantry, but from the very start of Operation *Overlord*, tanks and infantrymen suffered from a lack of communication seeing as they had no way of getting in touch with each other. The first way round the problem was to attach a metal .30 cal. ammunition box to the tank's rear on the right and put an EE8* inside it, linked by two cables to the interphone box of the tank commander.

It wasn't a very practical solution but it did enable the infantry to warn the tank of a change in their position, an unidentified target, or any obstacle along their line of advance.

It was only at the end of 1944 that the External Phone Box BC 1632 was put into service; an armored casing containing a handset and call pedal, the various extensions, a red warning light fixed under the outside

Above, left: An SCR 528 mounted on its FT 237 chassis.

Above, right: The BC 606 interphone box

Below, left: The WS M19 transmitter-receiver radio fitted to the British Shermans.

Below, right: The WS M17 radio transmitter.

Diagram of how radio frequencies were attributed to the different arms in the battle corps.

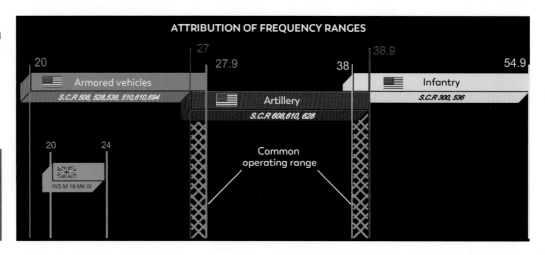

ATTRIBUTION OF FREQUENCY RANGES

| 20 | 27 | 27.9 | 38 | 38.9 | 54.9 |

Armored vehicles
S.C.R 508, 528, 538, 510, 610, 694

Artillery
S.C.R 608, 610, 628

Infantry
S.C.R 300, 536

20   24
WS M 19 MK III

Common
operating range

Using the interphone network followed the same rules but in practice it was common for the name or rank to be used in communications.

casing, and a second lamp on the tank commander's radio box. The BC 1632 system was tested first by the Marines in the Pacific in July 1944.

Using the military radio networks meant following clearly defined procedures comprising among other things:

A. Attributing the traffic frequency and the call signs

The traffic frequency was attributed within a range that the radios concerned would then use; the frequency used was called F1 and enabled all sets in a unit to exchange messages. Generally, the F2 frequency, called the clearance frequency, was used when there were communication problems, jamming by the enemy, a request for MEDEVAC, or an intervention for a technical problem.

A Sherman crew and all the gear carried by the tank. (US Signal Corps)

On a network used by the regiment or battalion there were in principle:

- a command frequency, used by the staff and unit commanders;
- a maneuvering frequency, used by regimental vehicles;
- a logistics frequency for handling fuel, ammunition and ordinary supplies,* breakdowns and evacuations.

Radio call signs were attributed to all vehicles equipped with radio sets. They were based on the phonetic alphabet used by all the units taking part in the fighting. From A-Alpha to Z-Zulu, these call signs consisted of two letters—ME for Mike Echo—or a letter and a number, like D-Delta 5. In the armored regiments, the common practice was to use the squadron color followed by a number.

The first squadron was blue, so the captain commanding it was called Blue 1 (pronounced "blue unit"), the commander of the 1st platoon was Blue 10, his second-in-command was Blue 11 and the subordinate tank was 12; the commandant of the 2d Group was blue 13. Blue 14 was his subordinate.

Some regiments used the combat number stenciled on the turret for their radio procedure.

B. Opening the radio network by the appropriate authority which fixed the rules for network use.

C. Contacting and confirmation

The station that was calling gave the unit's call sign followed by its own call sign, then followed the message followed by "Speak" or "Over to you."

D. Radio silence

This procedure was applied when the unit's advance had to be as discreet as possible because of the tactical situation. It could also be needed when one of the network users had a weak communication signal.

The radio means had different characteristics and performances depending on how they were used. The most important were the power (expressed in watts) delivered by the transmitter, the receptiveness of the receiver, the range of frequencies, the number of channels, and the power source (fixed, vehicles or batteries). These were the parameters allowing communications to be set up at more or less great distances; but they also enabled different types of radio sets to communicate among themselves, on condition that the frequency ranges overlapped at a particular threshold.

In the case of the SCR 508-538 models, the sets worked on FM (frequency modulation), within the 20 to 27.9-megacycle range; it comprised 80 channels split into 100-kilocycle segments numbered from 0 to 79. Antenna strength was 60 watts and it was pre-set for 10 frequencies, controlled by a push button.

The 508 group weighed 101 kg and had a range of 16 km. With the 508, using two receivers allowed two different networks to operate with the same transmitter.

In practice, the frequency ranges were attributed as follows:

Armored divisions: 20—27.9 megacycles for the SCR 508, 528, 538, and 694 sets on 80 frequencies, of which 10 were pre-set.

Artillery regiments: 27—38.9 megacycles for the SCR 608-628 on 120 frequencies, of which 10 were pre-set.

Infantry divisions: 38—54.9 megacycles for the ANVRC and ANPRC SCR 300 and 635.

In frequency modulation the SCR 610 model's power was a—low—2 watts with a range of 8 km in favorable conditions. It weighed 84 kg and had a frequency range from 27—38.9 megacycles split into 100 kilocycle sets numbered from 0 to 119.

The **SCR 510**: frequency range: 20—28 MHz FM, power 1 watt for vehicles equipped with batteries, 6v or 12v. Range 8 km.

The British WS M19 sets

These sets had a 2—9 watt power range and two working modes. In Mode A the range was from 2—9 mega cycles; in Mode B, it was from 22—24 megacycles. Its range was 25 km (A) and 1.2 km (B).

Apart from radio, there were other means of communication:

A set of red, yellow and green pennants. These were used to signal an incident or shooting, or to express tactical signals when a unit was moving under radio silence. In cases where the radio network could not be used (such as enemy jamming or radio silence), pennants were used. These pennants were stowed in a sheath, in the right sponson within reach of the gunner.

The air-ground panels. There were also three of these: red, green, and white. They were intended first for aerial recognition. According to which tactical plan was used, a colored panel was fixed onto the tank to enable the planes to tell it from the enemy tanks. These panels were stowed in a sheath near the radio sets.

There were different colors of **signal flares** whose use and codes were determined in advance.

The tank also had spare level M1 and M9 periscopes, binoculars, etc. Aiming and observation instruments, the gunner's telescopic sights, the exterior aiming instruments, binoculars, and various spares were also embarked aboard the tank.

Inside the Sherman were various extra items like maintenance parts, the crew's daily needs (e.g. rations), drinking water, blankets, etc., and every crewman carried some items and utensils needed for daily life on board the tank.

All these items were loaded aboard the tank and differed according to the missions to be carried out. The tank crews always took the strict minimum, seeing as space was at a premium. All these items were carried therefore in a compartmentalized bag or in a big bag, the "All Purpose Bag." This usually contained toiletries, sleeping bag, canvas half-tent, beaker, mess tins, and cutlery, as well as more personal items like cigarettes, lighters, and sometimes a camera.

The bags were hung on the outside where they wouldn't get in the way of the swiveling turret, firing the 12.7-mm machine gun, or opening the hatches completely.

As well as the bags, the crews took aboard combat rations which were stowed inside the tank, in a box situated at the end of the right-hand sponson. This box was marked "Combat Rations" depending on the M4 model.

The radio set Wireless Set Number 19 and its protective grid inside the turret of a Sherman tank. This is a turret armed with a British QF 17-pounder. *(Private Collection)*

Among them some were flares.

Tank M4 75: 12 signal flares mounted in their own box on the battery box. There were 3 white star parachute flares, 3 white star cluster flares, 3 amber parachute flares and 3 green parachute flares.

Tank M4 76: 18 signal flares mounted in their box on the turret floor. Fired with a flare pistol.

The supplies and packaging were the following:

- K-type rations: rations for two days for five men, 30 boxes.
- C-type rations: rations for two days for five men, 60 boxes.
- D-type rations: rations for one day for five men, two boxes.

The C-type rations were special in that they were packed in ½ daily rations, in a smaller semi-rigid packaging; the cover could be removed using a key into which a small tongue was inserted, rather like the way canned goods and ammunition boxes were opened.

Among the items of equipment aboard the M4 was a stove allowing the crew to heat up certain combat ration dishes (*see photos in the appendices*). The heater cover was used as a dish to contain the five crewmen's rations. The ration boxes marked "Type D1" contained two boxes marked "Dinner" and "Supper," which were the main courses.

To these dishes was added a whole series of packets containing salt, pepper, sugar, and powdered drinking coffee and soup; chocolate, biscuits, cigarettes, toilet paper, and matches were all part of the ration boxes, as were three condoms.

Packing subsequently evolved, especially when the French Army started to supply its troops with its own rations. Although the box dimensions were like the American rations, what they contained was radically different. There were two types of rations, the E-box for Europeans and the M-Box for Muslims. The latter didn't contain any pork or cognac (or anything resembling it); tea replaced the coffee and there was a lot more sugar.

Exterior Turret Arrangements

The Sherman turrets, although equipped with a variety of guns, gun carriages, and mantles, did have some items of equipment in common.

On the turrets fitted with a single access hatch, the cannoneer used a swiveling periscope and in front of this was the barrel of the smoke mortar, if the model had one. The searchlight and the ventilator extractor were located in the center of the turret.

At the front of the turret and before the gun shield was a lifting ring; on the right was the gunner's fixed periscope and the tank commander's outside aiming instruments. The gun shield was also fitted with two rings used for removing the gun. The AA machine-gun mounting and its barrel fastening system were on the upper part of the turret. This system folded down.

The mast base for the radio aerial and its protective cover was also at the rear of the turret. The tarpaulin, held in place by straps, the spare AA machine-gun barrel mountings, and an additional mounting for the AA machine gun were at the rear of the turret.

Various hooks, additional armor, the evacuation slot for spent cartridge shells, and the two lifting rings were all located on the turret sides. A bracket for the spare track links (non-regulation) was on the left-hand side of the turret.

Preparing the Hull

The emergency tools and spares were spread out over and inside the Sherman's hull. On the outside, on all the M4 models, starting at the rear, was the large-sized track tightening spanner. This tool was used for working on the bogeys or on the tracks (link changing or repairs when the track came off), and was fixed on the vertical panel above the exhaust. In certain cases, it was on the far side of the rear deck. It was also there that the sledgehammer (part of the pioneers' gear) and, for the M4 and M4A1 models, the starting handle were fastened.

On the rear part on the right were the spade, the axe, the pickaxe and its handle, and the crowbar. The towing cable was laid out on the left hand side, and inserted into the left shackle. On certain M4s (the M4 105 in particular) the ramrods were attached to a rack on this side. On other models, these rods were mounted on the rear panel in place of the track-tightening spanner.

On the tank's rear, depending on the model, the spare track links were fixed to the mudguards. On the "Late" models there was the external telephone box on the rear right-hand side. Certain tanks, usually the M4A3s and "Late" M4A1s, were equipped with folding racks on the rear deck. These racks could hold extra jerrycans or the tarpaulin and the camouflage netting. The ramrods were fixed under the horizontal part of this support, which was referenced as the "Blanket Rack."

Previous page: The crew of this Canadian 29th Reconnaissance Regiment (the South Alberta Regiment) M4A2 have a little rest before going back to the Normandy front in July 1944. (*Canadian Military Archives*)

Above: Cherbourg, June 1944. An M4A3E2 Jumbo and an M32 B1 breakdown tank; two 75-mm M4s, and in the background two 105-mm M4s, are all being prepared before being convoyed to the front-line units. (*NARA*)

On British armored vehicles, a big chest was often attached to the rear panel. In some cases, a similar chest was on the front glacis. The British tanks were often equipped with additional chests on the turret bustle or again on the front and/or rear mudguards of the tank.

The spare links were attached to the right-hand side of the turret, or, on the HVSS models, on the right and left-hand sides of the hull, just above the widening extensions for the T80 tracks.

In this case the spare road wheels were placed on the same side along with the first-aid kit cases. Some models were equipped with two spare crowns for the sprocket wheels attached to the sides towards the rear.

On the M4s, M4A1s, and M4 Hybrids the air filters were also at the rear. All the M4s had a towing hook with two shackles, the exhaust deflectors, and the engine doors at the rear.

There were two towing shackles on the transmission armor at the front of the tank. Its on-board gear comprised two spare shackles, an extra towing hook, and a spare road light. On the frontal glacis, depending on the models, there were one or two spare road wheels, the barrel transport cradle, and spare track links. These were very often used as extra protection and the glacis was often littered with bits of tracks. Sometimes protection of this type was added round the turret.

Among all the material aboard, one mustn't forget the tooling needed for servicing the tank stowed in compartmentalized or reinforced canvas bags containing among other things the "*grenouilles,*" special tools needed for working on the tracks.

The tank's gear also included torches fitted with three filters — green, blue, and red (Type TL 122) — a portable lamp for night maintenance, some spare parts for the auxiliary electric generator, oil to fill up the engine or for servicing the air filters, and a grease pump with extra grease.

A water bag and a jerrycan pourer spout were part of the standard equipment. The driver and assistant driver also carried spare periscopes and their respective weapons, ammunition, and radio accessories. Everybody carried rations and blankets. The M4's equipment also included a stove heater, a lamp with two lenses, and a magnetic bracket.

Life aboard and fighting in 1944

We have seen what was carried aboard the tank, the way the crew posts were laid out and, in another chapter, how they got out.

The fighting in the Normandy fields has also been looked at briefly. Tank combat was a much more complex process than can be summarized in a few situation analyses; neither can it hide behind the tactical plans or the instructions set out in the Field Manual, even if this was impressively precise and thorough.

We also have seen that the tank crews were trained, and prepared with the help of extremely rigorous documentation and experienced instructors, with training sessions and programs which we would qualify these days as "intensive," to say the least.

At the time, all this teaching material and all this accumulation of learning had only one aim: to prepare men for combat, without hiding from them the fact

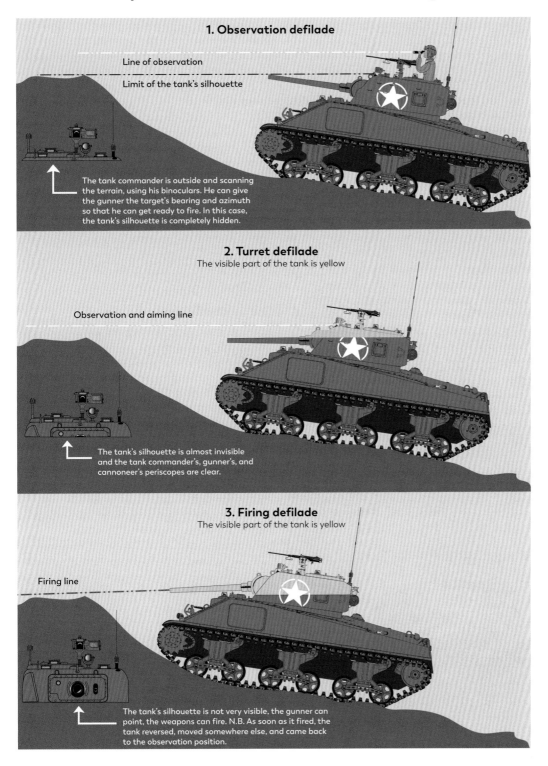

1. Observation defilade

Line of observation

Limit of the tank's silhouette

The tank commander is outside and scanning the terrain, using his binoculars. He can give the gunner the target's bearing and azimuth so that he can get ready to fire. In this case, the tank's silhouette is completely hidden.

2. Turret defilade
The visible part of the tank is yellow

Observation and aiming line

The tank's silhouette is almost invisible and the tank commander's, gunner's, and cannoneer's periscopes are clear.

3. Firing defilade
The visible part of the tank is yellow

Firing line

The tank's silhouette is not very visible, the gunner can point, the weapons can fire. N.B. As soon as it fired, the tank reversed, moved somewhere else, and came back to the observation position.

that the outcome of the fighting could be fatal, on one side just as much as the other.

All the dispositions which were taken or would be taken depended on one inevitable parameter: the crew that lived with the tank had to be alive to it and with its team spirit. If there wasn't any communion—the word was not too strong—of this sort, then the battle was lost, and not due to the enemy.

I was lucky because in the course of my career I worked with old hands who had taken part in these battles for the liberation of France. These were men who, at that time, had been servants in a Sherman, the very same who had freed Strasbourg or landed in Provence. Members of my family had also chosen to take up arms during this period of turmoil; the letters, memoirs, and accounts that they left behind are invaluable help today as irreplaceable eye-witness narratives.

These accounts were told without animosity and always placed first and foremost their enthusiasm and desire to win, but also showed that mixture of courage and insouciance that were the hallmarks of youth. So, what was it like being 20 years old in a Sherman in 1944?

"Life aboard" a tank was the same, no matter what side the crew was on, or where it came from. It became the cement that brought together the different members of the team. They discovered this life together, learnt it, and got used to it. Month after month, they trained together in a company, a squadron, regiment, or battalion. They learnt to land and then one day they embarked for the coasts of Italy or France. The adventure for some of them ended before they even set foot on the sand, beaten by a mine or a shell, or by capsizing. Others managed to get through the first anti-tank obstacles, charged the machine-gun nests or the PaKs; then some of them perished, burnt in their tank pierced by the shell from a Tiger or a Jagdpanther. Some pulled their comrades out of the inferno the tank had become, while others dropped from exhaustion dragging ammunition boxes.

For those who survived the battle it was then time to lick one's wounds, both physical and emotional, and look after the tank, fill it up, restock with ammunition, and carry out checks. Here again these movements had become automatic and reinforced the bonds among the crew. They finished what had to be done with that little gesture that could just save your life: weapons ready, therefore clean; radio equipment with all its accessories working; tools in place and well battened down.

Then there was the debriefing, a time to summarize the situation: they learnt that their neighboring tank had been hit by a *Panzerfaust* or an 88 shell; another had run over a mine which destroyed its sprocket and first bogey.

Fighting sequence

After that, the orders were given for the next part of the fighting, the next day or even the same night. They moved off. Never mind, they thought, we'll just sleep less—or not at all. Only after all that could the crew think of themselves, be elsewhere than in the crackling of the radio, the racket of the engine and the tracks, bumping around because of the tank's abrupt movements—it wasn't always on a road. The driver was sitting in the low-down position and his field of vision was limited. Orders sometimes followed each other very quickly: "Forwards, right quick, straight ahead fast, slowly, on the left, stop!" He changed down, pulled on a steering lever with both hands to take the bend tightly; a hillock, change down! "Speed up!"

Everything followed on from there. The assistant driver, one hand on the periscope and the other on the machine-gun handle, remained on his seat as best he could, his knees hitting the ammunition box mounting; he inserted a new cartridge belt and took the empties out of the bag, throwing them through the open hatch. His knee hit the spare machine-gun barrel: "Bloody barrel!" We'll deal with that later.

Up in the turret it wasn't much better. On the cannoneer's side, a smoke grenade was put on standby, the coaxial machine gun reloaded and armed. A glance in the 75-mm empties bag. "Okay! There's still room." He opened the pistol port to have a look around on the left. Then he looked ahead through his periscope.

Fitted with Duckbills and with its rear deck well laden, this Sherman is advancing through a snowed-in forest during the Ardennes offensive in December 1944 or January 1945.

A delicate position for this tank, and the driver has his work cut out. In the foreground, crates and £105-mm shell cases. (*Private collection*)

A series of shots was fired. Orders were shouted everywhere, quick, sharp, and precise.

The lives of others could depend on his reactions.

"Armor-piercing shell!"

He opened the breech and brought the lever back under the cannon. Half a turn in his reduced space and he pulled the emergency shell from its rack; he inserted it into the firing chamber then with a sharp shove, pushed the shell home into the barrel. The shell case closed the breech locks, the case extractors were in place, and the breech block closed with a sharp noise. He announced "Loaded!"

On the gunner's side, it was better if you didn't suffer from seasickness. The gunner's post was the lowest in the turret. As a result, he had no view of the outside, unlike all the other crew members. He used the periscope or the telescopic sights to see. When the tank was moving sometimes he saw trees, or a puddle of mud, depending on the terrain. He sat, stuck between the azimuth indicator, the pointing wheels, the hydraulic commands, and the canon's protective shield on the left. At his feet were the cannon and coaxial machine gun firing pedals, boxes of ammunition, and a shell caisson. The hand grenades were under his seat.

For him too, there were orders everywhere.

"Turret at 10 o'clock, 900 meters, armored target." Read: "Turret slightly to the left, 900 meters away, an enemy tank." The driver slowed down and then stopped. The gunner had his eyes stuck to the sights.

The firing distance came up on the reticule, taking into account the type of ammunition (armor-piercing, so it had a different muzzle velocity from the smoke or explosive shells).

He announced "Ready" and took the lock off the firing pedal.

"Fire!"

He rammed his foot down on the pedal. Percussion, the shot went off, the noise was deafening. The gun recoiled violently on its carriage, slowed by the firing brake. The ventilators got rid of the smoke; the spent case was ejected and fell into the spent shell box. The cannon returned ready to fire, braked by the retriever.

The tank commander, halfway out of the turret, looked with his binoculars and announced "Tank destroyed," then "Backwards, left. Stop! Forwards slowly."

Apart from the firing sequences, the tank commander followed the orders he received for the squadron's or the group's progress on the radio, watched the sky—or got an infantryman to do this, sitting on the turret—kept an eye on his tank's position in the platoon, and followed and anticipated what ammunition and fuel it needed.

Promiscuity noise and temperature were among many negative factors the crewmen had to put up with during the fighting, causing them stress. When they weren't in a danger zone (it did happen!), the atmosphere was more relaxed. Driver and assistant driver drove "heads out," the tank commander and the gunner would sit with their legs hanging down over the

Opposite, top: Pacific, 1944. Evacuating a wounded crewman from a damaged Marine Corps Sherman. (NARA)

Opposite, bottom: Italy 1944. A pitiably camouflaged Sherman M4 standing in a poppy field. (G. Silk, Private Collection)

edge of the hatch, and the radio operator sometimes took the gunner's place inside.

In this case the AA machine gun was locked in the "road" position, and even covered. During the resupply halts, the crews took advantage of the few minutes' respite to wash—when there was water—to eat something or look after their few belongings. These rare—but essential—moments of breathing space allowed them to talk, not only among themselves but with other crews. They could even—a small, much appreciated pleasure—eat their combat rations, which were sometimes "improved."

After combat, life and its hazards

These were the simple moments, together with the combat sequences, which forged the crew's team spirit discussed above. They didn't just eat their rations: they comforted a wounded comrade; they made fun of the driver who missed a gear change; they lent a pair of socks to the guy whose kit bag burst the last time the tank went through the undergrowth.

To these combat conditions had to be added the whole series of hazards and unpredictable factors the crews had to deal with as quickly as possible, and to confront these situations they possessed an almost unbeatable weapon: initiative. Sometimes, in the French Army, it was called the "*Système D*" ("*Système débrouille*" = resourcefulness), or "*la Débrouille*" or "*la Démerde*" (same meaning).

Deeply anchored in the French soldier's genetic heritage—even nowadays, fortunately—this reaction enabled the French tankmen to get out of all sorts of sometimes embarrassing situations.

Too hot …

Among the situations causing these contretemps was of course the weather. We saw for example that

during Operation *Overlord* (Normandy), the state of the sea caused a lot of problems for the disembarking troops. Landing craft capsizing caused loss of men and materiel that had to be replaced in an emergency, this in itself causing untold delays and extra losses. On the other hand, during Operation *Dragoon* (Provence), it was the very hot weather which caused inconvenience.

Whichever tank it was, it was still a mechanical object; it could always break down. The ambient temperature, added to that caused by the engine, in its compartment could rise very quickly beyond normal working temperature and cause overheating, breaking pipe-work, radiator damage, or even engine damage.

The driver had to keep an eye on the temperature and pressure gauges, and listen out for any unusual noises. A very nasty problem for these engines caused by the heat, and encountered frequently, was the "Vapor Lock." This was liquid fuel changing into gas in the pipes leading to the carburetors. The trick was to cover these pipes with wet pieces of cloth to keep the temperature down. When there was a vapor lock, however, the vehicle stopped and was no longer any good for fighting, and what was worse, it became a static target.

Too cold …

But if things could get bad when it was hot, the same was also true if it was cold. Neither the combatants nor their materiel were spared during the winter of 1944-45. With the machines the first chore was putting anti-freeze into all the cooling circuits, a long operation given the volume of these circuits. Moreover, this job was always carried out in the most difficult conditions: no heated garages, no maintenance pits, no ramps either.

With temperatures dropping below zero, the engines had trouble warming up. Sometimes part of the radiators had to be shut off. After a prolonged halt even the oil would congeal, even though the prescribed degrees of viscosity had been respected. But the cold also had a disastrous effect on the soldiers.

Combat clothing was not always designed well enough (for the period) for such icy temperatures. Furthermore, a tank was a draughty box through which the cold air dispersed quickly and lowered the inside temperature even more.

The tankmen in the Ardennes, Alsace, and Lorraine suffered a lot from frostbitten toes. Once again, the ineffectiveness of the equipment was offset by the crew fending for itself. The men learnt to make a shelter with the vehicle's tarpaulin, and a camouflage net became an insulating mattress. You could warm your hands up behind the exhaust. The tank crews in the ETO knew how to protect their belongings by tying them to the rear deck, and the heavy helmet could always be used as a pot for heating up water.

A Sherman M4A1 on the Pacific Front, probably at the end of 1942 or beginning of 1943, as the uniform and the tropical helmet the man standing behind the turret on the left is wearing seem to indicate. (Private collection)

On top of all this bother, the crewmen also had to deal with difficulties caused by the tank itself. In the snow, the running gear could get "stuck" and the tracks come off.

The tracks could slither; the holes were concealed and when a tank fell into one, it stayed there.

It would then still take three or four others to get it out, if the heavy breakdown recovery vehicle wasn't needed. Setting up the winches in those temperatures was not comfortable … frozen steel was difficult to handle. The mechanics were cold and were not able to do everything with their gloves on; winching operations became much more laborious and longer, lasting way into the night.

If it wasn't too hot or too cold, it could rain too. There again, the crews would be affected as mud was just as much a problem as the cold. The tanks got bogged down and sometimes toppled over onto one side, or even slid and fell into a large puddle.

The crew had then to deal with the problem of humidity. They had to go into the water to shackle up the tank so it could be towed. They got out soaked through and there was no question at all of hanging out the washing to dry: the advance had to go on.

All these situations contributed to reinforcing the bonds between the men in a crew.

Did these tankmen, who were 20 in 1944, only experience losses, setbacks, misfortunes, or wounds? Many did … but there was some cause for satisfaction. They became comrades, they became brothers-in-arms; they went through the places they'd "liberated" and it was there that they received their reward. It was there that the people in the village or the town welcomed them with what means they had: a flower, the kiss from a lovely girl, a glass of wine on the side of the tank; that was their reward. After all, they'd earned it. So they, too, smiled.

7 Evolution of the Sherman

The Sherman was an armored vehicle which evolved throughout its career, either transformed by the country that acquired it through Lend-Lease agreements like the United Kingdom, or because it was modified by the different manufacturers or at the request of the US Army. These modifications and improvements (Upgrades) were not to be confused with all the experimentations carried out, of which there were just as many if not more.

All these developments went to improving tank performance in various areas like powerplant, running gear, turret, firepower and ammunition, the optics, and the firing sequence. Some technical data didn't change at all right through to the end of production, such as the ground clearance or the diameter of the turret well, set at 1.75 m.

The British Shermans

The British codified their Shermans differently: tanks with a 76-mm cannon were given the suffix "A"; the 105-mm howitzers received "B," and those with the 17-pounder received "C." The Shermans with the HVSS suspension were coded with "Y."

This gave:

M4	= Sherman I
M4 105	= Sherman I B
M4 105 HVSS	= Sherman I BY
M4A1	= Sherman II
M4A1 76 W HVSS	= Sherman II AY
M4A1 76 W	= Sherman II A
M4A1 Firefly	= Sherman II C
M4A2	= Sherman III
M4A2 76 W	= Sherman III A
M4A2 76 W HVSS	= Sherman III AY
M4A3	= Sherman IV
M4A3 76 W	= Sherman IV A
M4A3 76 W HVSS	= Sherman IV AY
M4A3 105	= Sherman IV B
M4A3 105 HVSS	= Sherman IV BY
M4A3 75 W	= Sherman IV A
M4A4	= Sherman V
M4A4 Firefly	= Sherman V C
M4A6	= Sherman VI

The M4

This originated with the T6 prototype launched in 1941. Equipped with gyro-stabilization and an auxiliary electric generator, its hull was made of welded armor plates. The transmission armor was in three parts. The frontal glacis had a 57° slope.

In the autumn of 1944, Shermans—the foreground tank is an A1 and the one behind it is an M4—from General Patton's Third Army, advancing in eastern France. (Signal Corps, NARA)

M4E6: equipped with the M1 76-mm cannon.

M4 76 W: this model, equipped with a 75-mm M1A1 cannon or a 76-mm M1A2, was given the letter "W" for "Wet," because the reputation it had for being a Zippo mentioned earlier was totally justified.

The initial models did have acceptable armor on the front, but on the sides it was much too light. Welded reinforcements were therefore added to the sides and the way the ammunition was stowed was changed. To avoid fires, the ammunition compartments were thereafter protected by a double envelope containing 140 liters of water added to methanol or glycol as antifreeze together with an anti-corrosion product. Hence the designation "Wet."

The frontal glacis had a 47° slope.

M4 105: this version was armed with a 105-mm howitzer; 800 were made, some of which equipped French units (weight 31,500 kg). The 105 M4 cannon was placed on an M52 carriage with a supply of 66 shells; the turret controls were manual for elevation and bearing* (only the "Late" versions had hydraulic bearing controls). The 12.7-mm AA gun had 600 rounds, the two .30 cal. machine guns 4,000 rounds, and the smoke mortar 12 rounds.

This series did not have a turret basket: it was replaced by a suspended half-floor. The ammunition was not "wet" stowed, but the bins were armored. The frontal glacis had a 47° slope. The 105 howitzer versions could tow a Type M10 Ammo Trailer containing 44 105-mm shells.

M4 105 HVSS: the M4 was now equipped with HVSS (Horizontal Volute Spring Suspension). This included the T80 or T84 tracks with connectors and a guide tooth down the middle. The first examples of M4 were equipped with VVSS (Vertical Volute Spring Suspension) suspension. Some 841 examples were put into service. This model was equipped with a 12-round M3 smoke launcher fitted on the turret. The frontal glacis had a 47° slope.

As mentioned in the introduction, the M4A2s were fitted with the VVSS suspension, but some also came with the HVSS. Likewise, certain M4A3s were "Wet" and others not.

The M4A1

M4A1: this had a hull made of cast parts. 6,821 examples were produced between February 1942 and December 1943 in the Lima Locomotive Works, Pressed Steel Car Co., and the Pacific Car and Foundry Co. On the first M4A1 series, twin .30-06 caliber M1919 A4s were fitted on the frontal glacis. These machine guns were fired by the driver. They had a +8° to -6° elevation. They were suppressed on March 3, 1942. An M4A1 series was fitted with three .30 cal. machine guns.

In the summer of 1942, new bogeys were fitted with 20-cm diameter springs, 2.5 cm more than the preceding ones. In December 1943, a small oval hatch was installed over the cannoneer's post. The first M4A1 guns were 75-mm M2s; since they were shorter than the M3s, they needed twice the counter-weight at the end of the barrel to be compatible with the gyro-stabilization.

The frontal glacis slope could vary between 33° and 55°.

Above: A column of Shermans from the 4th Armored Division—the second is a 105-mm M4—advancing through Coutances in Normandy during the summer of 1944. (NARA)

The M4A1 E3 76 M1 cannon version, M4A1 76 W HVSS

Some 3,423 examples came off the production lines between January 1944 and July 1945 (weight: 32,000 kg; length: 6.20 m; width: 2.67 m; ground pressure: 1.002 kg/cm²). It was equipped with the 76M1 A1, M1A1C, or M1A2 cannon. This could fire HVAP

(High-Velocity Armor-Piercing) ammunition at 792 m per second. It was mounted on the M62 gun carriage. The tank carried 71 shells, of which six were in the emergency rack. The 12.7-mm AA machine gun had 600 rounds, the two .30 cal. machine guns 6,250, and the smoke-grenade launcher 12.

The tank's speed was 39 kph and it had a range of 190 km. Two bins on either side of the propeller shaft containing respectively 30 and 35 rounds were protected by 131 liters of the "Wet" mixture. The six emergency rounds inside the turret were protected by an envelope containing 8 liters of retarding mixture. On the W versions, the additional side armor was suppressed. Besides, in order to use up all the space available, the turret basket was arranged so that the ammunition could be reached at the bottom of the hull. On the W series, the cannoneer's hatch was bigger, equipped with pull-back springs, and a swiveling periscope.

The M1 A1 cannon was lengthened by 33 cm, enabling the firing brake to be moved forwards, balancing the gun better. Some M1 A1Cs had muzzle brakes and they were fitted to all the M1 A2s. These tanks were fitted with T80 or T84 tracks. These tracks and the new suspension increased the weight by

Right: This M4 76 W Sherman has been entirely covered with sandbags and camouflage nets. The shot was probably taken during the winter of 1944—45 in eastern France. (NARA)

M4-75 EARLY

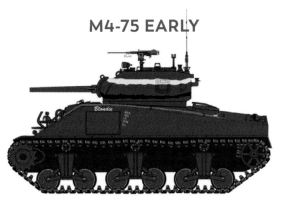

M4-75 Early from the 756th Tank Battalion, B Company, 1st Platoon, France, September 1944. Sergeant James Haspel's tank. Apart from the name of the tank ("Blondie"), the markings were those of the states the crew members came from. WVA: West Virginia; Tex: Texas; LO: Louisiana; IWO: Iowa; ILL: Illinois. No "Allied" star, but two black and white stripes on the turret to break the silhouette of the tank.

M4-105 HOWITZER

M4-105 howitzer from the 2/12 RCA. This tank landed in Normandy on August 2, 1944 from LST 1119. The markings on the sponsons indicate: GIUK: Green Island United Kingdom (where it landed); ORD II: Ordnance Department 2 (the sending organization); ADV: Advance (designating an advanced base); SD: Store Depot 341; CP: Command Post (Dispatching Post 375).

M5-105 HVSS WITH M10 AMMO TRAILER

M5-105 howitzer HVSS. As was often the case in American units, this howitzer towed an M10 Ammunition Trailer which could carry 54 105-caliber rounds. This ammunition was packed in light three-shell cases and the rocket nose cones were packed separately in the caisson attached to the shaft. These trailers could also carry 120 rounds of 75-mm shells, 18 rounds of 155-mm shells, or again eight 240-mm mortar shells.

M4A1 75

2e Cuirassiers, Escadron d'Etat-Major (HQ Squadron), Colonel Durosoy's tank. Registered 464,530. These markings date from 1946; the 1944 ones displayed the original MF Number, Allies' star, and Registration Number, not to be confused with the chassis number.

M4 HYBRID

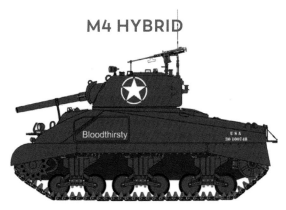

M4 Hybrid and 75-mm cannon on an M34A1 carriage. The tank belonged to the 44th Tank Battalion and took part in the capture of Manila (Philippines). Note the absence of the pistol port, so the turret was made between January and June 1943. It was fitted with lateral protective skirts which limited sand and mud projections.

M4A2 75

M4A2 with 75-mm cannon on M34A1 carriage. Glacis with 57° slope and "Twin Grey Marine" powerplant. Sloping rear panel and air intakes covered up. Turret with a single split hatch. Tank from 5e RCA, 4e Escadron.

M4A2 76

M4A2 with 76-mm cannon. Red Army tank with patriotic slogan on the sponsons. N.B. the American technical data still applied. M1C1 cannon on an M62 carriage.

M4A3 75 WET

M4A3 with 75-mm cannon and "Wet" stowage. Glacis with 47° slope and V8 Ford engine. 75-mm cannon on an M34A1 carriage. 104 shells, four of which in the emergency rack. Tank from the 2e Cuirassiers, 3e Escadron, fitted with a blanket rack at the rear. Chassis No. 49709 (made in May 1944), French registration 96012. Tank destroyed at Phalsbourg in northeast France in November 1944.

M4A3 E8

M4A3 E8 Easy Eight "Late," Germany 1945. Tank belonging to Colonel Creighton Abrams, commanding the 44th Tank Battalion. Armor on the front glacis, the sponsons, and the turret. M2 HB in traveling position. A4 .30 cal. machine gun in front of the tank commander's hatch. Colonel Abrams went on to command the US forces in Vietnam and was the Chief of Staff of the US Army.

M4A3 E2

M4A3 E2 "Jumbo," from C Company, 37th Tank Battalion, 4th US Armored Division, sixth vehicle. Ford V8 engine, 75-mm cannon on a T110 carriage. This tank was also equipped with a 76-mm cannon. The A3 E2 didn't have any road lights. First tank to enter Bastogne in the Battle of the Bulge. Type T48 tracks fitted with type 2 duckbills.

M4A4

M4A4 from the 2e Cuirassiers, 3e Escadron, glacis with 57° slope, and lengthened chassis (two guiding teeth between each bogey). Powered by the 30-cylinder Chrysler Multibanks. Radiator bulge visible on the rear deck. M1 75-mm cannon on an M34 carriage, 96 shells, 18 of which in emergency racks. N.B. many tanks in the 2e Cuirassiers had no additional sponson armor.

2,350 kg, but what it gained in ground pressure was important. The other advantage HVSS suspension had was to make servicing easier, as the bogeys no longer had to be taken off so that work could be done on the running gear wheels.

The glacis varied between 33° and 55°.

M4A1 E8: This version was equipped with the HVSS suspension and T80 tracks.

The M4A2

M4A2: 8,053 examples were manufactured between April 1942 and May 1944. The hull was welded. The powerplant comprised a General Motors 13.7-liter engine: the GM 6-71—two Greyhound bus engines twinned together.

The tanks were built by the Fisher Tank Division at Grand Blanc, Pullman Standard Car, American Locomotive Co., Baldwin Locomotive Works, and Federal Machine and Welder Co.

The A2 weighed 31,800 kg. It was 5.92 m long, 2.62 m wide, with a ground pressure of 1,001 kg/cm². This version was armed with the 75-mm M3 mounted on an M34 A1 carriage with M55 or M38 aiming sights. Ninety-seven shells were stowed away in the tank, eight of which were in the emergency rack.

The .50 cal. AA machine gun had 300 rounds and the two .30 cal. machine guns (coaxial and assistant driver) 4,750. It could get up to 48 kph on the road with its GM engine. In the turret, the M34 A1 gun carriage, compared with the M34, had an aiming sight whereas the other only had a periscope, which remained on the

M34 A1 version. With this carriage, there was a new shield which protected the sights and the .30 co-axial gun. On the M34 version, protection for the coaxial machine gun was separate. With the A2, fitting the new glacis plate with a 47° slope enabled the driver and assistant driver hatches to be enlarged.

The end transmission protection was subsequently a single piece. The frontal glacis had a 57° slope.

The **M4A2 76 W** was armed with the M1A1, M1A1C, or M1A2 cannon. Some 2,594 examples were built at Grand Blanc and 21 by Pressed Steel Cars between May 1944 and May 1945. The glacis had a 47° slope.

M4A2 E8: this was fitted with the HVSS suspension and T80 tracks.

This M4A1 75 Sherman, like the A3 in the background, was probably captured in Tunisia by the Germans. Here they are being evaluated by German tankmen in a series of tests. (NARA)

Germany, April 1945: this M4A3 Sherman belongs to the 9th Armored Division. (NARA)

An M4A3 E8 coming out of a tricky fording moment. A Browning 1919 .30 cal. machine gun has been installed in front of the tank commander's hatch. The tank belongs to the 11th Armored Division and is crossing the River Muhel, near Neufelden in Austria. In the background a Jumbo, together with another M4A3 76 VVSS, will soon be going through the ford.

THE M4A3

The Sherman was now equipped with the Ford V-8 GAAA-III liquid-cooled engine. From June 1942 to September 1943, 1,690 examples were built, and by Ford only. The hull was made of welded armor plates. The front part of the hull had also been entirely redesigned; the slope of the armored plate was reduced from 57° to 47° and it was thicker: 64 mm instead of 51 mm. At the same time the vision slots for the driver and the assistant driver were replaced by swiveling periscopes. The transmission casing was made of a single block.

Equipped with T48 or T51 tracks, its ground pressure was 0.959 kg/cm². Turret and armament were the same as the A2 model. Note the appearance of the 12-round 50.8-mm smoke-grenade launcher barrel angled at 35°.

All the A3s were equipped with reinforced bogeys with a return roller on the rear of the bogeys. They reached 42 kph on road and their range was 210 km, which put them in the lead of all the Shermans.

The big change to this model was installing a Ford engine, which reduced the height of the propeller shaft which now was hardly inclined at all. An extra radio could be mounted on the M4A3 in the assistant-driver's post. The driver's and assistant driver's seats were fitted with wide safety harnesses, but in combat they were not used.

M4A3 75W or M4A3W

Reinforced armor, "Wet" stowage and a 75-mm cannon were fitted to this version, of which 3,071 examples were built between February 1944 and March 1945 by Fisher Tank Arsenal. Equipped with the Ford V8 engine, it was the first model to be equipped with HVSS suspension and T84 E1 tracks. The tank carried 100 shells in 10 boxes at the bottom of the hull, surrounded by 140 liters of retarding mixture.

The four-round emergency rack in the turret was likewise protected by 3.8 liters of retarding mixture. This series was equipped with a twin-flap hatch for the tank commander and an oval one for the cannoneer. The gun was mounted on an M34 A1 carriage. The .50 cal. AA machine gun had 315 rounds, the two .30 cal. machine guns 4,750 rounds, and the smoke mortar 12 grenades. The frontal glacis had a 47° slope.

Unlike with the "Dry" stowage, there were no shell racks on the outside sponson, hence the suppression of the additional side armor. When "Wet," in the case of M4A3, the 75-mm shells were stacked vertically in the 10-shell racks under the turret floor. The emergency rack contained four rounds and was situated on the bottom, in line with the cannon; this enabled the cannoneer to get rid of the spent ammunition cases through the rear of the turret basket.

On the cannoneer's side, the turret floor had hinges, enabling him to get the ammunition as and when it was needed, and the turret sometimes had to be swiveled to get at the shells in the right-hand racks.

In the case of the M4A3 76W, the shell racks were also placed under the turret floor, stowed away in 13 five-shell racks. Because the projectiles were long, the racks were mounted diagonally. Each tank had three filler caps for the retarding mixture. A six-shell emergency rack was located transversally under the cannon; this rack was also "Wet" and had a filler spout.

M4A5 GRIZZLY

M4A5 Grizzly, made in Canada. The equipment and the layout were inspired by the British model, with typically, the big bustle chest. 75-mm cannon, nine-cylinder Continental radial engine. Turtle back chassis. The on-board gear and layout differed from the US version of the M4A1.

M4A4 FIREFLY

The M4A4 Firefly was equipped with the famous British 17-pounder. This tank didn't have a bow machine gun; the assistant driver's post was replaced by an extra ammo bin. The turret bustle was lengthened to house the radio. A bustle box completed the equipment.

TD M10 WOLVERINE

TD M10 "Mid-production" from the Régiment Blindé de Fusiliers Marins, 3e Escadron, 3e Peloton. Tank destroyer equipped with the 76-mm cannon firing HVAP ammunition. These were powered by the "Twin Grey Machine," and the TD M10 A1 models by the Ford V8 engine. The A1s were fitted with turret cover panels.

TD M36 B2

R.B.C.E.O. (Régiment Blindé Colonial d'Extrême Orient), at the time of the Indochina war. These tank destroyers were based in the Tonkin, the C.E.F.E.O. (Corps Expéditionnaire Français en Extrême-Orient) command fearing that China might supply tanks to the new Vietnamese Army.

M32 B3 TRV

US Marine Corps M32 B3 Tank Recovery Vehicle, model based on the M4A3 HVSS chassis. Korean War.

M74 ARV

M74 Armored Recovery Vehicle. Breakdown vehicle based on the M4A3 chassis, used in a lot of European armies from 1950 onwards. Recovery vehicle of the 2e RC-ECS/P.D.R.E.

M4A3 76 W

This version was armed with the 76-mm M1 A1 or M1 A2 cannon with M70F, M38 A2, M71 D, or M47 A2 telescopic sights. Some 525 examples were assembled at Grand Blanc and 1,400 by the Detroit Tank Arsenal (weight 32,320 kg, length 6.30 m, width 2.67 m). It could cover 161 km at 42 kph. The cannon, fitted on an M62 carriage, had a supply of 72 rounds, six of which in the emergency rack. The .50 cal. machine gun had 600 rounds, the two machine guns 6,250 rounds, and the smoke-grenade launcher 12 smoke canisters, making up the complete armament. The turret basket was completely suppressed on this series; the crew seats were hooked to the turret ring on side mountings. The frontal glacis had a 47° slope.

The **M4A3 E4** was a version equipped with the M1 76-mm cannon.

M4A3 E8 or M4A3 76 W HVSS

This was nicknamed the "Easy Eight": 4,542 examples came off the production lines between March 1944 and April 1945.

The letter E meant changes to the running gear—the horizontal suspension and the track width—to diminish the ground pressure (Tracks T66, T 80, and T 84). The nickname "Easy Eight" came from its greatly improved handling and explained the E8 designation. The glacis had a 47° slope. The M1 A2 76-mm cannon of this model was fitted with a muzzle brake from the German Panther!

M4A3 105

This was armed with a Type M4 105-mm howitzer. Detroit Tank Arsenal built 500. The armament was the same as the M4 105's (weight 31,730 kg). The series was equipped with the tank commander's revolving cupola on the "Late" models. The last series was equipped with a hydraulic turret motor (for swiveling). The frontal glacis had a 47° slope.

M4A3 105 HVSS: this was an M4A3 equipped with HVSS suspension; 2,539 examples were built by Detroit Tank Arsenal, with a 47° slope for the glacis.

M4A3 E2 Assault Tank

This tank was classified as an assault tank and nicknamed "Jumbo." Here the letter E meant a new type of armor. The frontal armor of the A3 E2 was better than that of the Tigers and Panthers, and this model took part in the Normandy fighting from August 1944 onwards.

It weighed 38,000 kg and was 6.27 m long and 2.93m wide, which made it the widest tank of the family. Armed with the M3 75-mm cannon on a T110 carriage, it carried 104 shots, four of which were in the emergency rack. It had M71G or M38 A2 (a model similar to the M38 but fitted with a lighting system for night vision) telescopic sights. The AA machine gun had 310 rounds and the two .30 cal. machine guns 4,750 rounds. There was also a 12-round smoke mortar.

The Jumbo was fitted with T51 tracks with connector extensions and could reach 35 kph over

161 km. It had a 22.5-m turning circle. It had a heavily armored front without lighting and a new transmission casing. The reduction gears were redesigned to compensate for the increased weight. A few "Late" Jumbos were equipped with a 76-mm cannon. The frontal glacis had a 47° slope.

The idea of a "heavy" M4 came originally from the British, suggested by the members of the British Tank Mission at the beginning of 1942. At the end of 1943 the US Ordnance Depot asked the General Motors Proving Ground to carry out weight tests on an M4A3, for 82,000 lb (41,000 kg).

A ballasted tank was tested over 500 miles and the results were considered satisfactory. The plans were drawn up in 1944 and the Ordnance Technical Committee designated this model as the M4A3 E2. Only 250 were to be built, plus four other examples for further tests.

The 250 E2s were kept for sending to the ETO and were delivered at the end of May 1944. Fisher Body and its sub-contractors used the A3 75 W chassis to build the E2s. Extra armor was welded onto the frontal glacis and the assistant driver's machine gun was retained. Thanks to this modification the frontal glacis armor rose to 12 cm.

The sponson armor reinforcements were assembled in two parts and welded down the center. The front of the transmission armor was new (it weighed an extra 1,200 kg) and protected the driver and the assistant

driver better. The same applied to the front part of the hull floor.

The engine plate armor was in two parts, a grid part and a rear part where the sledgehammer and the track tightening spanner were stored. The E2s were equipped with extensions for fitting sand screens (7.5 cm on each side), but the crews were not keen to fit these parts because they got damaged or destroyed too quickly. Besides, they had to fit smaller sand screens if they wanted to use duckbills.

An extra armored plate has been fitted to this M4A1 76 W's glacis. The Sherman belongs to the 3d Armored Division. The photo was taken near Korbach in central Germany on March 30, 1945. (NARA)

This M4A1 76 W and M4A3 E2 Jumbo are part of the 3d Armored Division. They are probably taking part in the battle of Hürtgen Forest. (NARA)

Right: This M4 Sherman is a command tank. It is recognizable by its extra antenna on the right-hand side of the hull. (*NARA*)

Pressed Steel Cars was the sub-contractor for the turret. The 75-mm cannon was installed in a 76-mm turret. The turret armor was 15-cm thick on the front, the sides, and the rear.

Two 2-cm plates were welded to the top of the turret to increase protection. This turret had no pistol port. The M3 75-mm cannon was installed on the M62 cradle of the 76-mm cannon. An extra 12-cm thickness of armor was welded onto the original shield and this new disposition protected 70 percent of the front of the turret. This assembly—gun, cradle, shield—was designated T 110.

The **M4A3 E9** was the VVSS suspension version with track wideners on all parts of the running gear, allowing duckbills to be fitted on both sides of the track.

The M4A4

The **M4A4** was produced by the Detroit Tank Arsenal—part of the Chrysler Group—and powered by a 30-cylinder Chrysler AC-57 Multibanks engine rated at 470 bhp. The engine compartment was lengthened to house it.

The hull parts were welded together. Note that the A4's running gear was modified because the hull was lengthened by bogey spacing and modifying the track tightening system (longer tracks). The Americans, who didn't really think its powerplant was reliable—it had nonetheless been installed in the M3—intended to send it to the Lend-Lease countries.

Later, at the beginning of the 1950s, the R975 replaced the Multibanks and powered the M4A4 Shermans in the French Army. These tanks were designated M4A4 T. This modification was carried out on the ERGM assembly lines at Reuil. This version weighed 31,600 kg in marching order with a ground pressure of 0.927 kg/cm². It was equipped with the 75-mm M3 cannon on an M34 carriage fitted with M38 telescopic sights, carrying 97 rounds, eight of which were in the emergency rack

inside the turret. The three machine guns used the same supplies as the A2.

Its top speed reached 40 kph with a 160-km range and it could wade through 1.07-m-deep fords (7 cm more than the others), though its turning circle was only 21 m against 19 m for the others.

The gap between the bogeys was increased to 162 cm on this version (145 cm for the others). There was some space in the compartment at the bottom of the hull which could house the engine ventilator. There was a bulge for the radiator filler spout on the rear deck.

The frontal glacis plate was simplified by using a model made up of five welded plates, compared with seven previously. All the M4A4s were assembled with the three-part transmission armor. The front glacis had a 57° slope.

M4A4 T: this was the French version equipped with the Continental radial engine. On this version, the M4A4's rear deck was replaced by the original one (M4), and the crankshaft hole became a rectangular opening in the rear armor. Extra supports and rear mudguards were added; the siren received a protective cover, and the turret was fitted with a periscope cupola with a revolving hatch instead of the split hatch. The front glacis had a 57° slope.

The M4A5

The **M4A5** was the designation given to the Canadian version of the tank, the **Grizzly**.

The **RAM 1** was a tank built in Canada using the American M3 as a base. It was armed with a British gun, the 40-mm QF 2-pounder. Two .30 cal. machine guns were mounted on either side of the cannon and another could be mounted on the turret for AA use.

The **RAM 2** was equipped with the British 57-mm QF 6-pounder gun, and carried 92 shells. The chassis was slightly modified compared with the RAM 1 and the engine was a Continental R 975 EC2. The best-known variants were the Kangaroo, the flame-thrower, and the six-man command vehicle with a false cannon.

One of the very first M4A4 Shermans built. (*NARA*)

At the beginning of 1945, this M4A3 from the 12th Armored Division is nearing the town of Schneeberg in Germany. It is equipped with a T23 D 82081 turret; the cannon is a 76-mm M1 A1 C with a small sleeve for fitting the muzzle brake. (NARA)

Eighty-four examples of these were built. The Montreal Locomotive works built 2,993 examples of the RAM 1 and 2 between 1943 and 1944.

The Grizzly was a tank assembled using the American M4A1 as a base; 188 were built in 1943, armed with a 75-mm cannon. Production was interrupted since the Americans were able to satisfy all the orders themselves.

The M4A6

This tank was powered by a Caterpillar RD-1820 diesel engine and had a cast frontal glacis. The rest of the hull was made of welded armored plates.

Production was cancelled after 75 examples were built because there were problems with the engine; this was also to limit the number of engines in service and the sources of fuel supply. The US Army always favored using a single fuel type. It is important to know, however, that Caterpillar equipped this model with a real multi-fuel engine. Dimensions, turret, and armament were all similar to the A4 versions, except for the 75-mm M3 cannon which was mounted on an M34 A1 cradle. All the A6s were equipped with the single-piece transmission armor. The turret armor was increased so it no longer needed any over-armor. The frontal glacis plate had a 33—55° slope.

The **M4A6** was put into service in a single American unit, the 777th Tank Battalion, in 1943. This was a training unit, and when the battalion was engaged in the ETO it was equipped with M4A3s.

A digression worth the detour

The data given below actually upset the official total production figures. The A2 HVSS and the A2 "with large

half hatches" were produced mainly for Lend-Lease, according to the following information: apparently Fisher Tank Arsenal built 1,000 M4A2 75s "with large half hatches" between November 1943 and May 1944, and knowing that the HVSS cost $2,000 more than the VVSS, the same firm built 1,594 M4A2 VVSSs and 1,300 M4A2 76 HVSSs between May 1944 and May 1945.

Pressed Steel Cars made 21 M4A2 76 HVSSs between April and May 1945.

The Soviets were the first to receive the M4A2 76; they acquired 2,073, of which 460 were M4A2 76 HVSSs. In the second quarter of 1945, the British received just five. In September 1945, a report indicated that there were 704 M4A6 76 HVSSs in depots across the USA, of which 133 had been earmarked for conversions and tests.

Canada bought 300 M4A2 76 HVSSs in 1946. These tanks remained in Canada and were used in training schools.

A Canadian M4A5 Grizzly Sherman in a tricky posture. The shot was taken in Italy in July 1944. (ARC)

8 | The Sherman Family

Without needing a great deal of imagination, it can be said that when built, the M4 was brought out in all forms conceivable and used in all likely circumstances. But there was even more to it than that!

Its chassis was used to develop a whole series of variants, some of which have indeed earned their place in our museums, such was the scope of their designers' creativity which sometimes bordered on the funny. The only risk we run here in writing this chapter is to miss some of them out, either through ignorance, or by inadvertence.

In the previous chapter, we mentioned the breakdown versions which were what logically followed on from a whole family of armored vehicles, everyone knowing that, mechanics and crews being fallible, these breakdown vehicles would some day be needed.

M3, M3B1 and M31B2 TRV

Although they did not use the M4 as a base, these breakdown machines towed and repaired Shermans in the American, British, and French armies.

A breakdown vehicle based on the M3A3 Tank chassis, the M31 was a Tank Recovery Vehicle. From October 1942 onwards, 296 were built by the Baldwin Locomotive Works.

A six-man crew set up the special equipment and the vehicle's armament comprised two .30 cal. 1919 machine guns. It was powered by the General Motors Twin 6046 engine. The tank was equipped with two fake guns, one 37-mm on the turret—which became the rotating mounting for the crane jib—and a fake 75-mm cannon installed on a support on the left-hand side.

The jib could lift up to 4,500 kg without the A-frame, 5,600 kg with its legs fixed to the frontal glacis, and 14,000 kg with its legs on the ground. The rest of the vehicle's equipment comprised a winch with 17-ton direct traction power.

M31B1

This used the M3 chassis and was put into service in December 1942; 506 were built, powered by the nine-cylinder Wright Continental radial engine.

An ARV Mk I Sherman of the British 3rd County of London Yeomanry from the 4th Armoured Brigade, most likely a few hours after landing in Normandy, as the Waterproofing equipment seems to indicate. (*Tank Museum*)

Unlike the diesel-powered TRVs, power take-off for the specific equipment items used the transmission and was situated at the rear left of the vehicle. The M31 was put into service after the M31B1.

M31B2

This tank was based on the M3A5 tank chassis with equipment like the B1.

The breakdown, dozers, and special Shermans

1. M31 ARV on a M3 chassis.
2. M32 ARV at Bône 1943 (photo by Alain Tomei).
3. M 74 Tank Recovery Vehicle (post World War II).
4. British BARV (Beach Armored Recovery Vehicle).
5. ARV Mk I, breakdown vehicle on an M4 chassis (British).
6. ARV Mk 2 (British).
7. Tank Dozer on an M4 105 chassis.
8. Canadian Kangaroo.
9. Sherman "Tulip" equipped with two rocket launchers (British).
10. Sherman Observation Command Post with fake cannon (British)
11. Demolition Tank on HVSS chassis.
12. Sherman CD.

An M4 Sherman and its motorbike are towed by no less than two M31 breakdown tanks on an M3 chassis. *(NARA)*

M31 TRV (Tank Recovery Vehicle)

This was a breakdown tank equipped with an A-framed jib and a winch with 28 tons direct traction power. The cable went through the front glacis cable guide or through the opening in the casemate (when used as a crane with jib deployed). The jib was operated by means of a cable which wound round a hub fitted to the right sprocket wheel.

The turret was replaced by a casemate armed with an 81-mm mortar firing smoke grenades. The casemate armament comprised a .50 cal. machine gun; a .30 cal. machine gun was installed in the billet nose cone cover. Some 163 examples were built.

M32B1

Based on the M4A1, 1,055 were built.

M32 A1 B1

The same as the B1 but with an HVSS running gear.

M32 B2

Based on an M4A2 chassis; 26 built.

M32 B3

Based on the M4A4 chassis; 318 examples built.

M32 B4

Based on the M4A4, only one built, not approved for production.

T14 E1

M32 B3 HVSS built for the Marines; 80 built.

M74 ARV

As far as the M4 breakdown tank family was concerned, the Recovery Vehicles survived longer than all the other versions of the M4. After the M32, a few examples of an intermediate version, the M34, were put into service. The best-known was without doubt the M74 Medium Tank Recovery Vehicle. It was developed using the M4A3 Easy Eight as a base but with improved lifting and winching equipment.

The main winch was increased to 40 tons direct pulling power, which was nonetheless not always enough in some situations. The jib used as a crane when deployed was bigger and an anchoring blade was also part of the equipment.

An oxyacetylene cutting post was also carried, the towing triangles were doubled, and specialized kits were loaded into the various stowage areas.

The M74 was powered by the V8 Ford engine, whose cooling system had been revised by increasing the volume of the circuit. The two-part engine shutters on the rear deck were hinged and pivoted on torsion rods. On the casemate side, the mortar was removed; the radio was one of the SCR 508/528 sets and the indispensable .50 cal. machine gun was still on its casemate mounting, like the .30 cal. in its billet nose cone. Armament also included a 3.5-inch (89-mm) caliber AT M20 (or M20 A1) rocket launcher. Built by the Bowen-McLaughlin-York Company between 1954 and 1955, a small series was built at the end of 1958 by the Rock Island Arsenal (60 examples). The French Army received some M74s after 1960.

This grandfather of all recovery vehicles made sure that broken-down vehicles were recovered up until the moment the M48 tank appeared, for which the Americans had to put the M88 Heavy Recovery Tank into service, breaking away completely from the M4 concept.

It's worth noting that this M88 is still in service in the US Army. This vehicle still carries out maintenance and towing operations for the M1 Abrams, showing that the American designers were still faithful to their boom, which is still used in exactly the same way as it was for the M32 B3, except on the M88 A2 version where all the equipment is hydraulic.

When you have encountered the Americans' know-how in the automation and hydraulics domains, you know that that boom just has to be reliable, to say the least.

Back to the M74: it was in service in French units until the end of the 1970s, so it towed M24 Chaffees, M47 Pattons, and AMX 30s, to mention just three.

Sherman ARV Mk I

This was the British version of the breakdown tank—the "Armoured Recovery Vehicle." It was equipped with a winch and an A-shaped boom, deployed mechanically. Its equipment comprised the Holmes-type anchoring system, a two-piece towing triangle (attached to the left outer sponson), cables, various pulleys, and all the tooling needed for taking out an engine or a gearbox. An oxyacetylene post was fixed on the rear right-hand side, in the turret well housing. A vice was mounted on the differential casing on the left-hand side and it could move across horizontally. The rear deck was occupied by two big coffers containing equipment and sheaving pulleys.*

Sherman ARV Mk II

This more elaborate version of the Mark I was developed using the M4A4 as its base. The A-shaped boom was carried in several parts; the legs were fixed on the left- and right-hand side sponsons. The vehicle was fitted with a fake cannon and a casemate was installed over the turret well. At the rear were the lifting hoist and an anchoring system with hydraulic commands.

The Sherman BARV

This was one of Percy Hobart's brainwaves—the "Beach Armoured Recovery Vehicle." Its purpose was clear: it operated on the beaches. Just from its appearance one could deduce that it was able to ford relatively deep watercourses, since the exhaust pipes were mounted high enough inside the hull's waterproof protection. The vehicle had no close-quarters defense weapons and

Normandy, July 1944. A turretless Sherman ARV towing a Sherman I from a British unit. (IWM B8910)

it had limited equipment: no towing triangle, no winch, just very long cables and a few pulleys. On the front was a pushing system made of log beams fixed to a metal structure intended to push the vehicles in difficulty.

It was first and foremost a rescue and recovery vehicle able to operate in water up to 2.9 m deep. Fifty-two were built for the Normandy Landings. Later a BARV was built on a Centurion chassis and used during the Falklands War in 1982. Today (2019) the Netherlands are equipped with a BARV version using the Leopard tank chassis.

After the breakdown vehicles, here's a brief look at some of the variants you could come across. Some of them were not produced in great numbers or were abandoned after unsuccessful trials.

M4 Dozer

This M4 was equipped with a bulldozer blade, with or without a turret, for the Engineers Corps.

Although hydraulically operated, the dozer blade was only used for pushing potential barriers, abattis, anti-tank obstacles etc. out of the way. It was not used for leveling but for filling in ditches, making embankments, or excavating so a tank could dig in. Several Dozer versions were equipped with the

A Sherman and its M1 bulldozer blade on a Normandy road. As one cannot distinguish the engine shutter stops or that the frontal glacis plate is at 57° with small hatches, it's probably an M4A2 or even an M4. (NARA)

Caterpillar D8 Bulldozer hydraulic system, especially for the landings in Italy in 1943. It proved very satisfactory, so the M1 Dozer blade was designed and put into production in 1944.

A second blade model, the M1A1, was designed to be mounted on the HVSS versions. It was fixed on both sides to the central bogey and was operated by the turret hydraulics. A short series of M4s was delivered with a permanent mounting for the blade dozer. These vehicles were intended for the Engineers and had no turrets.

Sherman OP Command

This version of the Sherman, used as an Observation Post, was created by the British. On these models there were up to three radios; they were easily identifiable by the number of aerials mounted on the superstructure.

These tanks were intended, among other things, for the "Operations" officers, artillery observers, and senior officers of the armored divisions. They were equipped with a WS M19 radio set in the turret and a WS M18 in the sponson, near the assistant driver or sometimes in the turret. The inside was laid out differently in these British tanks because of their special function, the main modification being the removal of the cannon and its replacement by a wooden fake; this freed a lot of space

Left: The Sherman ARV Mk II was perfectly set up. Unlike the M32, its American equivalent, the British breakdown vehicle was only armed with a bow machine gun. The cannon was a fake. (*Tank Museum*)

Below: August 14, 1944: Major-General Roberts on the right with Brigadier Harvey, commanding the 29th Armoured Brigade (11th Armoured Division), in front of the latter's tank. (*IWM B9184*)

in the turret. All this space was used for equipment, especially for the maps and firing tables. The turret used, the Firefly's, was easily recognizable because the radio caisson was emptied.

The AA weapon (.50 cal.) was kept, as were the two .30 cal. (coaxial and assistant driver's) machine guns, explaining the presence of metal ammunition cases in the turret. The equipment was made up with the usual spares for periscopes, combat rations, various lamps, pennants, first aid kits, fire extinguishers, ammunition, smoke grenades, hand grenades, and individual weapons. The OP Command versions were fitted with extra steps up the front glacis, offering easier access for the tank commander.

The M4 and Gap Clearing

M4 Fascine

This model was not really well known, though it was almost the precursor in the art of clearing gaps. Indeed,

the British had already brought out a system based on the Churchill which enabled it to cross obstacles such as very wide ditches.

The principle was rather simple: a tracked vehicle equipped with an overhead bridging element positioned itself at the bottom of the gap to be crossed

Opposite: This cross-section of a Norman hedge (the *bocage*) shows the difficulties encountered by the tanks while driving around in this environment. (Drawing by the author)

1. M34 Sherman equipped with the Fascine system.
2. M4 Sherman Twaby Ark
3. M4 Sherman Octopus
4. Mobile Assault Bridge

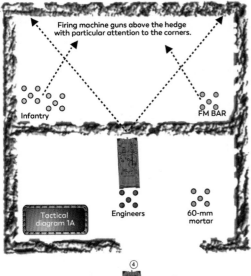

Firing machine guns above the hedge
with particular attention to the corners.

Infantry

FM BAR

Engineers

60-mm
mortar

Tactical
diagram 1A

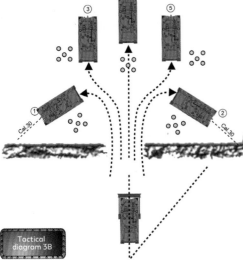

④

③

⑤

①

②

Cal.30

Cal.30

Tactical
diagram 3B

Diagrams of the different ways to go through a hedge in
the Normandy *bocage*. (*Drawing by the author*)

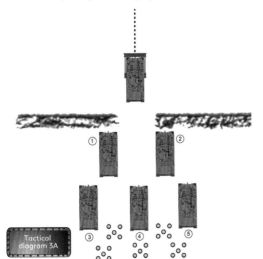

①

②

③

④

⑤

Tactical
diagram 3A

A British Churchill tank
crossing a gap with
the help of a Sherman
Octopus. (*NARA*)

and the tanks then drove over the bridging element.
In anticipation of Operation *Overlord*, the Americans
had wanted to improve on the principle by taking up
the idea of a bridge-laying vehicle—a bridge layer.* The
British came up with the Fascine.

The objective was to equip the Sherman with a light
and fast way of clearing gaps; in this case it was a metal
armature on a turretless tank. There were two of these
armatures, which were placed one after the other in
the gap, covered with planks and tree trunks, allowing
armored vehicles not exceeding 40 tons to get across.

The fascines slid down the metal ramps set up at the
front of the tank. An improved version used the turret
hydraulics and a rack, on which was fixed—instead of the
turret—a cradle enabling the first fascine to be placed,
then by swiveling through 180°, to place the second.

The M4 Sherman Twaby
Ark had shorter spans than
the Octopus. Here they are
folded. (*NARA*)

At the end of July 1944, an M10 Tank Destroyer (left) from the 702d Tank Destroyer Battalion, still equipped with part of its Fording Kit, being overtaken by an M4 of the 743d Tank Battalion fitted with a Cullin Type 2 hedge cutter. The shot was taken near Lonlay l'Abbaye in Normandy. (NARA)

This layout also turned out to be very effective during the fighting in the Pacific and in Korea. It was installed on a "Cannon" Sherman as well as on the tank destroyers.

M4 Mobile Assault Bridge (MAB)

This was the bridge-laying tank with a ramps fitted at each end and a boom for deploying them. This model was rather rare. The MAB was especially used in Sicily and Italy, like most of the bridge layers.

Sherman Badger

This was an M4A2 HVSS fitted with a one-piece bridging element. It was developed in Canada in 1945.

Sherman Twaby Ark

This gap-clearing version was designed round the British Churchill Ark, and was especially used for instructing and training crews.

Sherman Octopus

This tank was like the preceding one but with longer bridging elements.

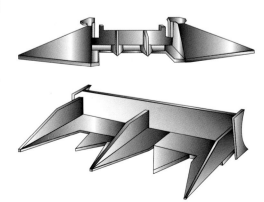

The Cullin Type 1 and 2, so-called "regulation" systems.

Sherman Plymouth

The Plymouth was a bridge layer using the structure of the Bailey bridge. These structures were in fact modular bridges which were set up quickly, transported by M4s.

The *Bocage* Tank

The M4 Cullin Hedgerow Cutter

This was a special for Normandy, an AOC almost, like the wine classification.

This was an M4 equipped with a tool at the front for getting through the hedges of the Normandy *bocage* (small fields surrounded by high, thick hedges and ditches). This version was also called the "Hedge Trimmer" (or "Prong"). Most of these tools were made from the anti-tank obstacles that the Germans had set up along the Normandy beaches. One version, the Hedge Buster, consisted of a molded tappet. This explains why the forms and the make-up of the Cullin system were so varied. Among the most widespread models there were two main variants.

The system was fitted in July 1944, a little more than a month after the landings. It was a surprise to learn that the lovely hedges of the Normandy *bocage* constituted such an obstacle for tracked vehicles of more than 30 tons, but nature is a formidable opponent. The American High Command had brought out a special booklet for armored units in Normandy called "Combat Lessons," with a chapter entitled "Fighting in Normandy." It gives an idea of how important these hedges were for the tankmen who had landed. The book begins by defining the hedges in question and their environment.

One read that the lines of penetration through the Normandy *bocage* went across a very slightly hilly terrain, comprising crop fields separated by hedges. These fields were of different sizes and set out in a higgledy-higgledy pattern which for the Americans resembled patchwork, which they called Crazy Quilt.

The hedges themselves consisted of a 2-m high, 1.6-m wide embankment; the crest was planted with tightly packed, stalwart bushes; the embankment slopes were strewn with spiny tufts of vegetation. At the base of the embankment, on both sides, was a little stream 30 cm wide and 50 cm deep which drained the water down to a collector at the end of the field.

Apart from the fact that the hedges were an obstacle which slowed progress, or even halted it, they were the ideal location for an ambush or for preparing an attack, all the more so as small country roads ran along these hedges. This caused a delicate situation for the infantry accompanying the tanks. Another drawback, and not the least, was the lack of visibility from one field to the next, except when there was a village nearby, in which case the church steeple or water tower acted as a landmark.

In Normandy, the Germans had a huge advantage: ever since 1940, they had studied and organized their whole coastal defense. They had mastered the art of using this terrain to their advantage. Caen, Falaise, Villers-Bocage and others were just some examples of the bitterness of the ensuing fighting.

In a memo, the general commanding the US XIX Corps wrote:

"The Germans have organized their defense around the 88-mm cannon used both for PaK and FlaK, the Tigers and their 88-mm cannon, and the Panthers with their 75-mm cannon with high-velocity shells.

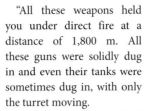

Top: Sergeant Cullin in Normandy, July 1944.

Right and below:
1. Making a Cullin Type 1 device on the front of a tank
2. A "Prong" device mounted on an M4
3. "Rhino" type mounting
4. A variant of the Cullin Type 2 device

"All these weapons held you under direct fire at a distance of 1,800 m. All these guns were solidly dug in and even their tanks were sometimes dug in, with only the turret moving.

"Add to that the work of the German snipers who didn't hesitate to remain in place four or five days after a position had been lost and then reveal themselves with fatal shots, incendiary grenades or carefully booby-trapped armored vehicles."

From there on, the Normandy *bocage* hedges became a really gaping wound for the Allies. It was essential to use the tank-infantry combination to break down the resistance and get through the hedges. The attacks took place according to a well-tested plan: 15 minutes of artillery preparation and then the armor (six tanks) opened the way by taking out the anti-tank weapons. Six other tanks accompanied the infantry company, and the last six tanks came up in cover.

Opposite:
1. Mine Exploder built by the USMC on the basis of a Dozer M1
2. T1 E1 Mine Exploder
3. T1 E4 Mine Exploder
4. T1 E3 Mine Exploder
5   T1 E5 Mine Exploder
6. T1 E6 Mine Exploder
7. T4 Mine Exploder
8. T2 Flail Mine Exploder
9. T3 E2 Mine Exploder
10. T3 E1 Mine Exploder
11. T4 Mine Exploder

1. Operation *Cobra* was the code name for the American offensive in the Cotentin in July 1944, to open up the way into Brittany and drive in the German lines of resistance which were still very strong in this sector.

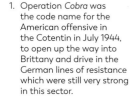

In 1943, during tests carried out with other Sherman "Scorpion" type mine-clearers in Sicily and Italy, the US Army used the T1 E3 "Aunt Jemima" anti-mine device fixed to an M1A1 Sherman. "Aunt Jemima" was a famous make of industrial pancakes whose publicity character was reproduced on the tank's hull. *(NARA)*

The tanks accompanying the infantry copiously sprayed the hedges all along the way. This combination advanced from hedge to hedge, therefore at walking speed. In certain cases, tank-dozers were called up to open a breach in the hedge, enabling the soldiers to deal with both sides of the hedge at the same time. In other cases, Engineer units dealt with the targets.

When the Cullin tools were mounted, whatever the materials used, the hedges were grasped as low as possible by the base, enabling the tanks to rip them out. If trying to cross a hedge without using this tool, the tank would lose power because of the slope, the nose would run into the vegetation on the embankment, and it would halt. The tank-infantry combination in Normandy was frequently supported by elements from the Engineers using explosives.

The hedgerow-cutting system was devised by Sergeant Curtis G. Cullin, who in fact took up an idea from a certain Billy Roberts who wanted to put big teeth on the front of the tank. This initial solution envisaged eliminating the problem of the Normandy *bocage* and was called "Salad Fork"; it comprised two big metal bars welded to the front of the tank, like two horns. The tank planted the fork in the embankment, leaving two holes which were then filled with explosives, thereafter creating an opening through the hedge.

In practice, this solution wasn't the best, as the metal bars often broke in the embankment. They were at first replaced by a blade with very large teeth, called "Green Dozer," but this wasn't very satisfactory either.

Sergeant Cullin's tool was finally adopted because when it lifted the earth and vegetation of the hedge with its teeth, this increased the tank's protection as it came over the top of the embankment, the most vulnerable moment. To get the most out of the system, the tanks tackled the embankment in third gear at 15 mph.

The Cullin Hedgrow Device was sometimes called "Rube Goldbergs" and the tanks which had one were called "Rhinos," referring to the animal's horns. The Americans made and mounted about 500 Cullin devices on their tanks, mainly M4s, M5s, and M10 TDs in the 2d Armored Division. The British produced about a thousand, of which 600 were in England. General Bradley did all he could to ensure that as many tanks as possible were equipped with these devices before Operation *Cobra*.[1]

The Mine-Clearers

There were a great number of M4 mine-clearers. The Germans had liberally scattered mines all over the beaches and their direct access routes, but also all the possible landing sites, in Sicily and Italy. The Americans had started to develop anti-mine systems on the M3 tanks.

The British had produced mine-clearing vehicles based on the M4, but also on the Churchill and Valentine tanks (Crab 1 and Crab 2). There were three types of mine-clearers: one model exploded the mines using rollers or spinning flails attached to the front of the tank; another used a device which unearthed the mines; and the third hit the mines so they'd explode.

It is worth knowing that, at least for the period, laying mines or a minefield followed very precise rules. For a minefield for instance, a laying plan established the tracks, the various markers and the mine-clearing sequences. The reasons for laying anti-vehicle mines along the (well identified) tracks was to put the tank out of action, making the anti-tank gunners' work easier.

The mine-clearers with rollers

T1 E1 Earthworm Mine Exploder

An anti-mine tank fitted with armored disks: a rare creature indeed. The set of armored disks was put together like a tricycle with each front "wheel" made

of six disks. These wheels were attached to an M32 Recovery Vehicle which pushed them, the disks being suspended and worked by the Recovery Vehicle's boom. The system was developed in 1943 and weighed 18 tons.

T1 E2 Mine Exploder

This was the T1E1 reduced to two seven-disk units. Designed in 1943, it remained just an experiment.

T1 E3 (M1) Aunt Jemima Mine Exploder

An anti-mine tank equipped with two units of five 3.3-m diameter armored disks. The disks were driven by a chain from specially adapted sprockets; 75 were made and were used in Italy and in Normandy. It was sometimes pushed by a second tank because of its weight.

T1 E4 Mine Exploder

An anti-mine tank developed in 1944 equipped with 16 disks on the front. These were mounted on a reinforced boom fitted to the tank hull.

T1 E5 Mine Exploder

An anti-mine tank based on the T1E3 and developed in July 1944. It was equipped with two units of six armored disks mounted on a central support instead of a boom. Drive came from the sprockets. It remained an experiment.

T1 E6 Mine Exploder

An anti-mine tank similar to the T1 E3 but with serrated disks. It remained at the prototype stage.

T2 E1 Mine Exploder

An anti-mine tank developed for the US Marine Corps (USMC) based on the M32 Tank Recovery Vehicle and using a boom. This unsatisfactory prototype was abandoned in October 1943.

T9 Mine Exploder

An anti-mine tank equipped with six rollers. It was difficult to steer.

T9 E1 Mine Exploder

An anti-mine tank, lighter than the T9, but not very effective because some mines didn't explode.

The Flails

T2 Flail Mine Exploder

This is the American designation for the British Crab 1 tank which was fitted with two metal arms on the front linked by a cylinder. Long chains were fitted round this cylinder and hit the ground when the drum was made to rotate.

When they hit an anti-personnel or anti-tank mine, the chains set it off. The explosions destroyed nothing on the Sherman, which simply carried on going across the minefield. Some examples were used by the US Army in 1944—45 in Northwest Europe.

T3 Mine Exploder

Designed in 1942, this anti-mine tank was base on the British "Scorpion" technique. The system consisted of hollowed-out drums and chains mounted on arms of American design. Drive was transmitted from a motor fixed on the right-hand side of the tank. When the chains moved they made a spiral.

On the front of the tank was a shield to protect it from falling stones or debris. Forty-one T3s were built by the Pressed Steel Car Company, but production of this version ceased in 1943.

T3 E1 Mine Exploder

A T3 anti-mine tank equipped with longer arms and a chain rotor whose drum was filled with sand. On this version, the flail drive was removed and it was the tank engine that drove the flail. This lighter system only weighed 2,500 kg and the rotation speed of the flail increased from 75 rpm on the T3 to 178 rpm on the E1.

T3 E2 Mine Exploder

An anti-mine tank based on the T3 E1 but with an armored drum instead of a chain rotor.

T4 Mine Exploder

American designation for the British anti-mine tank, Crab II. Only a few examples were tested by the US Army.

The Mine Excavators

T4 Mine Excavator

Developed in 1942, here the mines were no longer exploded but unearthed. On this model the Tank Dozer's blade was modified by fitting it with forks at the base of the tank. The blade was mounted on the front of the M4. The model was abandoned after several unsuccessful trials.

T5 Mine Excavator

Designed using a T4, on which an attempt was made to improve its reliability by replacing the blades with V-shaped spades. A later version was designated T5 E1.

T5 E2 Mine Excavator

A system designed using a T5 E1 and equipped with the hydraulics of the Tank Dozer to control the depth of the digging.

T5 E3 Mine Excavator

On this model, the angle and the shape of the blade were modified in order to unearth the mines and push them to the side. The blade was curved to prevent the mines from falling back between the blade and the tank. One hundred were made at Plante-Choate and shipped to the Pacific theater of operations.

T6 Mine Excavator

A model based on the T5 on which the shape of the spades was modified. Followed by the T6 E1 and TE E2 models. The system was abandoned because the depth of the digging could not be modified.

T7 Mine Exploder

This anti-mine tank was developed at the end of 1943. Its hull was equipped with little rollers each consisting of two disks. It was abandoned because it was thought unsatisfactory.

T8 Mine Exploder

An anti-mine tank equipped with steel spikes mounted on a swiveling chassis. These spikes hammered the ground in front of the tank, rather like a woodpecker.

This tank was difficult to maneuver, which earned it the nickname "Johnny Walker" (after the whisky). The spikes were driven by the left-hand sprocket on which was fixed a toothed rim. A set of pinions engaged on this wheel and drove a shaft which set the hammers moving. A T8 model with six hammers was tested.

T9 and T9 E1

The T9 was equipped with a spiked cylinder pushed in front of the tank using a big telescopic tube. This system by itself weighed 32 tons, or the weight of the Sherman pushing it. It was much too heavy and its successor, the T9 E1, had a similar but lighter cylinder. The telescopic cylinder that activated the drum measured 6 meters but this could be increased to 8 meters.

1. T5 E3 Mine Exploder
2. T5 E2 Mine Excavator
3. T7 Mine Exploder
4. T9 E1 Mine Exploder
5. T10 Mine Exploder
6. T8 Mine Exploder
7. T11 Mine Exploder
8. T12 Mine Exploder
9. T15 E1 Mine-Resistant Vehicle
10. Final Flail
11. Galloping Ghost

A Sherman Crab Mk II from the 1st Lothian and Borders Horse, a regiment in the 79th Armoured Division. At the rear are the guiding lights and the station keeping marker system to show the limits of the de-mined area. *(Tank Museum)*

Opposite:

1. The Lulu mine-clearer
2. On the Marquis mine-clearer, the turret had been replaced by an armored caisson containing the operating system for mine clearing.
3. The Scorpion Mk IV was equipped with two engines housed in the structure at the rear.
4. The Pram Scorpion
5. Crab Mk I, flail lowered.
6. Crab Mk II, flail lowered. Note the station keeping system and the spotlights at the rear.
7. AMRCR (Anti-Mine Reconnaissance Castor Roller) Mark I in action
8. The Lobster Mine Exploder preceded the Crab

Big Foot T10 Mine Exploder

An anti-mine system mounted on a tricycle unit under the tank, controlled at a distance by the following tank. The bogeys were removed; the hull floor was strengthened by an extra 25-mm plate of armor; the two front wheels were 2.4 m in diameter and the rear drum measured 1.82 m in diameter.

The T10 rode 1.4 m above the ground and weighed more than 58 tons. Its mine-clearing speed was 3 kph and its maximum road speed was 10 kph. It was difficult to control and was finally abandoned.

T11 Mine Exploder

An anti-mine tank armed with six mortars mounted on the front. The mortars were fired by a common control and were of the Spigot type. Unlike the classic mortar where the ammunition was dropped into the barrel mouth, the barrel of the so-called Spigot was surrounded by the ammunition. Experimental only.

T12 Mine Exploder

An anti-mine tank armed with 23 mortars. This model was effective but was nonetheless abandoned in December 1944.

T14 Mine Exploder

An M4 tank was fitted with ventral armor, reinforced tracks, and armored lateral protection. It exploded the mines by driving over them. Abandoned at the end of the war.

T15, T15 E1, T15 E2 Mine-Resistant Vehicles

These models were built after September 1944, and were improved versions of the T14. The turret was removed and the extra armor was increased on the running gear. The bogey wheels were coupled to armored disks and extra rubber shock absorbers were fitted above the wheels.

An armor plate covered the turret well and a closed position intended for the tank commander was fitted there. This weaponless and turretless version, built by Chrysler, weighed 36 tons. The T15 E1 was equipped with tracks with external teeth.

Snake equipment for M4s

A Sherman tank pushed an explosive charge in the shape of a serpent. It was used by the American infantry, especially during the Normandy Landings.

T59 10.75 inch

A system of rocket launchers whose task was to clear a passage through a minefield. The M4 towed a trailer on which the launching system, firing 1.98-m missiles weighing 160 kg, was installed.

The British mine-clearers

The British mine-clearers fitted to the Churchills and Valentines are not included here. The British mine-clearing devices were mainly flails. They were called Lulu, Scorpion, Lobster, Marquis, Pram, and Crab. The

The American mine-clearing flail tank on an M4, based on the British Scorpion model shown here, is being tried out in a desert area. (NARA)

AMRCR (Anti-Mine Reconnaissance Castor Roller) versions were fitted with the Roller Device.

The Scorpion and Pram Scorpion Mine Exploders

The Scorpion system was originally mounted on a Grant tank. It was powered by two Dodge engines installed in the rear. These engines drove the flail, with the transmission shafts fitted to the sides of the tank. The gantry of the flail—wide and fixed to the sponsons—made maneuvering the tank round tight bends and across bridges rather delicate.

The Pram Scorpion was a system installed on the M4 tank; the tank engine powered the flail and its arms were fixed to the central bogey. On the frontal glacis, between the flail's arms there were two armored rollers, pushed along by the tank during mine clearing.

Marquis Mine Exploder

The Scorpion system was mounted on an M4 whose turret was replaced by an armored caisson sheltering the engine driving the flail.

Lulu Mine Detector

A very nice detecting system with rollers. Unlike other models making use of the weight of the rollers, these were equipped with three light drums in which there were electric coils—this was the principal of the SCR 625 (more commonly known as the "frying pan").

Two drums were attached to the front in line with the tracks and a drum was fixed to the rear between the track lines. When a mine was detected, Lulu sent a sound signal inside the tank. A mine-clearing team was then brought up for the area.

The front and rear rollers could be folded down on to the rear deck so the tank could move around normally.

Crab Mk I and Mk II Mine Exploders

The Crab system was Sir Percy Hobart's creation: he devised a much simpler solution using the power take-off from the tank engine itself. A set of cardan shafts was chain-driven and the system could be moved by a hydraulic group. The 43-chain flail had a power of 285 bhp. The Crab Mk II copied the basic Crab Mk I but corrected one major defect: the Mk I had a flail which could only be lowered to a horizontal position in front of the tank, meaning that it could not go down any lower and thereby reach the bottom of hollows and potholes on the terrain or the track.

The Mk II versions were therefore equipped with a system which enabled the flail to follow the lie of the land more accurately. An adjustable counterweight was added to the left-hand arm of the flail so that it would follow the profile of the track or the road to be de-mined.

Another of the Mk II's improvements was the track markers on either side of the tank: two flat containers containing chalk powder were installed behind the arms of the flail. As the tank advanced, the two edges of the cleared zone were clearly marked out. All people had to do was keep between the chalk lines.

The de-mining speed of the Crab Mk II was 2 kph. These machines were entirely satisfactory and were assigned during Operation *Overlord* to the 79th Armoured Division, in which they served until the end of the war.

Lobster Mine Exploder

The Lobster was tested but could not better the Crab Mk II's performances. On this model, the flail comprised a series of spoked disks (unlike the drum flail of the Crabs) onto which the chains were attached. This was to improve vision during mine-clearing operations. The chains were attached to each other by horizontal rods in order to strengthen the stroke when hitting the ground. Two actuators attached to either side of the central bogeys activated the flail arms.

AMRCR Mk I Mine Roller Device

This was a mine-clearer with rollers. Four steel rollers were mounted on arms on the front of the Sherman—usually a Sherman V—each roller being made up of 18 armored disks. Fourteen of these disks were 49.5 cm in diameter and 25.4 mm thick.

The four remaining "separating" disks measured 66 cm in diameter and were 12.7 mm thick. The rollers, divided into two groups, were mounted in the axis of the tracks.

The Canadian CIRD

The Canadian Indestructible Roller Device was a mine-clearer equipped with two solid rollers, pushed in front of the tank, in line with the tracks. These rollers were equipped with suspension springs and were mounted on a frame which itself comprised two shock-absorbing springs in case of a mine exploding.

The suspension and the absorber springs enabled the rollers to rise and reverse when there was an explosion, then return to their initial position to continue mine clearing.

Mine clearing speed was 10 kph. There were two types of rollers: the 15.5-inch (63.5-cm for 487 kg) and 18-inch (71-cm for 762 kg).

The Flamethrower Versions

E4 R2-5R1, E4 R3-ER1, (M3-4-3) Flame guns

The flamethrower was mounted in place of the bow machine gun.

E4 R4-4R 5-6RC Flame Gun

This flamethrower was in the form of a periscope and mounted in place of the bow machine gun. The reservoirs were installed inside the tank and they lasted longer.

POA Flamethrower

A flamethrower tank whose injector was installed inside the barrel of the 105-mm cannon, whose breech block had been suppressed. This projection device was the Mk I. The napalm tank was in the turret.

POA-CWS 75-H1

A flamethrower tank whose injector was installed inside the barrel of the 75-mm M3 cannon. The flamethrower apparatus was the E13-13.

1. POA CWS 75H Sherman Flamethrower
2. E12 M4 Sherman Flamethrower
3. E4R2-5R1 Sherman Flamethrower
4. POA CWS H5 Sherman Flamethrower
5. Sherman Crocodile Flamethrower and its trailer
6. M3 4-3 Sherman Flamethrower

POA-CWS 75-H2

Flamethrower tank whose injector and additional barrel were installed on the right of the 75-mm cannon, so it could still be used.

E6R1

A flamethrower kit replacing the assistant driver's periscope.

E6-R7 Flame Gun

A flamethrower tank whose small diameter barrel replaced the cannon. The napalm tank was stowed in the turret.

M4 Crocodile

A flamethrower tank using the British Crocodile equipment. These M4s carried the napalm in a small cistern towed by the tank.

E1 Anti-Personnel Tank Projector

A specific version developed in 1945. This system comprised four little flamethrower tubes set out around the hull. They were fired individually or together from inside the tank. The aim was to stop suicide attacks very near the tank.

T33 Flamethrower

M4A3 tank equipped with an E12 R4 flamethrower. The tank was fitted with a special turret.

A few examples were used to the end of the war in the Pacific.

All these flamethrowers were used mainly during the war in the Pacific. The crews of these tanks used to protect the sides of these tanks with wood to prevent the Japanese from sticking magnetic mines on them. One can easily imagine the result of a mine exploding against a tank full of napalm.

Sherman artillery tractor and ammunition transporter

US M30 Cargo Carrier

Based on the M12 chassis, it transported the ammunition for the 155-mm howitzers and cannon. A 12.7-mm machine gun was mounted on a ring support fixed to the rear of the vehicle. This tank could tow an M10 ammunition trailer carrying 16 155-mm shells. It was fitted with a hook enabling another trailer, or a cannon (e.g. a 57-mm anti-tank gun), to be hooked up to it.

M34 and M32 B1 Full Track Prime Mover

The Recovery Vehicle fitted with a winch on which the boom had been taken off. It was used as an artillery tractor.

The Amphibious Shermans

The Deep Wading Sherman

This version of the Sherman was fitted with two air sleeves to allow air to reach the engine and to heighten the exhaust outlets, the aim being to enable the Sherman to ford deep water or to disembark before it reached the beach. It was especially studied for the Marines Corps and later extended to other units. These modifications proved their effectiveness during the landing phase in Normandy, but also in Italy. Naturally this system could only be temporary because it prevented the turret swiveling through 360° in both directions.

It had therefore to be dismantled easily and recoverable. On the other hand, when in place, the clearance was still enough to allow the gun to fire during this delicate and dangerous phase approaching the beaches. These clearing "appendices" were mounted on the M4A2s, the M4A3s, and the M10 and M10 A1 TDs, the armored vehicles equipped with the GM 60-71 engine or the Ford V-8 GAA engine.

Another system, the Wading Stacks, was especially studied to adapt to the grids and exhausts of the M4A2,

This M4A1 76 W flame thrower from the 70th Tank Battalion is going through a series of tests before going up to the front. The E4-5 flamethrower projects the flaming liquid some 22 meters. (*Signal Corps, NARA*)

powered by the Twin General Motors engine. The air inlet comprised an extra plate, fixed around the engine grids on which a heavy-duty 200-liter barrel (a barrel with two reinforcement hoops) was customized.

The exhaust was enveloped in an M3-like Deep Wading System which stopped on a level with the top of the upper armor. Here a second 200-liter barrel was installed. This system was used a lot during the war in the Pacific (Iwo Jima, Tarawa, etc.).

The details of the system

This was a system studied, tested, and standardized for Operation *Overlord* for installing on the Sherman chassis. These kits were voluminous and comprised a host of parts, and mounting them on the tank needed a lot of work. Installing the sleeves themselves required a lot less time. Preparing the tanks for an "offshore" landing was a very long operation that had to be carried out with great care. Preparing these tanks for disembarkation using this system was prescribed in the TM 9-2853, together with TM-9- 238.

The two main sleeves extended the air intakes and the exhaust outlets upwards, but that still didn't mean the tank was ready to go through any fords deeper than a meter. The water could still seep through non-watertight openings like the petrol, oil, or water filler spouts, the ventilations ports, the bow machine gun, the tank air intakes, the driver's and assistant driver's half hatches, the turret ratchet, and the various cut-outs for the electric cabling.

All these tanks based on the M4 chassis are equipped with water clearing systems with a view to the landings in Normandy. The M4s and M10 TDs only had one air duct to be mounted, whereas the M7 needed two. (*NARA*)

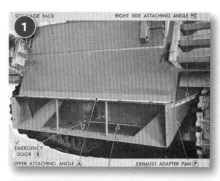

STOWAGE RACK — RIGHT SIDE ATTACHING ANGLE (C)

EMERGENCY DOOR (R)

UPPER ATTACHING ANGLE (A) — EXHAUST ADAPTER PAN (P)

FELT STRIPS — AIR INTAKE ADAPTER (N) — STOWAGE

EXHAUST ADAPTER (M)

RIGHT SIDE ATTACHING ANGLE (C) — EXHAUST ADAPTER PAN (P)

Supports for T6 device

Supports for Floating Device (brackets could also be used instead of supports.

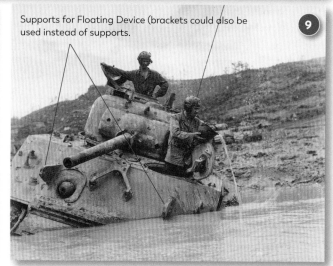

Water could also seep through the headlights, the siren, and the blackouts. The tank had therefore to be waterproofed either with special adhesive tape, with grease, or with a special waterproofing product. All these operations took the crew a lot of time, and this work was verified using an impressive checklist.

The T6 Floating Device

This device enabled the Sherman to move about in water and was called the "Ritchie Device." It consisted of four steel caissons (pontoons) fastened around the tank: two open-bottomed side caissons, one in front, and one caisson at the rear. Two rudders were fixed on the latter, and worked by hand. The front and rear pontoons were compartmentalized and filled with compacted plastic mousse, increasing its floatability. Moreover, this "filling" meant the caisson continued floating even if punctured by enemy fire.

The tracks, fitted with little cups, Duckbill-style, at the end of the connectors and turning inside the side caissons, produced forward movement. During the approach phase, the tank was able to use its cannon—thanks to the gyroscopic stabilization—unlike the Duplex Drive that prevented the turret cannon from being used. When the tank got nearer the beach, a pyrotechnic device detached the caissons from the tank. Tactically, the caissons abandoned on the beach were used as shelter by the infantry following, a consequence General George Patton appreciated very much.

This apparatus was used by the Marines at Okinawa and Iwo Jima. Launched by the LSTs 18 km from the coast, they took five hours to cover the distance. By the end of the war, in August 1945, 500 sets of these pontoons had been delivered for the Sherman, plus 250 for the M18 Hellcat (T7) and M24 Chaffee (T20). This device, presented to Patton in April 1944, was not retained for Operation *Overlord* because it was too cumbersome as it took up as much space as two Duplex Drives and the four caissons weighed 15 tons.

A system designated T8 was built for the M25 Pershing. On this model the two rudders were controlled from the driver's post by a cable and chain system. This was quickly abandoned but had already been designated M19.

As far as the M4 was concerned, there was also an M12 floating device made up of two inflatable "sausages," both equipped with an outboard motor. This device comprised the Deep Wading Trunk.

The Sherman DD

Its real name was the Duplex Drive although the initials DD did also make it known as Donald Duck! It was one of Sir Percy Hobart's adaptations—the original idea and conception were the work of the Hungarian

Nicolas Straussler. Hobart was a major general in the British Army and was responsible for thinking up the inventions people called "Funnies." This vehicle was, above all, very delicate to get going.

The plan was simply to make the Sherman amphibious.

Adaptations

First of all the tank was equipped with a floatation system attached to the hull so the tank could float while approaching the beaches. Next, the device had to be retractable when the machine reached *terra firma* so it could continue moving around and use its armament. A flexible skirt was therefore fitted round the tank; the lowest part of the skirt was attached to the hull by a welded sill. This fixation was waterproof and a duct came up from the exhausts inside the skirt. To cross the water, the skirt was lifted turret-high and was held in place high up by inflatable tubes installed around the hull and inflated by a pneumatic system.

The armature was made up of 36 inflatable tubes; three metal straps braced by 13 metal posts reinforced the system. Setting all this up took 15 minutes. The compressors—or compressed air tanks—supplying the pressure were placed in the front, on the skirt supports (for the later generations of models).

The top of the structure was made rigid by a light metal armature. When the skirt was lifted, the driver was blind. The tank commander therefore stood up

This M4A2 was christened *Fire ball*. It belongs to the 4th Marine Tank Battalion and is getting ready to land at Saipan. The top of the turret has been painted white to make air identification easier. (NARA)

Previous page:

1—3. The main phases of installing the Deep Wading Gear (RA PD 346685).

4. M4A1 equipped with a "homemade" Deep Wading Gear.

5. Pacific theater of operations, the tank is equipped with the Deep Wading Stacks (220-liter reinforced stacks).

6. Even with the fording kit, a hole does not forgive!

7. Rare shot of the T6 system.

8. The rear fixation points for the T6 Floating Device.

9. The fixation points on the frontal glacis for the Floating Device.

in the turret (a platform was added to this model) and guided the driver by radio. Subsequently, certain driver's posts were fitted with a periscope to replace the driver's episcope. During this amphibious phase, the rest of the crew was outside on the turret.

Two propellers drove it in the water; drive came from the two idler pulleys through a transfer box. It was engaged by a hydraulic system, the driver declutching before lowering the propellers.

The phase when the propeller casings lowered onto the transfer box pinion was controlled in the driver's post by a lever on the intrados of the glacis, above the dashboard. The driver had a control lever located on a level with the gearbox and by using a hydraulic system he could steer the tank right or left. The tank commander had a rudder with drawback bars commanded by a tiller.

In theory a hold pump was installed in the DDs, to pump out bilge water during the crossings. On some DDs you can see a flange added to the idler pulleys.

This device was used to secure the sprocket rim, the aim being to improve the performance of the tracks in the water. It was later suppressed. As it turned out, mud and gravel would block the track near the extra sprocket wheel and make the track come off.

The rear sprocket wheel was therefore suppressed but the fixation flange remained in place. Like on the Wading Trunk, the exhaust was channeled and came out in the skirt support, enabling the exhaust gases to escape above water.

The DDs were used during the crossing of the Rhine and for this operation the floatation skirt lifting mechanism was modified. This improvement consisted of reducing the lifting height at the front to allow the weapons to be used during the crossing. The rear part was raised as much as possible so as to prevent it filling up with water at the moment when the tank climbed out onto the river bank at the end of the crossing.

Where driving and the approach were concerned, the Duplex Drive was far from easy to use; these difficulties were known to the designers and the DD crews went through special training on Lake Fritton in Norfolk. The British had built an underwater caisson using an M4 chassis and the crews trained using the DEA—Davis Escape Apparatus—designed to enable the crew to escape from the tank in case it accidentally foundered. It gave seven minutes of breathing time.

This flotation equipment remained delicate to use. During the Normandy Landings, the results of using the DDs and the Deep Wading Tanks were mitigated, depending on the beach.

You can't talk about the Duplex Drives without mentioning D-Day, June 6, 1944, since it was on that day that they were used massively. D-Day was the consecration for the DDs. The LSTs which disembarked the DD tanks were fitted with special apparatus (longer ramps fixed to the landing beam), enabling the tanks to be already floating when the tracks left the ramp.

Sherman Topee

This was an improvement to the DD Sherman. The crews reported very early on how the flotation skirts were damaged when the tanks drove around "dry," subjected to rubbing against fences or trees when the tanks advanced through undergrowth, even though the skirts were correctly folded down. To avoid this damage the British equipped the upper part of the skirts with a hinged metal protection.

This—effective—protection was slipped into position on the skirt during operations without any handling beforehand. Subsequently the sponsons formed by the Topee system were used—experimentally only—to install electrically controlled machine guns which the tank could fire while swimming.

Another improvement was also envisaged by the British engineers: to protect the tank while swimming through burning water. This possibility, which could be dealt with without a lot of preparation, was taken very seriously. It consisted of a combination engine pump fixed onto the rear deck of the M4. This pump was driven by a power take-off on the upper part of the flotation skirts; a simple duct sucked in the water in which the tank was swimming and expelled it

This time this M4A3 christened *Calcutta* belonged to the 5th Marine Tank Battalion. *(NARA)*

through outlets all around the skirt, thereby pushing the burning surface of the water outwards.

The Normandy Landings: preparation and chronology

Apart from the M4 DDs and the DUKW 353s (made by GMC), which had their own amphibious capabilities, the other tanks and vehicles disembarked from barge-type vessels. Many of these were designed especially for the Normandy Landings. The main ones were:

- LCVP—Landing Craft, Vehicles and Personnel (USA).
- LCI—Landing Craft, Infantry (USA).
- LCM—Landing Craft, Mechanized (USA).
- LST—Landing Ship, Tank (USA).
- LCA—Landing Craft, Assault (GB)
- LCT Mk 4—Landing Craft, Tank (GB)
- LCT-R—Landing Craft, Tank-Rocket (GB)

These landing barges all had different functions and capacities. Among them two were of particular interest since they were intended for landing heavy materiel.

The LSTs were ships built in 1941 and used for the first time in 1942 for the landings in North Africa, then in Normandy and in Provence. They could carry 2,100 tons of equipment or 20 M4 tanks right up to the beaches. The LCT Mk IVs could carry three M4 tanks or 136 tons of equipment, and also served under the American flag during operations in Normandy, Korea, and Vietnam. These two types of barges, together with the DUKWs, transported men and equipment to the beaches. To do this they took

inward and outward lanes, which not only enabled the sea traffic to flow strictly but also allowed timing to be precise. Both these parameters were obviously decisive for the landing operations to run well, taking place as they did, one has to remember, under heavy enemy fire. This timing took into account what equipment was needed at a particular moment, "T," the number of units to be unloaded, the equipment, and structures necessary.

Let's look, for instance, at the schedule set up for the Omaha Beach landings.

This beach was made famous by the difficulties encountered and the number of lives it cost; it was subdivided into several sub-sectors from the Pointe

Swimming progress trials for this Sherman equipped with two exhaust hoods for the exhaust and air intake. They were fixed to the engine deck. (NARA)

Near Utah Beach on June 6, 1944, an M4A1 Duplex Drive from A or B Company of the 70th Tank Battalion. The lower strip of the flotation skirt is still attached to the tank. (NARA)

SHERMAN D D DUPLEX DRIVE

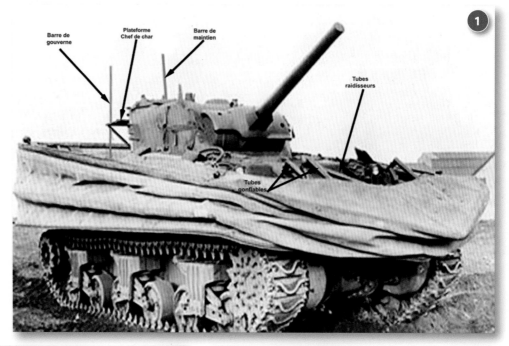

Barre de gouverne

Plateforme Chef de char

Barre de maintien

Tubes raidisseurs

Tubes gonflables

MK 2

DD TANKS AS SEEN BY AN AMERICAN BRIGADIER-GENERAL

On Utah Beach the 743d Tank Battalion launched 32 DDs; four sank with their LCT which struck a mine; the remaining 28 were able to reach the beach 10 minutes after the first wave of infantry.

On Omaha Beach the situation was much more delicate. Two LCTs carrying eight Deep Wading tanks struck a mine and sank. The wind was blowing at 18 knots and there were wave troughs 1.8-m deep. Because of the tides and the configuration of the terrain, the conditions turned out to be rather worse on Omaha than the other beaches. The maneuver turned into a disaster when it was decided to launch the 741st Tank Battalion's DDs from 5 km out! C Company lost 16 DDs out of 16 in the first 1,000 m, but most of the crews were saved.

B Company from the same battalion launched its DDs nearer in and two reached the beach, whereas three other DDs were dropped directly onto the beach by their LCT after the first one had been sunk.

The 743d Tank Battalion decided to land its tanks directly from the LCTs onto the beach: 32 DDs, seven Deep Wading Shermans, and two Tank Dozers, or 42 tanks out of 56, were able to reach the beach. Out of the 112 tanks intended for Omaha Beach, 58 were able indeed to take up their positions. These 58 tanks were decisive for the pursuit of operations on "Bloody Omaha." At the end of the day there were only three tanks from the 741st Tank Battalion left.

In a battalion of American tanks, A Company was equipped with Wading Gear cannon tanks, B and C Companies were equipped with Duplex Drive Shermans.

The American battalions were transported as follows: 741st Tank Battalion, B Company: the tanks embarked four by four in the LCTs 537, 599, 600, and 603. C Company embarked aboard LCTs 549, 598, 601, and 602. 743d Tank Battalion, B Company: LCTs 535, 586, 587, and 589. C Company on LCTs 588, 590, 591, and 713.

The US Army subsequently used the DDs successfully during the landings in Provence (756th Tank Battalion on Alpha Yellow Beach, Pampelone) then with the British during the crossing of the Rhine.

On Sword Beach, 24 of the 40 DDs were launched 5 km from the beach; three were very quickly submerged; out of the remaining 31, eight remained on the beach after their engines stalled, submerged by the backwash. The rising tide subsequently engulfed them.

On Gold Beach, some of the DDs were supposed to be launched 5,000 m from the beach, but the bad conditions meant that some of the DDs were launched only 1,000 m from the beach while the other DDs were dropped directly onto the sand by the LCTs. Out of the 16 planned, only two DDs took part in the first landing wave. The others were able to come up at the same time as the Flail tanks which landed first.

On Juno Beach, the DDs were launched at distances between 4,000 and 1,000 m. In places the shallow water even enabled them to advance using their tracks. On this beach the DD arrived after the first waves of infantry.

It is certain that the British and Canadian crews were far better prepared and mastered their Duplex Drive Shermans better, hence their lighter losses. For the HQ staffs, landing tanks to accompany the first assault waves turned out to be much more reliable when the tanks were equipped with the Deep Wading gear.

Previous page:

1. M4 Duplex Drive with flotation skirt down.
2. The propellers with their control rods.
3. Flotation skirt up and propellers lowered ready to drive.
4. The inside of the raised skirt; in blue, the inflatable tubes; in yellow, the metal tubes for rigidifying the structure; in red, the supporting armature or the flotation skirt.
5. Landing ramp of an LST. Note the positioning of the two extra ramps which enabled the DD to be afloat at the moment when the rear of the tank left the ramps.
6. Using the Davis Escape Apparatus.

A few hours after landing, the lower part of the exhaust hood is still attached to the hull of this Sherman from the 743d Tank Battalion. The other tanks in front of it have retained the DD's junction strip for the flotation skirt. (NARA)

du Ras to La Percée at Port-en-Bessin, about 5 miles, among which were Charlie, Dog Green, Dog White, Dog Red, Easy Green, Easy Red, Fox Green, Fox Red, Easy White, and Fox White.

The documents and maps referring to Operation *Overlord* sometimes mentioned the word Bigot—Top Secret Bigot or Neptune Bigot. The overall codeword for the Landings in Normandy was *Overlord*; it grouped

Legend		
I LCI	V LCVP	A LCA
M LCM	T LCT	DUKW ◇ DD

LANDING DIAGRAM OMAHA BEACH
(Sector of 116th RCT)
TOP SECRET BIGOT   *Note Plan as of 11 May*

	EASY GREEN	DOG RED	DOG WHITE	DOG GREEN
H-5			◇◇◇◇ ◇◇◇◇◇◇◇◇◇◇ Co C (DD) 743 Tk Bn	◇◇◇◇ ◇◇◇◇◇◇◇◇◇◇ Co B (DD) 743 Tk Bn
H HOUR	T T T T Co A 743 Tk Bn	T T T T Co A 743 Tk Bn		
H+1	V V V V V Co E 116 Inf	V V V V V Co F 116 Inf	V V V V V Co G 116 Inf	V V V V V Co A 116 Inf
H+3	M M M 146 Engr CT	M M M 146 Engr CT — Demolition Control Boat	M M M 146 Engr CT	M M M 146 Engr CT — A A Co C 24 Ranger BN
H+30	V AAAW Btry / Co M HQ Co E Co M / V AAAW Btry — 116 Inf	V V V V V V 2nd Bn CoM Co F CoM 2d Bn AAAW Btry — 116 Inf	V AAAW Btry / Co M HQ Co G Co M / V AAAW Btry — 116 Inf	A A A A A A A Co B HQ Co A Co B AAAW Btry — 116 Inf
H+40	M 112 Engr Bn	V V V V 112 Engr Co D 81 Cml Wpns Bn 149 Engr Beach Bn	V 149 Engr Beach Bn M 121 Engr Bn	HQ A A A M V V V V V 1st Bn 116 149 Beach Bn 121 Engr Co O 116 Inf
H+50	T T T T T Co L 116 Inf	V V V V V Co I 116 Inf	V V V V V Co K 116 Inf	M V V V V V V V 121 Engr Bn Co C 116 Inf
H+57		V V V V V V V HQ Co 3rd Bn — Co M 116 Inf —		V V V Co D 81 Cml Wpns Bn 112 Engr
H+60	T	V T T T 112 Engr Bn	V HQ & HQ Co 116 Inf	T T T A A A A A 121 Engr BN Co A&B 2nd Ranger Bn
H+65				A A A A A A A 5th Ranger Bn
H+70	I 149 Engr Beach Bn	I 112 Engr Beach Bn	I AH HQ & HQ Co 116 Inf	M T T A A A A A A A A 121 Engr Bn 5th Ranger Bn
H+90			T T T T T 58 FA Bn Armd	
H+100			I 6th Engr SP Brig	
H+110	III FA Bn (3 Btrys in DUKWs)	AT Plat 2nd Bn AT Plat 3rd Bn 29 Sig Bn		AT Plat 1st Bn Cn Co 116 Inf
H+120	T T T AT Co 116 Inf 467 AAAW Bn 467 AAAW Bn	T T T T 467 AAAW Bn AT Co 116 Inf 149 Engr Beach Bn	T T 467 AAAW Bn	T T T 467 AAAW Bn
H+150		— DD Tanks — T T T	I HQ Co 116 Inf 104 Med Bn	
H+180 TO 215	T T	461 Amphibious Truck Co	M T M T M T — Navy Salvage —	T T T T
H+225	461 Amphibious Truck Co	T	T	T

The general landing diagram for the Omaha Beach assault forces, June 6, 1944. *(NARA)*

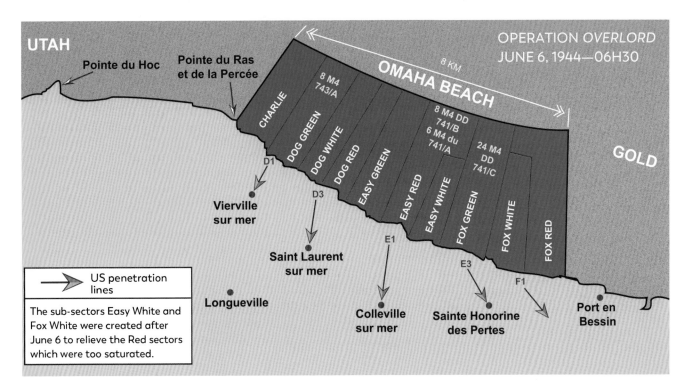

with it the naval operation, code-named *Neptune*. Bigot was the classification that came after Top Secret.

In fact Bigot was the anagram for "to Gib," an expression stamped onto the papers of officers heading for Gibraltar, to prepare Operation *Torch* (North Africa).

Reading the document "Landing Diagram Omaha Beach" shows that the zone for the 116th RCT (Regiment Combat Team) was made up of sub-sectors Easy Green, Dog Red, Dog White and Dog Green. The left-hand column gives the timing and starts at H-5 to finish at H+225, in other words, 3 hours and 45 minutes after the start of the landings.

H-5. The DDs in C Company, 743d Tank Battalion, were launched on Dog White whereas the DDs from B Company headed for Dog Green, in all 34 M4 DDs.

H-00. Eight LCTs launched the Shermans from A Company of the 743d Tank Battalion on Easy Green and Dog Red.

H+01. Six LCVP landed E Company of the 116th Infantry Regiment on Easy Green. Six LCVPs landed F Company from the 116th Infantry Regiment on Dog Red. Six LCVPs landed G Company from the 116th Infantry Regiment on Dog White. Six LCVPs landed A Company from the 116th Infantry Regiment on Dog Green.

H+03. Three LCMs landed elements of the 146th Engineers Battalion on Easy Green.

Three LCMs landed elements of the 146th Engineers Battalion on Dog Red; a fourth LCM was demolition Control Boat.

Three LCMs landed elements of the 146th Engineers Battalion on Dog White.

Three LCMs landed elements of the 146th Engineers Battalion on Dog Green, plus two LCAs which landed C Company of the 24th Rangers Battalion.

H+30. On Easy Green, two LCVs landed two AA batteries while three LCVPs landed E and HF Companies with HQ elements form the 116th Infantry Regiment. On Dog Red, eight LCVPs landed an AA battery, the 2d Battalion, its HQ, and F Company of the 116th Infantry Regiment. On Dog White, two LCVPs landed an AA battery, and three LCVPs landed F Company and the HQ of G Company of the 116th Infantry Regiment. On Dog Green, eight LCAs and an LCVPO landed A and B Companies, the HQ of A Company, and an AA battery.

H+40. An LCM landed elements of the 112th Engineers Battalion on Easy Green. Four LCVPs landed D Company of the 81st CMI and an LCM landed elements of the 112th Engineers Beach Battalion. On Dog White, an LCVP landed elements of the 149th Beach Engineers and an LCM landed elements of the 121st Engineers Battalion. On Dog Green, four LCAs landed the 1st Battalion of the 116th Infantry Regiment and elements of the 149th Beach Engineers; an LCM landed elements of the 121st Engineers Battalion and five LCVPs landed D Company of the 116th Infantry Regiment

H+50. On Easy Green, seven LCVPs landed L Company of the 116th Infantry Regiment. On Dog

This map shows the landing zones for the amphibious Shermans on Omaha Beach on June 6, 1944.

NEPTUNE
CT 18, DIV TRPS.
DIAGRAM

TYPE	SPEED in KNOTS		NOTE
	R/A L/D	D/L H	
RF	3.5	4	A TWO KNOT CURRENT IS ASSUMED BETWEEN R/A AND L/D, PERPENDICULAR TO THE TRUE COURSE.
D&DD	4	4	
I+T	5	6	
V.M	7	8	
LCI	10	10	

EASY RED

WAVE N°	LEAVE R/A	LEAVE L/D	LAND	REMARKS
1	H-161	H-55	H-10	...
2	H-124	H-18	H-00	B.Tanks, 4 TH Dozers Co."A" 741 TK. Bn.
3	H-86	H-12	H-01	Return to Henrico Co."E,F. 16th Inf.
4a	H-84	H-10	H-05	
4b	H-79	H-05	H-08	Engr. Spec. Task Force
4c	H-62	H+12	H-25	
5	H-57	H+17	H+30	All landing craft return

Detail of the American landings diagram for the *Easy Red* sector of Omaha Beach. *(NARA)*

four LCTs landed equipment for the 121st Engineers Battalion. On Dog White, a LCVP landed the HQ Company of the 116th Infantry Regiment. On Dog Green, three LCTs dropped vehicles of the 121st Engineers Battalion and five LCAs landed A and B Companies of the 2d Ranger Battalion.

H+65. On Dog Green, seven LCAs landed the 5th Rangers Battalion.

H+70. On Easy Green, an LCI landed the 149th Beach Engineers Battalion. On Dog Red, an LCI landed the 121st Engineers Battalion. On Dog White, an LCI landed the HQ Company of the 116th Infantry Regiment. On Dog Green, an LCM and two LCTs landed elements of the 121st Engineers Battalion; eight LCAs landed elements of the 5th Rangers Battalion.

H+90. On Dog White, five LCTs landed machines from the 58th Armored Battalion.

H+100. In sub-sector Dog White, an LCI landed elements of the 61st Engineers Battalion.

H+110. Thirteen DUKWs landed three batteries of the 3d Field Artillery Battalion on Easy Green; seven DUKWs landed anti-tank platoons from the 2d and 3d Battalions and elements of the 29th Signals Battalion. On Dog Green, 10 DUKWs landed an anti-tank platoon and the command company of the 116th Infantry Regiment.

H+120. On Easy Green, three LCTs landed elements of the 467th AA Battalion and an anti-tank company from the 116th. On Dog Red, five LCTs landed elements of the 467th AA Battalion, an anti-tank company from the 116th, and elements of the 149th Beach Engineers Battalion. On Dog White and

Red, seven LCVPs landed J Company of the 116th Infantry Regiment. On Dog White, six LCVPs landed K Company of the 116th Infantry Regiment. On Dog Green, an LCM landed elements of the 121st Engineer Battalion and seven LCVPs landed C Company of the 116th Infantry Regiment.

H+57. On Dog Red, nine LCVPs landed the command company of the 3d Battalion and M Company of the 116th Infantry Regiment. On Dog Green, four LCVPs landed B Company of the 81st CMI.

H+60. On Easy Green, an LCT landed equipment for the 121st Engineers Battalion. On Dog Red, an LCVP landed elements of the 121st Engineers Battalion and

Right: The Duplex Drive, its flotation skirt completely raised, measured 4 m. A ladder was indispensable for getting into the tank. *(Tank Museum)*

Opposite page: The Duplex Drives were also used during the landings in Provence in August 1944. The calmer Mediterranean waters were less problematic for the amphibious Shermans. *(NARA)*

Dog Green, four LCTs landed elements of the 467th AA Battalion.

H+150. An LCI landed the 104th Medical Battalion on Dog White.

H+180 to H+215. Two LCTs on standby on Easy Green. On Dog Red, three LCTs transported M4 DDs followed by DUKWs of the 461st Amphibious Regiment. On Dog White, three LCMs and three LCTs landed elements from Navy Salvage. In Dog Green sector, five LCTs were on standby.

H+225. Eighteen DUKWs from the 461st Amphibious Regiment reached Easy Green. An LCT was on standby at Dog Red and two LCTs at Dog White.

The timing was that used for Omaha Beach, in the sector of the 116th RCT. The other part of Omaha Beach had a similar schedule, and it was the same for all the other landing beaches. One can therefore imagine the number of movements along the Normandy coast in the first days of the landings, and especially during the first hours.

This diagram was an overall schedule; the subsections each had their own detailed diagram. On this diagram, you can see that the M4 DDs from the 741st Tank Battalion left LST 374, itself depending on the "master ship" USS *Henrico*. The Duplex Drives were embarked aboard LCTs 58, 599N, 57, 600N, 56, 537N, 55, and 603N. After the tanks were landed, the LCTs returned to the *Henrico* for another rotation. These tanks were part of the first assault wave.

LST 374 left *Henrico*, 2 hours and 40 minutes before H-Hour. The tanks left their LCT 55 minutes before H-Hour to reach the beach at H-10 minutes.

This diagram also gave information like the speed of the boats, the strength and the direction of the currents, etc. By 1230 hours on June 6, almost 19,000 men had been landed on Omaha Beach.

The Sherman Rocket Launchers

Sherman Callope: the rocket launchers

Here's the answer to the Russian *Katyushas*, or Stalin's organs. Among all the models we'll deal with, very few took part in the fighting and only a few reached the production stage.

T34 rocket launcher. This was a proper Sherman with hull and turret, on which the Americans added racks containing, in all, 60 4.5-in (114.3-mm) rockets. These racks were attached to the cannon by a mechanical linkage and were fired from the tank commander's post.

Depending on the needs, the first two 12-tube racks could be adapted on all M4s except the M4A1s. This system had been tried out satisfactorily in all the theaters of operations where it was used. Developed in small numbers starting in 1943, these rocket launchers were used in France by the 2d US Armored Division in August 1944.

T34 E1. Like the T34, but the first two racks had 14 tubes.

T34 E2. This was the preceding modified to fire 7.2-in (182-mm) rockets. It had 60 rockets. In an emergency all the rockets could be fired in one go.

Italy 1944. These M4 and M4A1 Shermans of the 752d Tank Battalion are equipped with the M17 rocket launchers with 20 18-cm projectiles. The tank numbered 34 has been painted with British-style camouflage. *(NARA)*

T39. This version comprised a caisson with lids holding 20 7.2-in rockets. Elevation pointing for the racks was at the rear of the turret. This was an experimental model.

T40. Same ammunition as the T39, but the pointing system was on the side of the turret and the cannon was removed. In an emergency all the racks could be fired at the same time. The rockets could be fired individually or in salvoes. This model was used in 1944—45 in Europe.

T40 Short Version. An experimental version equipped with shorter rockets. The 75 M1 was withdrawn and replaced by an elevation pointing mechanism. An opening was created on the side for the turret crew.

T72. A version of the T34 equipped with shorter tubes. Never used.

T73. Similar to the T40, but equipped with only 10 launch tubes. A system installed only on the M4A1s. Never used.

T76. M4A1 equipped with a launching tube for 182-mm rockets in place of the 75-mm cannon. This tank had an opening on the upper surface in front of the turret for getting rid of the gas and the smoke after

firing. The system was reloaded from the inside of the turret. Experimental in 1944. The same arms system installed on the M5 A3 HVSS was designated T76 E1.

T99. Two short racks with 22 114.3-mm rockets were mounted on each side of the turret of the 76-mm cannon-equipped M4s. Small production in 1945. This system was tested on the M25 Pershing.

T105. Single tube for 182-mm rocket installed in place of the 75 M1 on the M4A1 chassis. Developed from the T76 in August 1945, it got no further than the trials stage.

The AA Shermans

Tank AA, 20mm Quad, Skink. Anti-Aircraft prototype equipped with four 20-mm Polstein cannon—the Polish version of the 20-mm Oerlikon—the arms system mounted on Canadian M4A1 Grizzlies. It was called Skink.

T4 AA Sherman. Model equipped with a 40-mm cannon with large elevation and two 12.7-mm machine guns, on each side of the casemate.

T52 Multiple Gun Motor Carriage. Arms system installed on the base of an M4A2 and developed by Firestone; it was armed with two 40-mm Bofors cannon or one 40-mm Bofors cannon and two 12.7-mm machine guns. It was judged to be too slow for AA operations and was abandoned in October 1944.

T53 and T53 E1 90-mm Gun Motor Carriage. In 1942, a 90-mm AA gun was mounted on the rear of an M4 chassis and the engine moved to the center. A prototype was designed by Chrysler (Detroit Tank Arsenal) on the basis of an M4A4. Both running gears were redesigned and the bogeys reinforced and suspended to be able to absorb the recoil of the 90-mm cannon.

As the tests were positive, an agreement for 500 machines was signed but Chrysler had to move the cannon back to the center and put the engine at the back again. Thus equipped, it took the designation T53 E1 and was referenced as an AA and anti-tank vehicle.

Tested as a tank destroyer, it was not really much better than the M10 TD Wolverine. On the other hand, the AA artillery cancelled the project because its rate of fire was too slow.

Production was halted definitively and cancelled in May 1944.

Opposite page:

1. T34 Sherman rocket launcher
2. T40 Sherman rocket launcher
3. T40 Short Version Sherman rocket launcher
4. T72 Sherman rocket launcher
5. T75 Sherman rocket launcher
6. T42 Sherman anti-aircraft gun
7. T53 E1 Sherman anti-aircraft gun
8. The "Skink" Sherman anti-aircraft gun

Detail of how the Model T34 Calliope ramp was installed, at the moment the crew was reloading the tubes. *(NARA)*

The Sherman Firefly

This was another of Sir Percy Hobart's "funnies."

At the beginning of the conflict in Europe the Allies were all aware of the weakness of the Sherman's 75-mm cannon. The British already had a gun that was much better, and the ammunition to go with it. This was the QF 17-pounder (76.2 mm) gun (QF for Quick Firing). In British terminology this variant of the tank was called the Sherman IIc, but this new M4 was better known as the Firefly. The Fireflies were equipped with the big extra chest; the cannon road cradle was located on the left-hand side of the rear deck; on the rear right- and left-hand sides there was a portable fire extinguisher (2 kg); the smoke generator, together with two towing hook mountings, was on the engine compartment doors.

An M4A3 75 W equipped with its T34 Calliope ramp fires its rockets.

The Fireflies no longer had a bow machine gun, the assistant driver's post having been suppressed and replaced by a stock of ammunition (the 17-pounder shells took up more space than the 75s). The Fireflies were also equipped with two extra towing hooks at the rear for pulling a trailer, even with the Wading Gear in place.

It was a Firefly that destroyed German panzer ace Michael Wittmann's Tiger during the battle of Villers-Bocage in Normandy.

Villers-Bocage

Michael Wittmann was born in April 22, 1914 in the High Palatinate. When World War II broke

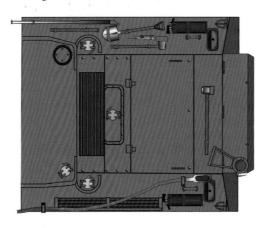

out he took part in the Polish, French, and Greek campaigns, in command of a StuG III assault gun. Wittmann served on the Eastern Front in a Panzer III before becoming a Tiger platoon commander during the battle of Kursk in 1943. On January 14, 1944, SS-Hauptsturmführer Wittmann was awarded the Knight's Cross of the Iron Cross.

When Overlord started, Wittmann's battalion arrived in Normandy on June 12 and was ordered to fill the breach on the left flank of the German disposition. Wittmann's 2d Company placed itself on Hill 213 in front of Villers-Bocage. He was accompanied by five tanks, of which two were damaged; he decided to charge alone, ordering the other tanks to hold the position. Enemy fire destroyed one of his running gears, so Wittmann and his crew evacuated the tank and managed to regain the platoon on Hill 213 on foot.

On August 8, during Operation Totalize, Wittmann took part in a counter-attack. He was at the head of a group of tanks in the schwere SS-Panzer Abteilung 101 and was ambushed in a fight during which his Tiger, which bore the number 007, was destroyed by one of the tanks of B Squadron of the 1st Northamptonshire Yeomanry. The hollow charge armor-piercing shell started a fire that spread quickly and the ammunition exploded, blowing off the Tiger's turret.

Wittmann and his crew were killed. Identifying the body was difficult, and Wittmann was only identified thanks to a gold tooth and the shreds of his leather jacket. The heat given off by the fire melted the dog tags. The five members of the crew were buried in a common grave. Their remains were uncovered in 1983 by some workers building a road. They were buried a second time, this time in the German military cemetery at Cambe.

At the time of his death, Michael Wittmann was credited with the destruction of 138 tanks and 132 anti-tank guns. The absolute record was held by Hauptsturmführer Max Wünsche, with 219 Allied tanks destroyed to his credit during the battle of Normandy.

Artillery On M4 Chassis

Motor Carriage M7 Priest self-propelled gun

Priest was the British name given to this variant of the M4. It was the British habit to give religious names to

One of the very first Sherman Fireflies converted on the chassis of a Sherman V. The M34A1 mantle was barely modified: six big bolts to attach it and the disappearance of the little armored cheeks at the base of the cannon. *(Tank Museum)*

This Firefly Vc of the 3rd Royal Tank regiment, 11th Armoured Division mounts guard on the Meuse at Namur. (NARA)

their guns, like the Bishop, Sexton, and Abbot. The first M7 accepted in February 1942 by the US Army was a variant of the M3 "Lee" and was initially called T32. Some 3,490 M7s were built and it was a real success in the American Army. It was armed with the M2 howitzer and carried 44 rounds. After some initial modifications, the M7 was able to carry 69 105-mm shells.

M7B1

This version was based on the chassis of the M4A3. It was standardized in September 1943 and only became an official version in January 1945.

M7B2

The elevation of the barrel was limited and the M7B2 was considerably modified because it was used in a particular theater of operations. During the Korean War, the elevation was increased to 65°. The mounting of the machine gun was also improved, allowing it to swivel through 360°. These improvements were in response to the hilly terrain frequently encountered in

Korea. The North Koreans deployed their artillery on the summits of the hills to the north of Seoul.

M12/M30: the artillery pair

This was a self-propelled gun on the M3 Lee, then on the chassis M4. The engine was moved towards the center of the tank and the tank was equipped with a French 155-mm cannon from World War I: 100 were produced by the Baldwin Locomotive Works between 1942 and 1943. These self-propelled guns were accompanied by M30 tanks, which were M12s whose 155-mm cannon had been removed. This increase in space enabled it to carry 40 155-mm shells and the two crew which could not get into the M12. There was one M30 for every M12.

M35 Prime Mover

Before the M6 High Speed Tractor became available, the US Army needed a new artillery tractor for the 120-mm cannon and the 240-mm howitzer, and the M35 was the answer. A few M10 TDs had their turrets removed to become the M35 Prime Mover.

The crew of this M7—with a 105-mm cannon—from the 69th Armored Field Artillery Battalion resting in the Anzio sector in February 1944 when the troops of the VI US Corps took up their defensive positions. (NARA)

1. The M7 105-mm howitzer motor carriage. This howitzer was mounted on an "Early" type chassis.
2. M12 howitzer motor carriage
3. M10 gun motor carriage
4. TB3 155 gun motor carriage
5. US M30 ammunition cargo
6. M4A2 HVSS transformed into an ammunition carrier by the Russians. Note the two impressive hooks replacing the shackles and the transformation of the revolving hatch.

M40

Based on the M4A3 chassis with HVSS suspension, its hull was lengthened to make a compartment for the 155-mm howitzer. The tank was divided into three parts: the driver's post at the front, which was equipped with two observation cupolas on the roof and a manhole cover; the engine in the center; and at the rear the combat compartment, taking up half the length of the tank.

The M40 crew consisted of eight men, including the driver and assistant driver who sat in the front part. The others were in the combat post or moving ammunition. The M40's armament consisted of a 155-mm M1 A1 or A2 howitzer on an M13 gun carriage. This artillery piece had a maximum range of 23 km. The M40 carried 20 155-mm projectiles. A large folding door at the rear with a loading ramp gave access to the six crew of the gun who could operate at their ease, loading the ammunition also being made easier.

Like the M12, the self-propelled howitzer was fitted with a large spade anchor at the rear which, when dug in, prevented the tank from bounding backwards with the recoil caused by the gun firing.

A total of 418 M40s were built in 1945 by Pressed Steel Car Co.; 24 were later converted into M43s. The M40 gradually replaced the M12s and their old 155-mm cannon.

M43

The M43 was based on the M4A3 chassis with HVSS suspension. The hull was lengthened to make the combat compartment bigger to take the 8-in howitzer. There was a crew of eight. The M43's armament consisted of an M1 203.2-mm howitzer. The M43 was equipped with a large anchor at the rear. In all 48 M43s were built in 1945 by Pressed Steel Car Co.; 24 were converted M40s.

Above: M10 "Wolverine" tank destroyer with its turret turned rearwards. *(NARA)*

The Tank Destroyers

The TD M10

The need for having a tank destroyer became obvious to the Allies very quickly. They had to confront the Tiger, but also the Jagdpanther tank destroyer. The chassis of the M4 was tried and ready, so it was decided to use it as the base for the future M10 Wolverine. The M10 tank destroyer was born.

Although it came from the TD 35 prototype, it mustn't be confused with the Tank Dozer TD M4, even though their designations begin with the same letters: one was a tank destroyer, the other was an engineers' version equipped with a bulldozer blade on the front. The tank destroyers were grouped together in constituted units, whereas the Fireflies were assigned to medium tank units, one or two per squadron.

The US Army deployed its tank destroyers in the Tank Destroyer Battalions. The British Army put them in the Anti-Tank Regiments, and the French Army in the Régiments de chasseurs de chars. The latter were the RCA (Régiments de chasseurs d'Afrique) because most of them were made up and trained in North

Africa. There were also units like the RBFM (Régiment blindé de fusiliers marins—navy fusiliers armored regiment), the RCCC (Régiment colonial de chasseurs de chars—colonial tank destroyer regiment), but also a dragoons regiment, No.2, the old "Condé Dragons."

The French units were equipped mainly with TD M10s and more rarely with M10A1s. Usually a regiment was equipped with 42 tank destroyers; they were in three squadrons, each made up of three four-tank platoons. It was only later in Indochina that the TD M36s appeared in constituted units in the RBCEO (Régiment Blindé Colonial d'Extrême Orient—Far-East Colonial Armored Regiment) among others.

In the US Army, the tank destroyer units were regrouped in battalions with numbering starting with 600, 700, and 800. All these battalions had a common insignia showing a panther biting into a tank.

The TD M10 based on the M2 chassis had an open turret, easily recognizable by the beveled shape of the rear of the turret (in fact this was the counterweight for the gun). This counterweight weighed 1,134 kg and was partly hollowed out to make storage space. The 76.2-mm cannon with its M51

Opposite: The insignia of the Tank Destroyer Battalions. *(drawing by the author)*

telescopic sights was installed in the turret. The on-board armament comprised a .50 cal. machine gun mounted on the rear of the turret. The tank carried 54 76.2-mm shells. This ammunition had a muzzle velocity of 892 m/s, still not enough to pierce the armor of a Tiger or a *Jagdpanther*. The turret was moved manually up and down and sideways. Part of the turret roof on the "Late" A1 models was made of light armor hinged panels with side openings. The bow machine gun had disappeared and the driver's and assistant driver's hatches were rectangular with a new closing system. The lateral armor sloped like on the turret so the shells would glance off at the moment of impact.

The TD M10s were powered by the General Motors 6-71 engine (twin six-cylinder engines); the fuel tanks contained 625 liters, giving it a range of some 320 km. The suspension was the HVSS type.

The tank destroyer armor was thinner than on the Shermans to increase mobility, a determining factor in tank warfare. The tank destroyer was therefore in the 28-ton category. The sloped armor sides nonetheless had threaded holes for bolting on additional armor, and supports for spare track links, jerrycan holders, or ramrod handles. The pioneers' gear and the track tightening spanner were placed on the rear deck.

The turret counterweight, indispensable because of the new cannon, was in two parts on the "Mid" models, and a single piece on the "Late" models.

1. TD M10 "Early" turret. On the rear of the turret, the track grousers were used as a counterweight.
2. TD M10 "Mid" turret. A modification to the counterweight in two parts.
3. TD M10 "Late" turret. The counterweight is cast this time.
4. TD M10 "Achilles" turret. The British version was equipped with the 17-pounder cannon.
5. TD M10 A1 turret. Light armor panels were placed on the turret. This one was powered by the Ford V8. The other turrets were driven by the M4A2's Grey Marine.
6. TD M36 B2 turret. The tank destroyers were equipped with the 90-mm cannon and were driven by the Ford V8 engine.

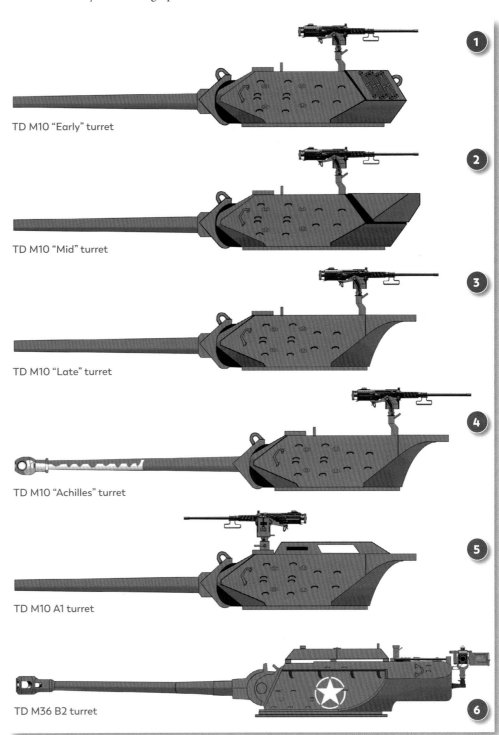

TD M10 "Early" turret

TD M10 "Mid" turret

TD M10 "Late" turret

TD M10 "Achilles" turret

TD M10 A1 turret

TD M36 B2 turret

The mechanics and armorers of a tank destroyer battalion replacing a 76-mm cannon of a TD M10. (NARA)

The remainder of the cannon ammunition was stowed in the right and left-hand sponsons; the shells were "cocooned," held in place by a strap on the racks. The TD M10 crew had US M1 .30 cal. carbines (five) with 450 rounds. The BMG M2 HB had 1,000 rounds. The tank also carried 12 hand grenades and four smoke canisters. The radio was an SCR 610 set. The "Late" M10s fired ammunition with a muzzle velocity of 900 meters per second.

TD M10 A1

This was the same as the M10 but using an A3 chassis. The TD M10s and TD M10 A1s could be equipped with the Deep Wading system or Wading Stacks, but reduced to a single chimney for the exhaust. The intake stack could not be mounted because of the turret counterweight. The A1 models were powered by the Ford V8 GAA. The running gear was still the VVSS type, but equipped with reinforced bogeys.

TD M10 Achilles

This was the British version of the Wolverine. The main difference was the famous British 17-pounder, replacing the M7 cannon. This gun was already fitted into the M4 Firefly versions and was certainly the best

The TD M10 Achilles, the British version of the TD M10, was armed with the famous 17-pounder cannon. (IWM B6006)

of the period. In any case it was the only one to rival the German 88s installed in the Tiger tanks until the American 90-mm came out.

TD M10 Sonic

A variant of the TD M10 on which the cannon had been removed and replaced by a fake cannon (like on the OP Command Fireflies). The space thus gained was used to install a loudspeaker system installed on a rack which folded down into the turret well when

the tank moved around. The idea was to reproduce false armored vehicle sounds and to trick the enemy into mistaking the type and number of vehicles. This system was used in France and in Italy. Twenty-four TD M10 were equipped as "Sonics."

TD M36

The tank came from the T71 Gun Motor Carriage prototype. It was based on the M10 A1 chassis and equipped with a 90-mm cannon mounted on an M4 gun carriage. The bustle chest was bigger and was used, among other things, for stowing ammunition (11 rounds of 90-mm shells); in all the M36 carried 47 shells. In total, 1,413 examples of the M36 Jackson were built, powered by the Ford V8 GAA engine.

The M36 fired shells with a muzzle velocity of 1,170 m/s. In the ETO, the fastest shell was the 75-mm shell fired by the Panther, at 1,200 m/s.

TD M36 B1 and B2

These were hastily designed models without any significant improvements. On the B2 the turret closed in using light armored plates. The M36 B1 was mounted on an M4A3 W chassis. In total, 187 were built by Fisher Tank Division between October and December 1944. The tank was equipped with a bow machine gun with 1,000 rounds, just like the HB M2.

Some 672 M36 B2s were built by American Locomotive Corporation and 52 by Montreal Locomotive between April and May 1945. They were powered by the GM 6071 engine. All the TD M36s were equipped with an SCR 610 radio set.

Left: The inside of a TD M10 turret. (*NARA*)

Above: The TD M36 Jackson. (*NARA*)

Bottom: A TD M36 Jackson from the 703d Tank Destroyer Battalion of the 3d Armored Division advancing in the Ardennes forest. (*NARA*)

1. The M4A3 E1.
2. The T23 tank.
3. The Sherman Sledge: an experiment for towing a train of armored sledges, with an infantryman in each sledge ready to go into the attack.
4. Sherman ballast trials.

After the battle of the Bulge, the HB M2s were placed on the left-hand side at the front of the turret where the .30 cal. machine gun was mounted.

Experimental M4s and Prototypes

Tests, trials, experiments: the Sherman went through many of them; it was even the origin of American tanks built after the end of the conflict. One could say that the Americans dared anything and everything and in all the domains concerning armored vehicles. Here are some of them.

Chrysler A 65

Here we have an enormous V12 that Chrysler developed at its own cost. This 1,568-in3 (or 25,695-cc) petrol engine was rated at 650 bhp. Nowadays we would say that such an engine was catastrophically uneconomic, but in 1944 it was very powerful. This water-cooled engine had been tested on an M4A4 for which the hull had to be lengthened once again by 9½ in (almost 23 cm). The tank's weight increased and its mobility, acceleration, and clearing capabilities were reduced. After a 650-km test run the engine was taken out

and apart, and examined: it was in perfect condition. The Ordnance Service asked other engine builders to continue their studies on engines with the same power and capacity. The Chrysler engine wasn't chosen.

General Motors Corporation V8-184 diesel engine

Unlike the V8 GAA, GMC studied this engine as a tank engine from the start. Based on a marine diesel engine, the impressive 1,470-in3 (or 24,089-cc) engine was rated at 600 bhp and the compression ration was 16.8/1. A version was tested on a M4A3 chassis, and designated M4Y. Once the Ordnance Department had taken over the test, it became the M4A2 E1.

To house this beast, the hull had to be lengthened by 11 in (28 cm) at the rear. Ground clearance was reduced since a bulge had to be made in the engine compartment floor to house the V8. This engine was tested over 3,000 miles and revealed no major defects or deterioration.

High-speed reverse transmission

This modification of the Sherman transmission increased the tank's speed in reverse, with a gear having a ratio of 5.65/1 (like first gear) and a maximum speed of 5 kph. The advantage of this configuration was

that the tank could if needs be climb a steep slope in reverse. The first modification carried out consisted in increasing the gear ratio, which reduced its slope-climbing capabilities. It was therefore decided to fit an auxiliary gearbox equipped with a planetary drive at the entry of the existing gearbox. This system enabled the five Sherman gears to be used in reverse. The reverser system provided the sprockets with an extra 25 bhp. This system needed a shorter driveshaft, so less vibrations and a longer life for the lengthened universal joints. Tested for a year, the system was entirely satisfactory. One could even say that it was approved! So why was it never seen on a Sherman? Very simply, because the war ended and production was stopped.

The Spicer 95 transmissions, General Motors 3030B Torqmatic and 900T

These three transmission models were tested on Shermans, though they were planned in the medium tank study programs to come.

The T20 was given the Spicer 95 transmission, based on a hydraulic torque converter, coupled with Hydramatic transmission. It was tested at the end of the war. The T23 was equipped with 3030B electric transmission, then with the 900T which already equipped the Hellcats. In mid-1944, two M4A3s

were modified—M4 A3 E3s—and were sent to the Aberdeen Proving Ground to be tested against M4A1 E3s and M4A3 E1s already being tested with the Spicer 95 transmission. The end of the war, but above all the arrival of the Cross Drive transmission, meant the end of all these transmission types which, anyway, had oil leaks or overheating problems.

The Cross Drive transmission systems

This type of transmission was under study in 1943. It brought together all the gearbox, clutch, steering, and sometimes braking functions in a single casing Originally designed for the Sherman, it was then intended to be the transmission that was to equip all tanks after the war.

The Cross Drive EX 100 was tested on a M4A3 on which a large opening had to be cut out of the transmission armor. The opening, fitted with armored plate to close it, was called the manhole cover by the technicians.

This transmission worked on the principle of the hydraulic torque converter, linked to electric braking and steering systems. The group was more compact than the original M4 gearbox and differential. Implementing this transmission took more time than planned—the reason why it was never put into the Shermans.

5. The M4A2 T.
6. The M4A3 E5.
7. The M4A2 HVSS.
8. The M4A2 E4.

The torsion bar

In 1943, the Ordnance Service recommended making running gear with torsion bars and wide tracks, like the running gear in use on certain German and Russian armored vehicles. Two M4A2 E4s were used for the tests, equipped with Model T20 E3 24-in-wide tracks. The advantage of this running gear was that it resulted in very low ground pressure.

Leaf spring

As its name indicates, this was a spring made of leaves. There were six on either side, mounted on the bogeys. The results were disappointing and the system was abandoned.

The Centipede suspension

This was a half-track suspension system adapted to the M4. It was out of date and too weak and quickly abandoned.

The Odograph

This was a combination of mapping and navigation working with the help of a magnetic compass coupled to the vehicle's tachymeter. The system was satisfactory on a Jeep-type vehicle but much less so on a tank, where the metallic mass was much greater. As the fighting in

desert zones was over, the program was stopped. It was used, however, for future developments.

Air conditioning for the combat compartment

This project saw the light of day and was tested on an M4A1, designated M4A1 E2. All the interior of the combat compartment was covered with insulating liner and equipped with an evaporation refresher. As with the odograph, the end of fighting in the desert put an end to the project.

Infrared driving system

An infrared night driving system was tested in 1942 and consisted of a group of infrared headlights invisible to the naked eye. An infrared light detector was mounted in place of the driver's periscope. The principle worked but it was not thought good enough for driving at normal speed. It was only a decade later that the first effective systems appeared.

M4 E1 (I)

This was in fact an M4A1 equipped with a 76-mm T1 cannon in the standard turret (M4) tested in July-August 1942; the turret was too small—despite the bustle modifications—for the resilient link and the 76-mm breech. Later the T23 was used.

9. TD T35, unfinished project.
10. T53 AA tank with a 90-mm cannon.
11. T53 E1 and its 90-mm AA cannon on an M4 chassis.
12. M4A3 E9 with wider suspension.

On the mudguards of the vehicle can be read for example:
1st Armored Division (1 + empty triangle),
28th Engineer Battalion (28e)
White Star
Headquarters Company (HQ)
12th vehicle in the unit (12)

Holland, October 1944: the population of Breda expressing its thanks after the town was liberated by Polish tanks. (*Private collection*)

Shipment markings

Preparation for overseas movement

The code POM was created for the TQM (Transport Quarter Master). These shipping logisticians not only had heavy responsibilities but had to manage a huge flow of materiel during the loading, transshipping, and landing operations. Take as an example one of the landings on a Normandy beach, where a lot of men and a quantity of different materiel for a variety of specific missions had to be disembarked. There was no question of piling all the gear into a landing craft and dropping it all on the beach. The first assault waves were not made up in the same way as the ones following. For example, along with the infantry came the Engineers elements with their specific equipment.

Support armor had to be landed as near in as possible, and the medics, those stretcher-bearers of the impossible, had to follow with all their gear. All these different people and equipment were to be found on the same naval unit and had to be identifiable quickly and without mistakes.

Moreover, part of the equipment followed the men according to different schedules. For example, certain radio communication equipment, ammunition, packaging, and blankets could be loaded in disorder in another barge but everyone had to be able to find things quickly without taking someone else's.

All the vehicles and machines in the US Army had specific markings identifying them. Moreover, each unit—right down to company level—had a five-figure code. For example, 42283 meant the 1st Engineers Battalion of the 1st Infantry Division. Although everybody could decipher them, these markings were not always sufficiently visible and clear when the vehicles were embarked or embarking.

It was not possible to check all the additional material mentioned above, so the American logisticians set up a color barcode system enabling them to identify surely and quickly all the material at a glance.

It was decided to use 10 colors with painted stripes 2-in high and 20-in long. There was a number from 0-10 for each color. The colors chosen in 1943 were changed in January 1944 to the following: 1, chamois; 2, olive drab; 3, yellow; 4, light green; 5, neutral grey; 6, dark blue; 7, brown; 8, red; 9, white; and 0, dark brown.

These colors could therefore generate 100 million combinations, which was easily enough to build up a POM code; the last two numbers of the unit codes were used. The penultimate figure gave the color of the upper stripes. The last figure fixed the color of the intermediate stripe.

So in the case of the Engineers battalion with the code 42283, we keep the 8 and 3 which gives us a red upper stripe, a yellow intermediate stripe and a red lower stripe. No other unit could have this code, and all the company's material and articles bore the same three-stripe code.

All types of vehicles which had been specially transported or gone by sea had a specific shipment marking. This marking was painted on the vehicle until 1944, then took the form of a plate, giving the vehicle's relevant technical information. It was placed on the right-hand side of the vehicle most of the time and was intended for the Navy and the Engineers to help them organize the transport. The plate was inside the cab.

All American vehicles had unit markings which enabled the vehicle to be identified and its place in the combat flowchart recognized. The first group of figures gave the highest level of the unit: army, army corps, or division. The second group identified the brigade, the regiment, or the battalion. The third group gave the company's identification. The fourth group was used to identify the vehicle within the company (see for example the photo at the bottom of page 172).

It goes without saying that the letters differed with each unit. Thus the armored division's triangle could be replaced by the letters AB for Airborne or I for Infantry. One particularity was that the brigade headquarters vehicles were identified by the letter X in the second group.

Example: 3A-X HQ-1: the vehicle No.1 of the HQ company of the Third Army.

The American armored divisions were represented by a triangular tactical sign, but their insignia were also triangular. In fact all American armored divisions had one common insignia; only the motto changed (*see the plate of American markings*).

This insignia—rarely painted on the tanks—was a triangle resting on a dark yellow stripe. The triangle was made up of three colors: yellow in the upper part, blue and red on the bottom. These three colors represented the components of an armored division (cavalry, yellow; campaign artillery, red; infantry, blue).

In the upper part was the divisional number. In the centre, a stylized running gear represented mobility and armor. The silhouette of a cannon symbolized firepower. Crossed with the cannon, a red lightning streak represented the shock action. These insignia came from the symbols used by the 7th US Cavalry Brigade which was the first to be changed into an armored division at the beginning of World War II.

In the band under the triangle was the name or the motto of the division. The insignia were as follows:

1st Armored Division—Old Ironsides
2d Armored Division—Hell on Wheels
3d Armored Division—Spearhead
4th Armored Division—Breakthrough
5th Armored Division—Victory
6th Armored Division—Super Sixth
7th Armored Division—The Lucky Seventh
8th Armored Division—Thundering Herd
9th Armored Division—Phantom Remagen

An LM4 with a composite hull in the Philippines in 1944. This tank, except for its name and its "hull art," has no markings on the flanks or the turret enabling it to be identified. (NARA)

10th Armored Division—Tiger
11th Armored Division—Thunderbolt
12th Armored Division—Hell Cat
13th Armored Division—Black Cat
14th Armored Division—Liberator
16th and 20th Armored Divisions—no stripe
27th Armored Division—Empire, on a dark-blue band
30th Armored Division—Volunteers
40th Armored Division—Grizzly, on a dark-blue background, a star at each end of the stripe
48th Armored Division—Hurricane
49th Armored Division—Lone Star, with a star between the two words
50th Armored Division—Jersey Blues

Some of these armored divisions were created after World War II. The 15th, 25th, and 39th Armored Divisions were the "ghost" divisions for Operation *Fortitude*.

Tonnage classifications

This indication was put in black letters on a yellow disc. There were two types of identification possible: a single vehicle or one with a trailer.

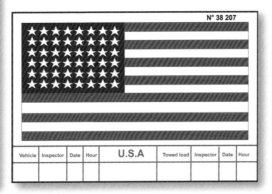

On any vehicle taking part in a landing, a US flag was put on the bottom left-hand side of the windshield. On the reverse side were details about landing vehicles. At the bottom of the flag were the vehicle's number, date, and time of embarkation, etc. (drawing by the author)

ARM AND SERVICE SYMBOLS
WEHRMACHT SYMBOLS OF WORLD WAR II

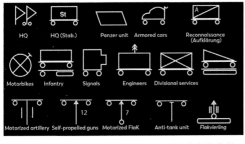

NATO SYMBOLS—POST-WORLD WAR II

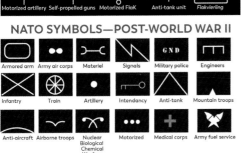

Sherman AVRE Bobbin from the 79th Armoured Division under Major-General Hobart, June 6, 1944. The division's bull's head insignia was painted on the left-hand side of the glacis. The white figure 40 in a black square in the centre indicates that the tank belonged to the divisional HQ. (*IWM*)

Following page, top: Sexton self-propelled gun, a 25-pounder on a Sherman M4 chassis from the British 11th Armoured Division (the Charging Bull insignia). The tactical sign (a white number in a half-red, half-blue square—the artillery colors) is here hidden by the camouflage netting. The field artillery regiment of the division this tank belongs to cannot be identified. (*IWM B9807*)

In the second case the figures were written as a fraction. The top figure indicated the weight of the vehicle with the trailer; the bottom one the vehicle by itself.

For the White 666 Breakdown Truck, for instance, the markings were 38-17 and for the Dodge WC 56, 6-4 (*see the plate "American markings"*).

The American flag

The 48-star American flag was located on the bottom left of the windscreen of any vehicle taking part in a landing. On the other side was all the information and details about vehicle landing: these procedures obviously concerned transfers by LCT and other landing barges to the beaches. These details were to make it easier for the TQMs (Transport Quarter Masters), the logistics officers, but were also used as a checklist for the personnel in charge of the landings, the crews, or the Engineering personnel. At the bottom of the American flag were some details like the number of the vehicle, the date and time of embarkation, and similar details for the landing.

On the other side of the flag was a 10-point checklist for the crews, including spark plugs and cabling, watertight ignition coil and distributor, watertight carburetor controls and battery, starter and battery contacts, and position of the front axle levers and jaw clutching. These markings, only valid for the transshipment, were removed, but it did happen that they weren't and then they lasted until they faded.

During Operation *Husky*, American tanks were identified by colored stripes on the barrel. For example, a red stripe designated the 2d Tank Company, two red stripes the 2d Platoon and so on. The company commander was identified by colored semi-stripes on the cannon.

Vehicle and machine symbols

On maps and tactical drawings, the US Army—like all armies in the world—used a variety of symbols to recognize the categories of vehicles, the artillery units engaged, and the materiel used.

These symbols were used in principle by the HQ staffs during large-scale operations.

Identifying large units and arms also depended on the markings, and the French Army was inspired by this for its own markings. A number of symbols were to be found in common, like the armored arm, signals, train, materiel, artillery, and engineers.

The first to use these symbols were the Germans in 1939 (*see opposite*).

British Markings

On the other side of the Channel the vehicles were identified by a Unit Serial Number issued by the War Department (WD) written on the side of the vehicles as they were in the USA. This five- or six-figure numbering (depending on the vehicle, etc.) was painted white and started with the letter T for armored vehicles (tanks). For the other categories the letters were as follows:

A—Ambulances
C—Motorbikes
E—Specific engineer vehicles
F—Armored cars
L—HGVs (heavy goods vehicles) more than 15 tons
M—Liaison vehicles
P—Amphibious vehicles
S—Self-propelled guns
V—Shelters
X—Trailers
Z—HGVs less than 15 tons

Regimental markings

These were colored squares inside which two white figures gave the indications. The tank regiments bore

A Squadron
13/16th Royal Hussars Rgt,
Senior Regiment,
Guards Armoured Division,
vehicle No.6

UNITED KINDOM

ACHILLE

T 624 059

1° British Armoured Div.	2° British Armoured Div.	5° British Armoured Div.	7° British Armoured Div.	8° British Armoured Div.	Guard Armored Div.	27° British Armoured Brig.
11° British Armoured Div.	9° British Armoured Div.	79 British Armoured Div.	HQ 8° British Armoured Div.	3° Royal Tank Rgt	Staffordshire Yeomanry	5° Royal Tank Rgt

a red square; the infantry regiments a green one; the light artillery battalions a black square; the square was separated into two colors for the artillery regiments—red on top and blue on the bottom. The Engineer squadrons' number was on a blue square and the reconnaissance regiments' square was green on top and blue below.

For example: the 5th Armoured Brigade of the British Guards Armoured Division comprised five armoured regiments numbered from 50 to 54. They all began with a five:

- 50 for the divisional HQ;
- 51 for the 2nd Armoured Battalion, Grenadier Guards (Senior Regiment);
- 52 for the 1st Armoured Battalion, Coldstream Guards (Middle Regiment);
- 53 for the 2nd Armoured Battalion, Irish Guards (Junior Regiment);
- 54 for the 1st Motor Battalion, Grenadier Guards.

Unlike with the French and the Americans, the traditional insignia were reproduced on the armored vehicles and painted on the frontal glacis, in the center or on the left and often repeated onto the rear mudguard, or on the rear panel when the mudguards were occupied by extra boxes, the outside telephone, or the first aid kit.

Christening names were stenciled on the front or the sides. In a squadron the names all started with the same letter. These names were in theory painted white, but could be pale blue.

The various squadrons could be identified by motifs like a lozenge for the HQ, a triangle for the 1st Company, a square for the 2nd Company, and a circle for the 3rd Company. These signs were colored differently depending on the regiment's seniority (date of creation). The senior regiments had red markings, the next senior yellow, and the most recent blue. For the British, bridge classification was written in black on a yellow background but painted on the right-hand side of the transmission armor.

On certain tanks, after 1942, the maximum speed was painted in mph. This marking was reproduced on the driver's side and consisted of a red disc inside which the speed was written in black letters. After 1943 these markings were marked on a khaki base, with red numbers for the front and black figures for the rear.

For blackout night-driving a white disc was fixed to the rear and bottom of the vehicle so it could be seen by the driver of the following vehicle. With some units, the two-figure brigade or divisional abbreviation was added for easier identification.

On later generations of vehicles, this plate was lit up by the driver with a separate light. This night-time help was also used by the Germans. It consisted of an escutcheon with a black cross; the closer the following driver, the more distinct was the cross.

Recognizing friendly vehicles from the sky always preoccupied the Allied General Staffs. In North Africa in 1942, British, New Zealand, South African, and

A Kangaroo from the 1st Canadian Armored Personnel Carrier Regiment on the chassis of a turretless Canadian RAM in Holland during the winter of 1944. This machine belonged to A Squadron (emptied-out white triangle on the tank side behind the tank's christening name). *(Tank Museum, Bovington)*

Canadian vehicles were recognizable by the roundel painted on the bonnet, the rear deck, or the turret top.

After June 1944, all Allied vehicles were identified by the white five-pointed star painted on the top or the bonnet and on the side of all vehicles.

The Transport Quarter Masters' embarkation codes

The British identified their vehicles by means of a two-colored rectangle surmounted by a four-figure number. These codes were assigned to a regiment and the color/figure combination allowed for a vast number of combinations. The abbreviations were put on the bottom of the turret towards the front and were, in theory, removed after each landing (see plate for British markings).

Canadian Markings

The Canadian Army adopted most of the British markings. Squadrons were thus identified by the symbols (lozenge, inverted triangle, square, and circle) in which was marked the number of the vehicle in order. The color indicated the rank of the regiment in the hierarchy—red, Senior Regiment; yellow, Middle Regiment; and blue, Junior Regiment.

The background of the geometric figure in some units was black. The names were painted in smaller letters than

on British tanks and placed on the additional armor along the sides and on the front of the tank, in the centre, low down. This position was more by default, since a string of track links was mounted on the front of the tank.

Serial numbers started with the letter T, inscribed in white on the sides towards the rear. The vehicle was a rebuild if the number ended with R.

The divisional or brigade insignia was on the front left-hand side and the regimental number on the right-hand side. This number was white on a square and repeated on the rear right-hand wing, with the divisional insignia painted on the rear left-hand wing of the tank.

The white and red markings on British tanks were painted on the right- and left-hand flanks of the tank (these markings disappeared after 1942). Like all vehicles in the ETO, Canadian tanks bore a white star theoretically without a circle. Bridge classification was marked by a black number 30 surrounded by a yellow circle without background (see plate of Canadian markings opposite).

The New-Zealand tanks were recognized by the emblem of their country, the fern leaf, painted on the rear right-hand wing with the divisional insignia. Generally, they adopted British-style markings like the other countries in the Commonwealth.

As with all the tanks engaged in British units, the cannons were painted white underneath to reduce visibility—the special case of the Firefly.

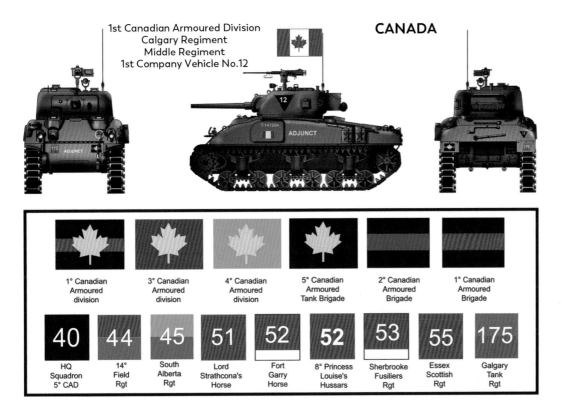

1st Canadian Armoured Division
Calgary Regiment
Middle Regiment
1st Company Vehicle No.12

CANADA

1° Canadian Armoured division	3° Canadian Armoured division	4° Canadian Armoured division	5° Canadian Armoured Tank Brigade	2° Canadian Armoured Brigade	1° Canadian Armoured Brigade

40	44	45	51	52	52	53	55	175
HQ Squadron 5° CAD	14° Field Rgt	South Alberta Rgt	Lord Strathcona's Horse	Fort Garry Horse	8° Princess Louise's Hussars	Sherbrooke Fusiliers Rgt	Essex Scottish Rgt	Galgary Tank Rgt

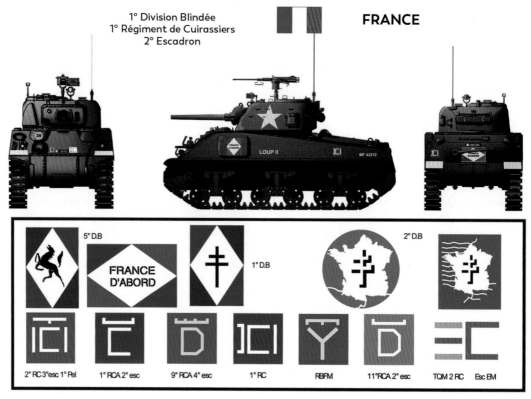

5° D.B

FRANCE D'ABORD

1° D.B

2° D.B

2° RC 3°esc 1° Pel   1° RCA 2° esc   9° RCA 4° esc   1° RC   RBFM   11°RCA 2° esc   TQM 2 RC   Esc EM

The Free French M4s

A Sherman M4A4 from the 2e Regiment de Cuirassiers, near Aubagne, France, on August 20, 1944. *(ECPAD)*

The Free French used different versions of the M4 Medium Tank, and the French armored divisions copied the American model of the times (Light Armored Division). In 1942, the French decided to create new divisions in North Africa and to equip them with new American materiel.

The 2e DB (2e Division Blindé—2d Armored Division), equipped with, among other things, M4 105s and M4A2s, landed in Normandy. The 1st and 5th French Armored Divisions landed in Provence equipped with M4A2s and M4A4s, whereas the 3d DB was used as a reserve for organizational and training purposes for the other divisions and was equipped with light tanks, about 200 of them, including some M3s and then M24s before they served in Indochina and Algeria.

Some A1 versions were also put into service in the French Army; this version was used by units of the armored arm.

Other versions of the Sherman like the M4 Hybrid were supplied—one only—to the 12e Régiment de Cuirassiers (Cuirassiers Regiment), to the RBCEO, or an M4A3 Jumbo to the 2e RCA and an M4 105 HVSS to the 2e RC. The Shermans subsequently equipped squadrons of Gendarmerie Mobile, while others were put into reserve-mobilization. As a battle tank, the Sherman took part especially in Indochina. In Algeria it was replaced mainly by the M24 and a few M7s.

A little digression now on the subject of the Croix de Lorraine, the symbol of Free France, which was on all units' markings. Unlike what is popularly believed, the idea did not come from de Gaulle. It was Lieutenant-Commander Thierry d'Argenlieu—commanding the CEFEO*—who suggested adopting the Croix de Lorraine as the Free France symbol, in memory of Joan

of Arc's perseverance but also in reaction to another cross, the Swastika.

In his general order dated July 3, 1940, Vice-Admiral Emile Muselier, who had been in command of the Free French naval and air forces for two years, created the French flag with a red *Croix de Lorraine* occupying the central white part.

A roundel using the Croix de Lorraine was also created. This cross was also the insignia for an American infantry division, the 79th, which distinguished itself in France during the fighting in World Wars I and II. The insignia represented the Croix de Lorraine on an azure escutcheon edged with silver.

The Sherman was in service from 1942 in the French Army and in the three French armored divisions:

1er DIVISION BLINDÉE (Armored Division)
Landed in Provence—Operation *Dragoon*
3e Régiment de Chasseurs d'Afrique
Reconnaissance, M8s, and half-tracks
9e Régiment de Chasseurs d'Afrique
Tank destroyers, TD M10s
2e Régiment de Cuirassiers, CC 1 (Combat Command 1)
M4A2s, M4A4s, M4A1 76s, M4A3s, M4A3 105s, and M5s

2e Régiment de Chasseurs d'Afrique CC 3
M4A4s, M4A1 76s, M4A3 105s, and M5s
5e Régiment de Chasseurs d'Afrique CC2
M4A2s, M4A1 76s, and M5A1s
RCCC
Tank destroyers, TD M10s
2e DIVISION BLINDÉE
Landed in Normandy—Operation *Overlord*
1er Régiment de Marche de Spahis Marocains (RMSM)
Reconnaissance, M8s, half-tracks, and M8 howitzers
Régiment Blindé de Fusiliers Marins (RBFM)
Tank destroyers, TD M10 then TD M10A1, and M8 armored cars
501e Régiment de Chars de Combat
M4A2s, M4A3 105s, and M3A3
12e Régiment de Cuirassiers
M4A2s, M4A4s, and M5A1s.
12e Régiment de Chasseurs d'Afrique
M4A2s, M4A1s, M4A3 105s, and M5A1s.
5e DIVISION BLINDÉE
Landed in Provence—Operation *Dragoon*
1er Régiment Etranger de Cavalerie
Reconnaissance, half tracks M8s
1er Régiment de Cuirassiers CC4

The 79th US Infantry Division insignia bore a Croix de Lorraine too. *(Private Collection)*

Sherman M4A4 *Fabert* from the 2e Régiment de Cuirassiers, 1er DB, in Marseille on August 21, 1944. *(ECPAD)*

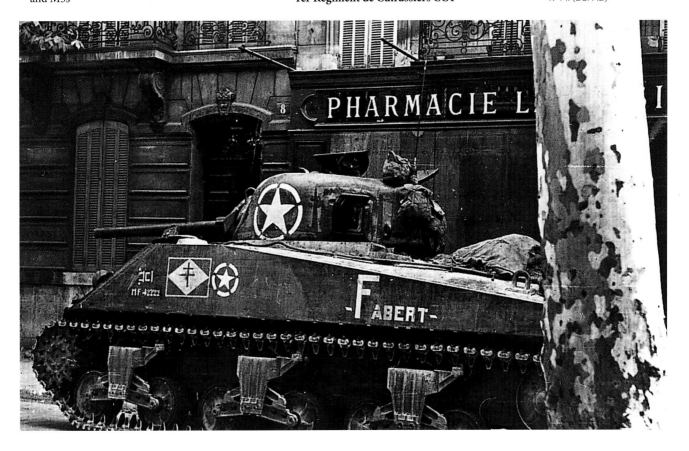

M4A4s and M5s

1er Régiment de Chasseurs d'Afrique CC5

M4A4s and M5A1s

6e Régiment de Chasseurs d'Afrique CC6

M4A4s and M5A1s

11e R.I.A.

Tank destroyers, TD M10s, and half-tracks

3e Division d'Infanterie Algérienne

Landed in Provence—Operation *Dragoon*

9e Division d'Infanterie Coloniale

Landed in Provence—Operation *Dragoon*

During Operation *Dragoon*, this division comprised two cavalry regiments, the 3e RSAR and the 7e RIA, both equipped with M8 light armored vehicles and half-tracks. The RCCC* and the RCIM* were part of the 9e DIC at that moment. Operation *Dragoon* was sometimes called *Anvil*, which was the name initially given by Eisenhower, but Churchill didn't like it: he'd have preferred a landing in the Balkans so as to get to Berlin before the Soviets. He was therefore *dragooned* into accepting, and *Anvil* became *Dragoon*.

French Markings 1943–63

This is another domain where the debate is still heated, everyone claiming to know everything about everything.

In the following lines we will use the regiments that participated in the campaign for France, the 5e RCA, 2e RC, or the 501e TCC, as a reference. When you look at the subject closely you see that even the witnesses who served on the Shermans can't agree among themselves. If we are to succeed in defining these markings, this chapter will have to approach the subject in two parts, sticking to real life as closely as possible.

Part No.1: the technical, tactical, and logistics markings.

Part No.2: the traditional markings.

The technical markings relate to information or data that the tank had to furnish. They were common to all tanks from the same country. They are for instance, with French tanks, the registration number, that ought really to be called the identification number.

These numbers comprised a combination of figures that gave the vehicle's role (light vehicle, lorry, armored vehicle, etc.), when it was put into service, and finally its place in the production.

For the Americans, for instance, all tanks had a number starting with 30. This identification number on French tanks was visible at the front and the rear of the vehicle. It was written in white figures on a black background, preceded on the left-hand side by the French tricolor flag in a black rectangle.

All French military vehicles put into service during 1943 received a registration number beginning with "4"; during 1944, they began with "95"; and then "96" in 1945.

Another marking: the tactical code

It gave the arm of the army the vehicle belonged to (engineers, infantry, cavalry, etc., or headquarters); a combination of horizontal or vertical stripes set out in squares or along the diagonals.

These signs were painted white on the rear and on the sides of the vehicles (*see plate about French markings*).

MF markings and TQM codes

The MF code was made up of five figures preceded by the letters MF (for *Materiel Français*). The first two figures indicated the division, the third the arm, the fourth the unit, and the fifth the squadron.

This gives us for example for the 2e Régiment de Cuirassiers the code No. MF42220 for the headquarters, the 1st Escadron (Squadron) being MF42221, then 42222, and 42223 and so on. We therefore have the codes for the 1e DB, 42; armored arm, 2; the 2e Cuirassiers, 2; then 0 for the HQ.

These markings came from the Americans. For the French divisions, the codes were as follows: 1re DB, 42; 2e DB, 49; and 5e DB, 44.

The codes for the different arms were as follows:

- 1 for the infantry
- 2 for the cavalry
- 3 for the artillery
- 4 for the engineers
- 5 for the signals
- 6 for the train
- 7 for the AA artillery
- 8 for the medical service
- 9 for the BPM
- 0 for the headquarters

All French units that had taken part in the French campaign were transported by the US Navy or the Royal Navy. They embarked with a POM code for the TQMs. In the French units, the POM code was called the TQM code, but the way it was determined followed the same principles as in the US Army. Taking the same example of the 4th Squadron of the French 2d Armored Division mentioned above gives us upper and lower stripes: olive green and the middle stripe light green.

The French units placed the first letter corresponding to the arm, in this case C for cavalry, on the right of the bar codes. The letter was painted the same color as the upper and lower stripes.

These TQM codes were painted directly on the front and rear of the vehicles. In the case where the code had olive drab colored stripes, the TQM code was painted on a white background.

Bridge-crossing classification

The tonnage was painted in black figures on a yellow circle depending on the weight of the vehicles. The abbreviation was painted on the front of the vehicle. In the case of a vehicle with a trailer, the markings were still on a black background but as a fraction, the weight of the tractor above and the trailer below.

Dimensions for train transport (after 1946)

Depending on whether a vehicle had the right dimensions or not when transported by rail, it bore a red or white grenade painted at the base of the turret, on both sides of the gun mantle, or again above the mudguards on certain wheeled vehicles. In the case where the vehicle needed to be prepared to make it compatible with the specified dimensions, the

THE MARKINGS ON THE TANK *JEANNE D'ARC*

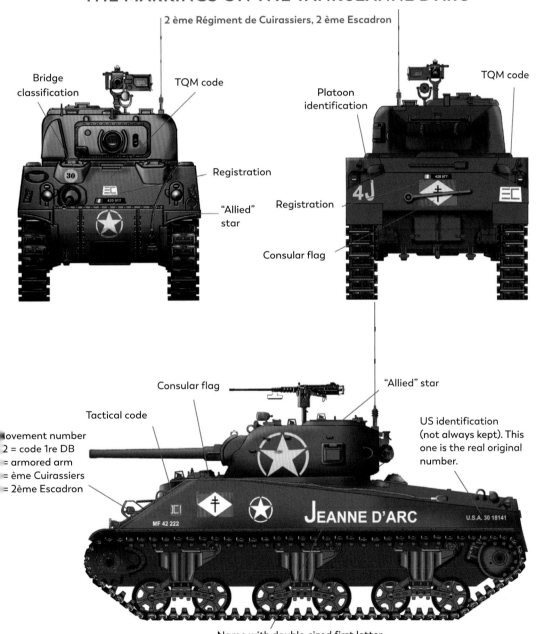

2 ème Régiment de Cuirassiers, 2 ème Escadron

Bridge classification

TQM code

Platoon identification

TQM code

Registration

"Allied" star

Registration

Consular flag

Consular flag

Tactical code

"Allied" star

Movement number
2 = code 1re DB
= armored arm
= ème Cuirassiers
= 2ème Escadron

US identification (not always kept). This one is the real original number.

JEANNE D'ARC

U.S.A. 30 18141

MF 42 222

Name with double-sized first letter

Destroyed at Marseilles during the battle for Notre Dame de la Garde. The chassis number of this M4 A4 was 17837; it was built by Chrysler Corporation, Detroit, Michigan.
Contract No. W.ORD.461 in the series between 16555 and 20554. Ref SNLG 104 Part 11
NB: Not every tank bore the Croix de Lorraine; others had a star without a circle. As with a lot of M4A4s in the 2e RC, the *Jeanne d'Arc* did not have additional armor plates on the sides.

3 ÈME DIVISION D'INFANTERIE ALGÉRIENNE ET RÉSERVE

Regimental insignia, TQM codes, tactical markings

7 ÈME RÉGIMENT DE CHASSEURS D'AFRIQUE (RCA)

HQ and AM&SS	2560		**R**	**D**
1st Squadron	2561		R	D̄
2d Squadron	2562		**R**	D̄
3d Squadron	2563		R	D̄
4th Squadron	2564		R	D̄

8 ÈME RÉGIMENT DE CHASSEURS D'AFRIQUE (RCA)

HQ and AM&SS	2570		**R**	O̅
1st Squadron	2571		R	O̅
2d Squadron	2572		R	O̅
3d Squadron	2573		R	O̅
4th Squadron	2574		R	O̅

2 ÈME RÉGIMENT DE SPAHIS ALGÉRIENS DE RECONNAISSANCE (RSAR)

HQ and AM&SS	44502		C	R̄
1st Light Tank Squadron	44503		C	R̄
2d Recce Squadron	44504		C	R̄
3d Recce Squadron	44505		C	R̄
4th Recce Squadron	44506		C	R̄

3 ÈME RÉGIMENT DE CHASSEURS D'AFRIQUE (RCA)

HQ and AM&SS	2255 G		**G**
1st Light Tank Squadron	2256 G		**G**
2d Recce Squadron	2257 G		**G**
3d Recce Squadron	2258 G		**G**
4th Recce Squadron	2259 G		Ⓖ

2 ÈME RÉGIMENT DE DRAGONS (RD)

HQ and AM&SS	44514		C	D
1st Squadron	44515		C	D
2d Squadron	44517		C	D
3d Squadron	44518		C	D
4th Squadron	44519		C	D

RÉGIMENT COLONIAL DE CHARS DE COMBAT (RCCC)

HQ and AM&SS	44506		C	D
1st Squadron	44507		C	D̄
2d Squadron	44508		C	D̄
3d Squadron	44509		C	D̄
4th Squadron	44510		C	D̄

grenade had one or two red dots. Certain units kept the American identification number.

This number was stenciled onto the sides of the vehicle towards the rear. The way these numbers were made up is dealt with in the chapter "American Markings."

In some units, the tanks had a combat number on the turret. It was painted in big figures on the sides.

Unit markings

These markings, unlike the technical or logistics markings, were particular to each individual regiment or unit.

Among them there were the "Allied" star, the divisional insignia or symbols, the regimental insignia, the names, and some private off-the-cuff inscriptions. There were not many of these among the French markings.

The history of the American star has been dealt with in the chapter on American markings. It was painted on the large majority of French vehicles.

This white star was painted on all Allied vehicles for recognition, especially by aircraft. Although it was supposed to be painted on all vehicles, some Sherman photographs show tanks without a star, neither on the sides nor on the upper surfaces. Was there not enough time when preparing? We don't know, but they were an exception.

Although the star's dimensions were generally respected, the location could vary from one unit to another. Thus in theory the 12e Cuirassiers tanks were supposed to have a circled star on the upper turret surface.

Photographs of various tanks in this regiment show them with a star on the sides of the turret or even no star at all, or again a star without a circle. But one has to remain pragmatic and imagine that at a given moment a turret might have been repainted, or the star rubbed off by the weather. The American star could be by itself, or surrounded by a full or an incomplete circle.

The markings for the big units were different: a map of France with the Croix de Lorraine in the centre (2e DB); the Consular flag with the Croix de Lorraine in the centre (1er DB); and the Consular flag with the motto "*France d'abord*" (France first) (5e DB). Subsequently the motto was sometimes replaced by a rearing horse recalling the arms of Stuttgart.

These markings were painted on the sides of the tanks, usually on the additional side armor. Showing the Consular flag—or the 1804-model flag—gave rise to several discussions.

This flag was made up of a white lozenge in the centre surrounded by red and blue. The blue was always at the top on the shaft side, which gave the red on the top on the right, blue at the bottom on the left and red at the bottom on the right. As with all flags, this layout was identical both on the obverse and reverse sides, whichever side it was seen from.

On the other hand, it is common practice to consider a flag as blowing in the wind, held by the shaft, and this applied to all flags of all countries. In the case of a flag shown on a tank, whichever side you are looking at, the flag shaft will always be at the front of the tank, in the direction of movement. The Consular flag was painted with blue at the top and left (shaft side and in the direction of movement), be it on the right or left. Any other representation is a mistake!

Imagine simply the American flag with the stars shaft-side on the obverse side, and the stripes shaft-side on the reverse side. In that case the French flag will have the blue shaft-side on the obverse side and the red shaft-side on the reverse side: unthinkable!

In all the cases, the Consular flag was not a divisional insignia. Some units painted a Croix de Lorraine in the centre of the lozenge, a common practice in the 1er DB, in particular in the 2e Cuirassiers; others painted the motto "*France d'abord*" inside the white lozenge. This flag, which was originally inspired by the cavalry pennant (therefore square), could be painted as a horizontal or vertical rectangle, in the case of the RCAs.

Vehicle names

In use in all the units, the names were painted on the sides of the hull or the turret.

The size of the letters varied. In some cases the first letter of the name was double the size of the others. Knowing that within a unit all the tanks had a name beginning with the same letter meant you could tell at a distance which tank it was. Certain regiments used writing edged with a different color or shadowed. After 1945, the regimental insignia could be painted onto the tank.

During certain operations all the markings were painted over or hidden by mud. But certain markings were far too visible and could be spotted by the enemy from a long way off and make targeting easier.

This 76-mm cannon M4A3 from the 12e RCA of the 2e DB has kept its US serial number; the combat number is on the side of the turret. There is no star.

1 ÈRE DIVISION BLINDÉE — ARMORED REGIMENTS

Regimental insignia, TQM codes, tactical markings

3E RÉGIMENT DE CHASSEURS D'AFRIQUE

HQ and AM&SS	42250	C R
1st Squadron	42251	C R
2d Squadron	42252	C R
3d Squadron	42253	C R
4th Squadron	42254	C R
5th Squadron	42255	C R

2E RÉGIMENT DE CUIRASSIERS

HQ and AM&SS	42220	C
1st Squadron	42221	C
2d Squadron	42222	C
3d Squadron	42223	C
4th Squadron	42224	C

2E RÉGIMENT DE CHASSEURS D'AFRIQUE

HQ and AM&SS	42210	C
1st Squadron	42211	C
2d Squadron	42212	C
3d Squadron	42213	C
4th Squadron	42214	C

5E RÉGIMENT DE CHASSEURS D'AFRIQUE

HQ and AM&SS	42230	C
1st Squadron	42231	C
2d Squadron	42232	C
3d Squadron	42233	C
4th Squadron	42234	C

9E RÉGIMENT DE CHASSEURS D'AFRIQUE

HQ and AM&SS	42260	C D
1st Squadron	42261	C D
2d Squadron	42262	C D
3d Squadron	42263	C D
4th Squadron	42264	C D

3 ÈME DIVISION D'INFANTERIE ALGÉRIENNE ET RÉSERVE

Regimental insignia, TQM codes, tactical markings

1ER RÉGIMENT DE MARCHE DES SPAHIS MAROCAINS

HQ and AM&SS	49871	C	R
1st Squadron	49872	C	R
2d Squadron	49873	C	R
3d Squadron	49874	C	R
4th Squadron	49875	C	R
5th Squadron	49876	C	R

The 6th and 7th squadrons were created after 1944, and have no barcode

501E RÉGIMENT DE CHARS DE COMBAT

EM (HQ)	49809	C	C
EHR (AM&SS)	49810	C	C
1st Company	49811	C	C
2d Company	49812	C	C
3d Company	49813	C	C
4th Company	49814	C	C

12E RÉGIMENT DE CHASSEURS D'AFRIQUE

EM4	9830	C	C
EHR	49831	C	C
1st Squadron	49832	C	C
2d Squadron	49833	C	C
3d Squadron	49834	C	C
4th Squadron	49835	C	C

12E RÉGIMENT DE CUIRASSIERS

EM	49820	C	C
EHR	49821	C	C
7th Combat Co.	49822	C	C
2d Squadron	49823	C	C
3d Squadron	49824	C	C
4th Squadron	49825	C	C

RÉGIMENT BLINDÉ DE FUSILIERS MARINS (RBFM)

EM	49877	C	Y
EHR	49878	C	Y
1st Squadron	49879	C	Y
2d Squadron	49880	C	Y
3d Squadron	49881	C	Y
4th Squadron	49882	C	Y

The Shermans *Austerlitz, la Moskowa, Romilly, Montmirail, Montereau II* (a 76-mm), and *Arcis-sur-aube* in front of the Arc de Triomphe, at the top of the Champs-Elysées, during the grand parade on September 8, 1944. These tanks belonged to the 501e Régiment de Chars de Combat. The four Shermans bearing the names of battles of the 1814 French campaign were from the 1/2 501 RCC. *(Private Collection)*

The plate on page 183 gives an example of the markings in 1944. This was an M4A4 from the 2e Régiment de Cuirassiers, whose tank commander was the Maréchal des Logis Keck. During the battle of Marseille, in the fighting on the hill near Notre Dame de la Garde, the tank was set ablaze and three crew members (in the turret) killed.

The names were placed variously in the RCCs, especially in the RCA, the RBFM, and RCCC. It was frequent in these units for the name to be painted on the gun shield, but sometimes the names were painted in gothic script as they were in the 7e RCA. In certain units the names obeyed stricter rules, like in the 2e RSAR where the first letter of the vehicle names had to designate the squadron:

- T for the 1st Squadron;
- P for the 2d Squadron;
- B for the 3d Squadron;
- R for the 4th Squadron.

The second letter designated the platoon. So for the 1st Platoon of the 4th Squadron, the letters were RE, so the tanks were all christened *Résistante, Revenante, Resplendissante*, etc.

RO was for the 2d Platoon, so *Rôdeuse, Rogneuse,* etc. RI was for the 3d Platoon, so *Rivale, Risque-tout,* etc. The final choice of name was left to the crew.

In the 2e RD (Régiment de Dragons), the names of the tanks and armored vehicles all had a name linked to the French capital. The corps commander's M8 SPG was called *Paris* and the other tanks bore names of the capital's monuments, like *Notre-Dame, Arc-de-Triomphe,* etc.

The armored cars had the names of the city's quarters like *Passy* and *Champs-Elysées.*

The jeeps used names of squares, streets, or underground stations, such as *Alma, Bastille, Rue de la Paix,* etc.

The half-tracks bore names of stadiums or velodromes, including *Parc des Princes, Buffalo, Vel'd'Hiv,* etc.

The command cars used the names of racecourses, like *Longchamp, Auteuil, Saint-Cloud,* etc.

The motorbikes had names such as *Tabarin, Maxim's, Garnier,* etc.

Trucks were called after the working-class suburbs like *Pantin, Billancourt,* or *Suresnes.*

Another custom was recording the "kills" (enemy tanks destroyed). These were shown by a swastika painted on the barrel. In the 11e RCA, for instance, a black rectangle with a white edge was painted on the barrel, near the shield; in the RBFM it was the silhouette of a tank painted on the outside sponsons.

Polish Markings

What follows is a brief summary of the Polish units, often forgotten in the accounts of the Liberation of Europe.

The 1st Polish Armored Division (1 Dywizja Pancerna, 1942–47)

A unit re-formed in Scotland in 1942, it numbered some 13,000 men and during World War II it took part in the fighting equipped with M4A2s and Fireflies, replacing them progressively with other models including M4A1

5 ÈME DIVISION BLINDÉE — ARMORED REGIMENTS

Regimental insignia, TQM codes, tactical markings

1ER RÉGIMENT ETRANGER DE CAVALERIE

EM	44270	C	R
EHR	44271	C	R
1st Squadron	44272	C	R
2d Squadron	44273	C	R
3d Squadron	44274	C	R
4th Squadron	44275	C	R
5th Squadron	44276	C	R

1ER RÉGIMENT DE CUIRASSIERS

EM (HQ)	49809	C	C
EHR (AM&SS)	49810	C	C
1st Company	49811	C	C
2d Company	49812		
3d Company	49813	C	C
4th Company	49814	C	C

1ER RÉGIMENT DE CHASSEURS D'AFRIQUE

EM and AM&SS	44221	C	C
1st Squadron	44222	C	C
2d Squadron	44223	C	C
3d Squadron	44224	C	C
4th Squadron	44225	C	C

6E RÉGIMENT DE CHASSEURS D'AFRIQUE

EM and AM&SS	44283	C	C
1st Squadron	44284	C	C
2d Squadron	44285	C	C
3d Squadron	44286	C	C
4th Squadron	44287	C	C

11E RÉGIMENT DE CHASSEURS D'AFRIQUE

EM and AM&SS	44228	C	D
1st Squadron	44229	C	D
2d Squadron	44280	C	D
3d Squadron	44281	C	D
4th Squadron	44282	C	D

76s. In Normandy, during Operation *Overlord*, the division was commanded by General Maczek, with unit commanders Stefanewicz, Koszutski, and Zgorelski. From Falaise (in Normandy) to Breda (Holland), the men in this division distinguished themselves in all the celebrated battles of the campaign, often paying a very heavy tribute.

After he was demobilized, General Maczek decided to remain in Scotland and settled in Edinburgh. The British authorities withdrew his rights as a former combatant and his military pension. In the 1960s he was a barman in an Edinburgh hotel, and he died in 1994. According to his last wishes, he was buried with his men in the Polish military cemetery in Breda.

The first Polish tank regiments were formed in Palestine to take part in the landings in Italy. Among these was the *4 Pulk Pancery* (2d Polish Armored Brigade), whose insignia was a scorpion.

Polish armored vehicles adopted the British-type tactical markings, identifying squadrons and companies by geometrical figures, with color codes for arms and divisions. The technical markings were classic, like the serial number (beginning with a T), and bridge classification by black figure on a yellow background. The traditional markings were the most current ones, i.e. the divisional marking and the name.

Sometimes the letters PL were added on the tank. The armored regiments were named *Pulk Pancery* whereas the lancer regiments were the *Pulk Ulanow*.

When the Polish freed the town of Breda, the Dutch population immediately expressed its gratitude by inscribing messages of thanks on the liberating tanks. Every year the anniversary of the liberation of Breda is the cause for important festivities.

Soviet Markings

Military vehicle markings of the Soviet period are rather difficult to define and classify, for one good reason: no document dealing with these inscriptions has come down to us. The markings nonetheless existed and some were indispensable when the tanks fought and got separated far from one another. After 1955, the Soviet Army started codifying and standardizing all the markings. Like all armies, the Red Army (the name disappeared in 1946 to become the Soviet Army) used recognition signs on its armored vehicles. At the beginning, as with the Americans, there was a white stripe around the turret, a sign meaning friendly tank or vehicle.

Later the Soviets added a white cross painted on the top of the turret for easier aerial recognition. Within the units, the vehicles were identified by a system of squares and triangles containing an order number.

It happened that in certain units, identification was by means of a three-number base, as it was with the panzers. The first figure gave the company or squadron, the second the section (or platoon for the Americans), and the last figure the position of the tank (section head, assistants, subordinates).

The Russians did not use a tactical code very much, and often the name was replaced by a patriotic or partisan slogan, bearing in mind that there was only one Party. In most cases the red star was *de rigueur*. Sometimes the hammer and sickle was also present. The slogans often sung the praises of the founding fathers, Lenin or Stalin.

Within the tank divisions, the Soviets had battalions (an organization not used in the west). In this case, the recognition markings consisted of a split lozenge, the upper part containing the battalion number and the lower part the number of the tank in the battalion. Another type of marking consisted of a lozenge and three triangles with an identification number; these markings were sometimes painted red with a white edge.

The letters CCCP were sometimes painted on the frontal glacis. The crews inscribed their kills by painting small stars on the turret, adopting an air force custom but also one used by the German panzers, one star meaning one enemy tank destroyed (*see the plate of Soviet markings opposite*).

German Markings

When discussing the markings in use during World War II, it is necessary to mention the Germans. The reasons for doing this are many and logical, because the Wehrmacht and the Waffen-SS (not to be confused with the Allgemeine-SS) used a number of tactical recognition symbols. The Germans, moreover, were the precursors where marking arms and services were concerned. The Allies had to wait for NATO to establish these symbols before using them in a more or less uniform manner on combat vehicles. The Allies used drawings to represent vehicle categories a lot, in particular when establishing tactical or strategic plans.

The identification of bigger units, as well as the classic markings (combat no., serial no., registration no., specified dimension, or unit no.), was all originally of German conception—the Germans were the precursors in many applications, innovations, techniques, and tactics in military matters.

This aspect of the fighting, although interesting, is too far removed from the M4 Sherman to be treated in detail in this book. The plate on page 177 gives an insight into the symbols and markings used between 1940 and 1945 in German units.

1st Armored Division
24th Lancer Regiment
Junior Regiment
C Company
Tank No.14

POLAND

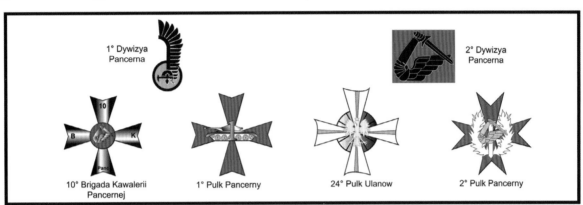

1° Dywizya Pancerna

2° Dywizya Pancerna

10° Brigada Kawalerii Pancernej

1° Pulk Pancerny

24° Pulk Ulanow

2° Pulk Pancerny

6th Division
Battalion 154
Tank No.17
2d Armored Battalion
Kirov Factory

SOVIET UNION

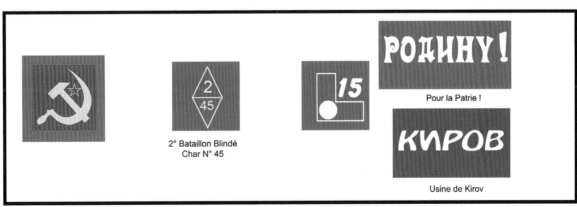

2° Bataillon Blindé
Char N° 45

РОДИНУ !

Pour la Patrie !

КИРОВ

Usine de Kirov

Unit Composition and Organization

Quite obviously, the composition of armored regiments varied according to their missions. Reconnaissance regiments were usually equipped with light tanks, armored cars, or half-tracks. Tank combat regiments were equipped with medium tanks; tank destroyer units were equipped with tank destroyers (TD M10s, TD M10A1s).

Nonetheless, light tanks and half-tracks were to be found in the medium tank regiments, just as the British tank units were sometimes equipped with a platoon of Firefly-type tank destroyers.

The Americans organized their tanks in battalions, just like the Soviets, whereas the French and British organized theirs in armored regiments. In general, in the French tank regiments, the 1st squadron was equipped with light tanks, type M3s or M5s. These tanks were equipped with a gearbox with an overdrive which increased mobility considerably, not to mention ease of driving.

The American tank battalion was subdivided into six companies: a regimental HQ and a HQ company, a service company, three companies of medium tanks (A, B, and C Companies), and a company of light M5 tanks (D Company). The HQ section was equipped with jeeps and half-tracks, plus two medium tanks: one for the battalion commander and one for the second-in-command.

In the services section, the HQ company comprised a reconnaissance platoon equipped with jeeps armed with machine guns on mountings, an 81-mm mortar platoon on half-tracks, and a platoon of assault tanks made up of M4 105s with M10 ammo trailers. The battalion's service company comprised a breakdown and repair platoon and a transport and supply platoon.

The breakdown and repair platoon was tasked with recovering and repairing damaged vehicles from the battlefield, whereas the transport and supply platoon provided all food supplies, ammunition, fuel, materiel, and other necessities.

Each combat company was equipped so it could function on its own for short periods at a time, and each had its own maintenance and administration unit.

As far as the TED personnel were concerned, a tank battalion consisted of 39 officers, 709 soldiers, 53 M4 tanks, six M4 105s, 17 M5A1 light tanks, six M32 TRV tanks, 15 half-tracks, 23 jeeps, one ambulance (replacing the two original half-tracks), four 6x6 Dodge trucks, 39 GMCs, two Wreckers, 17 M10 ammo trailers, 26 Bantan T3 ¼-ton trailers, and 27 Ben-Hur-type 1-ton trailers (*see the TO&E on the following pages*).

American units

Throughout the war, American tank battalions served either as organic units within a larger division, or as "separate tank battalions." The separate tank battalions, although independently numbered, rarely fought as stand-alone formations. Indeed, most of the separate tank battalions were attached to infantry divisions, providing an armored thrust to break through enemy

4th US Armored Division
704th Tank Destroyer Battalion
Company B—tank No.10
Jackson M36 B2 Tank Destroyer

BREAK THROUGH

U.S. TANK BATTALION TO&E 17–25 SEPTEMBER 1943

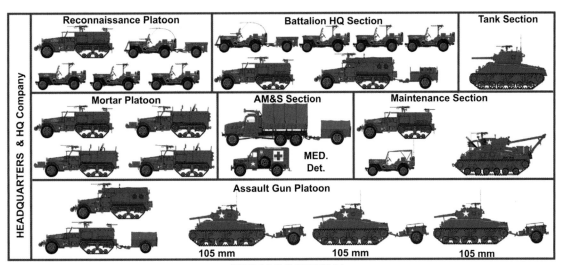

HEADQUARTERS & HQ Company

Reconnaissance Platoon

Battalion HQ Section

Tank Section

Mortar Platoon

AM&S Section

MED. Det.

Maintenance Section

Assault Gun Platoon

105 mm   105 mm   105 mm

SERVICE COMPANY

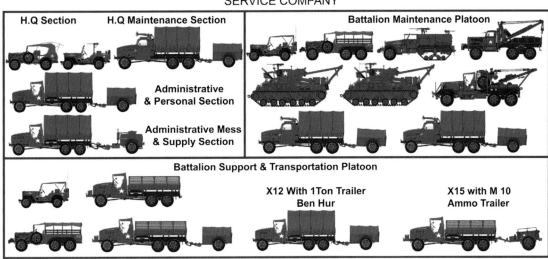

H.Q Section

H.Q Maintenance Section

Battalion Maintenance Platoon

Administrative & Personal Section

Administrative Mess & Supply Section

Battalion Support & Transportation Platoon

X12 With 1Ton Trailer Ben Hur

X15 with M 10 Ammo Trailer

MEDIUM TANK COMPANY A B &C

H.Q Section

Maintenance Section

AM&S Section

1st Platoon X 15

2nd Platoon X 15

3rd Platoon X 15

LIGHT TANK COMPANY D

H.Q Section

Maintenance Section

AM&S Section

1st Platoon X 15

2nd Platoon X 15

3rd Platoon X 15

Opposite page, left: Repairing a track for this crew. In the foreground, the connectors with guide teeth; at the rear, a frame (grenouille) is waiting to be used.

Opposite page, right: The 7th US Armored Division, 37th Tank Battalion. Changing the Continental engine for

this M4. In the foreground, the old engine. An operation carried out with the help of a Ward la France M1A1. (*Private collection*)

Opposite page, bottom: Transmission change in the undergrowth. (*NARA*)

U.S. TANK DESTROYER BATTALION

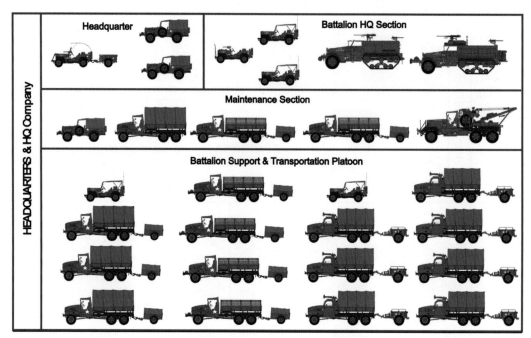

HEADQUARTERS & HQ Company

Headquarter

Battalion HQ Section

Maintenance Section

Battalion Support & Transportation Platoon

RECONNAISSANCE COMPANY

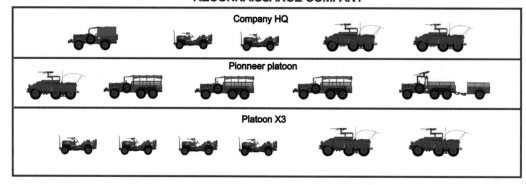

Company HQ

Pionneer platoon

Platoon X3

TANK DESTROYER COMPANY A B &C

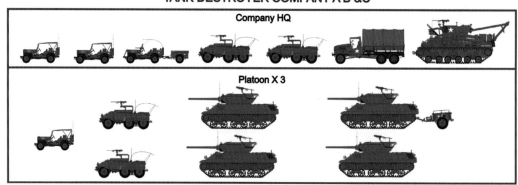

Company HQ

Platoon X 3

This M4A3, recognizable by its shaft supports on the rear sponson, going through an Alsatian village towing its M10 Ammo Trailer.

"Blown up" is the right word for this Dry Stowage M4 without side armor—the result of a bull's eye in the ammunition coffer causing the other racks to explode. The turret and driver's hatch have been blown off.

objectives. The 746th Tank Battalion was one such example. Throughout most of its time in Europe, the 746th supported the 9th Infantry Division.

The 746th Tank Battalion was organized according to the standard structure of a medium tank battalion. There were, however, minor variations to the unit's organization, tactical employment, and the comparative armaments aboard its combat vehicles.

For example, the battalion's HQ company was supposed to have a platoon of M4 Sherman tanks with 105mm guns. This platoon was known as the "assault gun platoon." However, the 746th did not receive any 105mm tanks until the first week of July 1944. Interestingly, this 105mm tank platoon was occasionally detached to the Division Artillery of the 9th Infantry Division, where it served as an *ad hoc* artillery battery. It was one of the few times in history where a modern-day "direct-fire weapon" (tank) became an "indirect-fire weapon" (howitzer). On other occasions, however, the HQ tank platoon provided general fire support and security.

While attached to the 9th Infantry Division, the battalion's Sherman-based line companies (A, B, and C) spent most of their time supporting different infantry regiments. Company A, for example, often supported the 47th Infantry Regiment. Company B was often attached to the 60th Infantry Regiment. Company C, meanwhile, frequently supported the 39th Infantry.

Company D, however, equipped with M5 Stuart light tanks, saw comparatively little action. Because they lacked the armor and firepower of the Sherman, the Stuarts were often relegated to supporting roles. Throughout most of June 1944, as the 746th pushed farther inland towards Cherbourg, Company D was often held in reserve and assigned "security" missions protecting the 9th Division's rear echelon, or along its flanks.

On July 5, 1944, the 746th Tank Battalion (while temporarily attached to the 83rd Infantry Division) helped repel a counterattack from the German 6th Parachute Regiment near Carentan. The German's

U.S. TANK BATTALION 18 NOVEMBER 1944

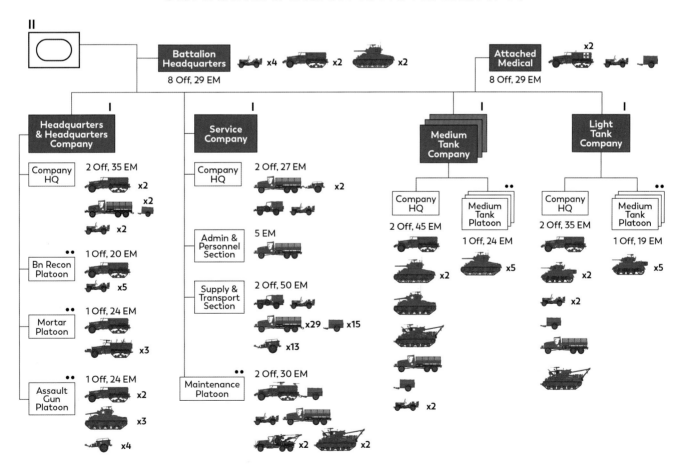

M4A4, perhaps it had the nickname "Chianti"? The co-driver is standing on his seat and pointing his Thompson submachine gun and the tank commander is directing his .50 caliber machine gun to the right.

A Marine posing in front of an M4 about to transport a Japanese T94.

Saint-Fromond, Normandy, 1944. This First US Army M4A1 Duplex Drive without its equipment is crossing a river, the Vire, preceded by a sniper armed with a Springfield 1903 rifle with telescopic sights. The second soldier is carrying an SCR 536 Handy Talkie.

A makeshift shelter with the tank's tarpaulin for the crew of this M4 105 and its M10 trailer.

Above: This MP (white stripe on his helmet) has parked his WLA 42 equipped with the standard issue M1 Garand rifle in its sheath. He is directing a unit of M10 tank destroyers through the streets of this Norman village.

Below: Soviet Wet M4A2 75 in the streets of Berlin. The cannon is fitted with a muzzle brake.

counteroffensive had been an attempt to disrupt the US VII Corps supply lines. Because the M5 Stuart tanks in Company D were considered "too light" for independent operations in Normandy, the commander of the 746th Tank Battalion decided to parcel out each of the M5 Stuart platoons to the medium tank companies for flank security. While attached to the Sherman tank companies, the Stuarts maintained security along the Allied lines of communication. Stuart tanks also provided mobile security to regimental and battalion command posts while serving as a general-purpose tactical reserve.

Soviet units

Meanwhile, the Red Army made great use of the M4 Sherman in battles against the Wehrmacht on the Eastern Front. Under the Lend-Lease Program, the Soviets acquired more than 4,000 M4A2 Sherman tanks. Of these tanks, approximately half were equipped with the original 75mm main gun, while the other half mounted the more capable 76mm gun.

By 1945, many Soviet armored units—including the 1st, 3rd, and 9th Guards Mechanized Corps – preferred the M4 Sherman to their own T-34. Soviet tank crews generally held the Sherman in high regard—commenting on its reliability, firepower, armored protection, and ease of maintenance. The Soviets also commented that the Sherman was less prone to premature ammunition "cook-offs" and less likely to roll over when making sharp turns on rough terrain.

On the Eastern Front, the Red Army organized its Shermans under the standard structure for Soviet armored units. For example, the 1st Guards Mechanized Corps was one of the premier operators of the M4A2 Sherman. Under Soviet doctrine, the mechanized corps was a flexible armored asset to be used during the "exploitation phase" of an operation. After 1942, the Soviet mechanized corps were comparable in size to the latter-day German panzer division. Unlike many of their Panzer-based contemporaries, however, the Red Army's mechanized corps were true combined-arms formation—striking a good balance of armor, mechanized infantry, and artillery. These mechanized corps units were structured similarly to their "sister formations"—the Red Army tank corps units. Indeed, the standard mechanized corps and standard tank corps both contained four maneuver brigades. Under the mechanized corps, the balance of forces was three mechanized brigades and one tank brigade—along with an anti-tank regiment, artillery regiment, and mortar regiment. By contrast, the tank corps had three tank brigades and one mechanized brigade.

Subordinate to the 1st Guards Mechanized Corps were the 16th, 17th, 18th, and 19th Guards Tank Regiments. By 1944, the standard Soviet tank regiment consisted of a Regimental HQ, each containing one tank and three armored cars, and four successively number tank companies. Each tank company had ten tanks.

SOVIET TANK REGIMENT 1944

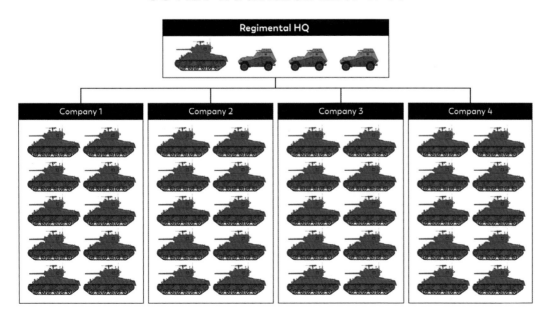

The British (serial number beginning with T) M4A4 (the radiator bulge clearly visible and the exhaust deflector specific to the A4 model) was distinguished by the extra coffer attached to the left-hand sponson, an extra jerrycan carrier on the rear, and a luggage rack on the rear deck. Note the sliding traces on the ground from the metal tracks.

British and Commonwealth units

The British Army likewise benefitted from the arrival of the Sherman tank. Although the British Army already had its own well-developed armored force, the UK nevertheless accepted 17,184 Sherman tanks under the Lend-Lease program. These numbers accounted for nearly 78% of all American Shermans provided under Lend-Lease. The first M4A1 Sherman given to the UK featured twin-mounted, driver-operated fixed machine guns and carried a 75mm tank main gun. The British later acquired the M4A2 and M4A4 variants of the Sherman—many of which they subsequently lent to the Free Polish and non-Axis Czechoslovakian armored units.

Under British service, the M4 Sherman units were organized according to the parameters of the British armored corps. However, the structure and organization of the British armored division frequently changed between 1939 and 1945. By 1944, the standard armored division consisted of three brigades – armor, motorized infantry, and artillery. The armored brigades contained three armored regiments and a motorized rifle battalion. The regiments themselves had been organized according to two parameters: those equipped *exclusively* with American tanks, and those equipped with a mixture of American and British tanks.

In a similar vein to the British Army, the New Zealand forces made considerable use of the M4 Sherman. Indeed, New Zealand's 4th Armoured

77th Anti-Tank Regiment—senior regiment
11th British Armoured Division
A Squadron—tank No.17
Achilles M10 A1 Tank Destroyer

Brigade distinguished itself in combat while mounted atop the diesel-powered M4A2 Sherman. Arriving on the front lines in Italy on October 23, 1943, the 4th Armoured Brigade saw its first combat action along the Sangro front. As part of the 2d New Zealand Division, the 4th Armoured Brigade worked alongside the British 78th Division, the Indian 4th Division, and a Combat Command (brigade-sized element) from the US 1st Armored Division—forming the so-called "NZ Corps."

While participating in the battle of Monte Cassino, the 4th Armoured Brigade used their Shermans primarily as infantry support weapons. Some tanks however, found their way onto static gun lines, becoming makeshift howitzers for artillery units that were short on ammunition.

Throughout the fall of 1944, the 4th Brigade assisted the British Eighth Army in the latter's assault along eastern end of the Gothic Line. During that campaign, the 4th Brigade's 18th Regiment captured the airfield at Rimini. The German defenders at Rimini had constructed a network of pillboxes, cleverly armed with Panther turrets.

In April 1945, the New Zealand armored units once again resumed their role as ad hoc artillery in the campaign to capture the city of Trieste. The German garrison surrendered, but the New Zealand brigade unexpectedly met the Yugoslav partisans who had also occupied the city. Although the New Zealanders and Yugoslavs were fighting for the Allied cause, the Yugoslavs' resented the New Zealanders' presence. The partisans now considered Trieste to be "their" city—and wanted exclusive access to its resources. Tensions escalated between the New Zealanders and Yugoslavs, resulting in a brief stand-off between the Shermans of the 4th Brigade's 19th Regiment and some 25 Yugoslav T-34 tanks. Luckily, cooler heads prevailed and the Yugoslavs quietly exited the city. At the end of the war, the New Zealand 4th Armoured Brigade surrendered most of its equipment to a British Army depot before disbanding on December 2, 1945.

The New Zealand armored brigades were structured similarly to their counterparts in the British Army. The 4th Armoured Brigade, for example, was composed of three armored regiments—the 18th, 19th and 20th. The New Zealand armored regiments were almost identical to the British regiments, but with fewer tanks (52 in total). Regimental HQ had a troop of four tanks. Subordinate to HQ were three squadrons, each containing sixteen tanks. The squadron was composed of a Squadron HQ (four tanks) and four troops (three tanks each). The regiment also had a reconnaissance troop ("recce troop") comprised of three reconnaissance vehicles.

NEW ZEALAND 4TH ARMORED BRIGADE

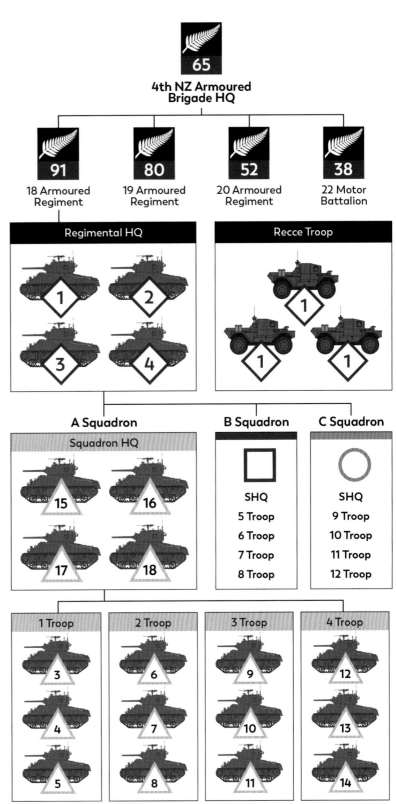

M4 Shermans from the 3d Squadron of the 2e RC entering a liberated town in the east of France. (ECPAD)

Below: Sherman OP from the 5th Royal Horse Artillery Regiment of the 7th British Armoured Division. The nice impact mark was caused by an 88-mm shell fired by Michael Wittmann at the turret in the summer of 1944. In the foreground are the wooden dummy cannon and the cannon shield.

Originally, the recce troop was equipped with the Daimler Dingo scout car. The Dingo, however, was quickly replaced by the Canadian-built Lynx, as the latter vehicle offered better cross-country handling. The Lynx, in turn, was replaced by the M3A3 Stuart tank.

French units

The equipment of the French Army in 1944 was defined by the TED/G or TED/P (*Tableaux d'Equipements et Dotation/Guerre* or *Paix* = War/Peace Equipment Distribution Tables). The French armored divisions were nonetheless created along the lines of the American light armored divisions, though there were some differences.

General Giraud signed the order setting up the Armored Divisions, in Algiers on 24 November 1942. A French armored division consisted of three regiments of medium tanks plus a reconnaissance regiment, a regiment of tank destroyers, a three-battalion motorized infantry regiment, a divisional artillery group (three units of 105 M7 Priests), an AA artillery group (equipped with 40-mm Bofors guns installed on a CCLW platform), an Engineers battalion, and all the other services like the Medics, repair units and fuel, ammunition, postal supply units, etc.

As these were French and American units, the way they were structured and used had to be the same since the French units were attached to the American Combat Commands. The American battalions corresponded to the French regiments. T/O &E 17-25 together with by FM 17-33, published by the War Department in December 1944, defined the make up of the American Tank battalions.

French armored units consisted of:

1. **Tank regiments**—the Cuirassier regiments, combat tanks, or Chasseurs d'Afrique.
2. **Tank destroyer units**—which were in the Chasseurs d'Afrique, Fusiliers-Marins, Dragons or the Régiment Blindé Colonial. The Chasseurs d'Afrique were set up in 1942 in French North Africa, so they had nothing to do with regiments like the Spahis, the Goumiers or the Méharistes, units which were formed on a traditionally local basis.

3. **Reconnaissance regiments**—Spahi regiments or Foreign Legion cavalry regiments organized according to the distribution tables in force, no matter what division they belonged to. The composition and the equipment would, however, vary depending on the period. The number of squadrons or companies could be increased; this was the case, for example, in the RMSM. Or an extra element was created, a mortar platoon for instance, as in the RBFM.

The modifications were mainly carried out between 1944 and 1946, enabling the unit's operational capability to be improved, or even to enable it to be incorporated into a Combat Command.

The organization of the 2e Régiment de Cuirassiers was typical for a cuirassier regiment (see TEDG on page 216). It had a headquarters with four M4 medium and four M5 light tanks. An AM&S squadron for all the logistics (kitchens, ammunition transport, recovery and breakdown means, medics).

2e Division Blindée RBFM
Régiment Blindé de Fusiliers Marins
2d Squadron
Wolverine M10 Tank Destroyer

T.E.D.G.* OF THE 2E RC IN 1944

(*Tableaux d'Equipements et Dotation Guerre = War Equipment Distribution Tables)

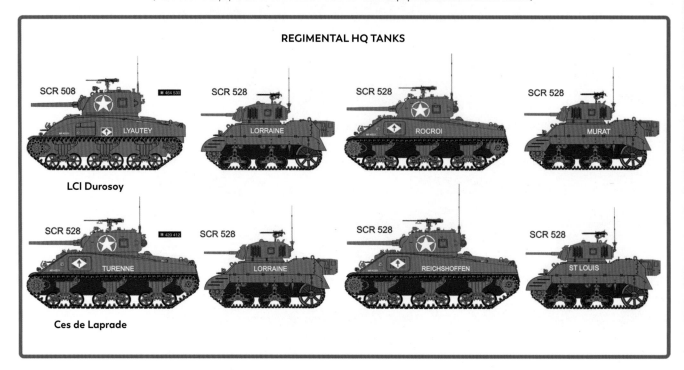

REGIMENTAL HQ TANKS

SCR 508 — 464 530 — LYAUTEY
LCI Durosoy

SCR 528 — LORRAINE

SCR 528 — ROCROI

SCR 528 — MURAT

SCR 528 — 420 412 — TURENNE
Ces de Laprade

SCR 528 — LORRAINE

SCR 528 — REICHSHOFFEN

SCR 528 — ST LOUIS

AMS&S PLATOON (one per squadron)

COMMAND GROUP

SCR 5

SERVICE GROUP

Paquetages

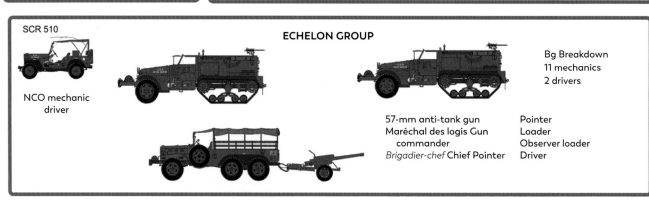

ECHELON GROUP

SCR 510

NCO mechanic driver

Bg Breakdown
11 mechanics
2 drivers

57-mm anti-tank gun	Pointer
Maréchal des logis Gun commander	Loader
	Observer loader
Brigadier-chef Chief Pointer	Driver

216

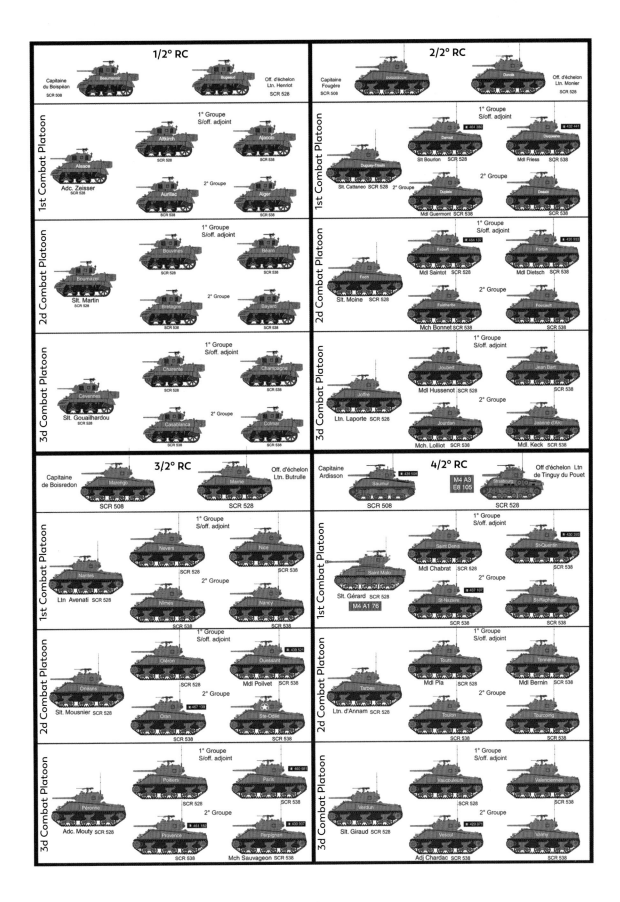

1/2° RC

Capitaine du Boispéan SCR 508 — Beaumanoir — Bugeaud — Off. d'échelon Ltn. Henriot SCR 528

1st Combat Platoon
Alsace — Adc. Zeisser SCR 528
1° Groupe S/off. adjoint — Altkirch SCR 528 — Ajaccio SCR 538
2° Groupe — Aurillac SCR 538 — Alger SCR 538

2d Combat Platoon
Bournazel — Slt. Martin SCR 528
1° Groupe S/off. adjoint — Bouvines SCR 528 — Béarn SCR 538
2° Groupe — Bretagne SCR 538 — Bayard SCR 538

3d Combat Platoon
Cevennes — Slt. Gouailhardou SCR 528
1° Groupe S/off. adjoint — Charente SCR 528 — Champagne SCR 538
2° Groupe — Casablanca SCR 538 — Colmar SCR 538

2/2° RC

Capitaine Fougère SCR 508 — DUGUESCLIN — Dunois — Off. d'échelon Ltn. Monier SCR 528

1st Combat Platoon
Slt. Cattaneo SCR 528 — Duguay-Trouin
1° Groupe S/off. adjoint — ✹ 464 380 Devout — Slt Bourlon SCR 528 — ✹ 432 441 Duquesne — Mdl Friess SCR 538
2° Groupe — Duplex — Mdl Guermont SCR 538 — Desaix SCR 538

2d Combat Platoon
Foch — Slt. Moine SCR 528
1° Groupe S/off. adjoint — ✹ 464 137 Fabert — Mdl Saintot SCR 528 — ✹ 430 933 Forbin — Mdl Dietsch SCR 538
2° Groupe — Faidherbe — Mch Bonnet SCR 538 — Foucault SCR 538

3d Combat Platoon
Joffre — Ltn. Laporte SCR 528
1° Groupe S/off. adjoint — Joubert — Mdl Hussenot SCR 528 — Jean Bart SCR 538
2° Groupe — Jourdan — Mch Lolliot SCR 538 — Jeanne d'Arc — Mdl. Keck SCR 538

3/2° RC

Capitaine de Boisredon SCR 508 — Marengo — Marne — Off. d'échelon Ltn. Butrulle SCR 528

1st Combat Platoon
Nantes — Ltn Avenati SCR 528
1° Groupe S/off. adjoint — Nevers SCR 528 — Nice SCR 538
2° Groupe — Nimes SCR 538 — Nancy SCR 538

2d Combat Platoon
Orléans — Slt. Mousnier SCR 528
1° Groupe S/off. adjoint — Oléron SCR 528 — ✹ 439 521 Ouessant — Mdl Poilvet SCR 538
2° Groupe — ✹ 467 139 Oran — Ste-Odile SCR 538

3d Combat Platoon
Péronne — Adc. Mouty SCR 528
1° Groupe S/off. adjoint — Poitiers SCR 528 — ✹ 460 581 Paris SCR 538
2° Groupe — ✹ 461 182 Provence — Perpignan — Mch Sauvageon SCR 538 — ✹ 430 937

4/2° RC

Capitaine Ardisson SCR 508 — ✹ 439 509 Saumur — M4 A3 E8 105 — Strasbourg — Off d'échelon Ltn de Tinguy du Pouet SCR 528

1st Combat Platoon
Saint Malo — Slt. Gérard SCR 528 — M4 A1 76
1° Groupe S/off. adjoint — Saint Denis — Mdl Chabrat — St-Quentin SCR 538 — ✹ 430 393
2° Groupe — ✹ 437 107 St-Nazaire SCR 538 — St-Raphael SCR 538

2d Combat Platoon
Tarbes — Ltn. d'Annam SCR 528
1° Groupe S/off. adjoint — Tours — Mdl Pla SCR 528 — Tonnerre — Mdl Bernin SCR 538
2° Groupe — Toulon SCR 538 — Tourcoing SCR 538

3d Combat Platoon
Verdun — Slt. Giraud SCR 528
1° Groupe S/off. adjoint — Vaucouleurs SCR 528 — Valenciennes SCR 538
2° Groupe — ✹ 420 071 Vesoul — Valmy — Adj Chardac SCR 538 — SCR 538

RBFM/Regimental HQ

LA BALEINIERE	ONDINE	METZ	GHISLAINE	PIGOULIERE	LE COTRE
95 715	400 195	400 285	445 737	445 774	95273

LA FREGATE	LA BISQUINE	SANS SOUCIS	L EVEILLE
419 390	90462	L 101 3002	400 197

RBFM/AMS&S/HQ Platoon

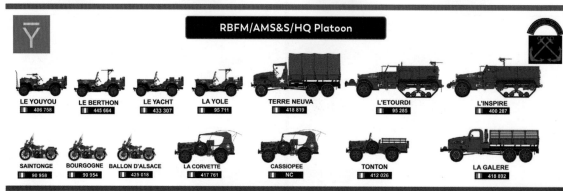

LE YOUYOU	LE BERTHON	LE YACHT	LA YOLE	TERRE NEUVA	L'ETOURDI	L'INSPIRE
406 758	445 664	433 307	95 711	418 819	95 285	400 287

SAINTONGE	BOURGOGNE	BALLON D'ALSACE	LA CORVETTE	CASSIOPEE	TONTON	LA GALERE
90 958	90 954	425 018	417 761	NC	412 026	418 892

RBFM/AMS&S/Unit platoon

TOURANE	ESCOFFIER		DOMINIQUE	LA GOELETTE	SAINT BERNARD
409 798	412 050	90 479	442 819	90 962	440 596

AMS&S/Supply platoon—Fuel

BEARN	FLEURET	ARBALETTE	X 9		X 12		
90 8892	433 317	N.C					

PANTAGRUEL	**GARGANTUA**	**DARTAGNAN**	**JOYEUX**	**PROF**
429 195	429 194	415 929	427 268	418 900
BALISTE	MOUSQUET	PORTHOS	TIMIDE	ATCHOUM
414 322	427 896	427 227	445 536	418 866
ARQUEBUSE	COULEUVRINE	ATHOS	GRINCHEUX	DORMEUR
428 931	428 932	418 925	427 267	405 024
TROMBLON	BOMBARDE	ARAMIS	SIMPLET	BLANCHE NEIGE
427 895	90 477	418 888	427 195	418 690
	LANCE			
	400 478			

AMS&S/Medical Platoon

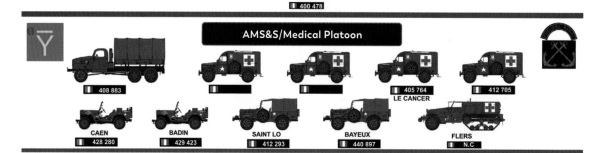

408 883			LE CANCER	412 705
			405 764	

CAEN	BADIN	SAINT LO	BAYEUX	FLERS
428 280	429 423	412 293	440 897	N.C

Four combat squadrons each comprising:

- a command platoon;
- an AM&S platoon;
- a service group;
- an echelon platoon;
- 17 combat tanks, M4s or M5s.

This organization takes into account tanks replaced after being destroyed.

The A4 models were replaced by A2s, sometimes but more rarely by A1s with 75-mm M1A1 cannon, sometimes by M4A3 E8 105-mm howitzers.

There was also an M4A3 E2 Jumbo in the 7e RCA, as well as an M4A3 75 W in the 12e RC—the "Bourg-la-Reine."

During Operation *Dragoon* (1944), tank destroyer unit Régiment Colonial de Chasseurs de Chars (RCCC) was equipped with five squadrons, each comprising:

A headquarters equipped with a jeep and an armored car.

An AMS&S platoon comprising a command group and a platoon echelon.

Three platoons each comprising four TD M10s in two groups, plus a jeep and a Dodge for the protection group.

1st Squadron

AM M8 and M20-Reco
Platoon 1: *Aïr, Adrar, Arrouenit, Aquellal.*
Platoon 2: unknown.
Platoon 3: unknown.

2d Squadron

Platoon 1: *Bangui, Chari, Congo, Ogoué.*
Platoon 2: *Fort Trinquet, Fort Crampel, Fort Largeau, Fort Archambaud.*
Platoon 3: *Douala, Yaoundé, Abéché, Bangui.*

3d Squadron

Platoon 1: *Afert, Tindouf, Bou-Denib, Azoul.*
Platoon 2: *Messifré, Souéda, Rayack, Aïn-Tab.*
Platoon 3: *Kissoué, Raphsaîl, Taza, El-Hadras.*

These five Shermans (in the second row) from the 12e RCA (No.29 Maurienne, No.28 Tarentaise, No.27 Valserine, No.26 Iseran, and No.25 Morvan) lining up at the assembly point at Vély after landing in Normandy.

The M10 tank destroyer "Cyclone" from the 4th Squadron, Platoon 3 during the fight for the liberation of Paris, in August 1944. (*Private collection*)

Under the watchful eye of two children, this M32B2 crew is getting ready to heat up their standard issue rations. Note the presence of the 3.5-in mortar, in place on the frontal glacis. (*NARA*)

Below: A cannon has to be looked after, even a 105-mm howitzer. While waiting to repair the right track, the crew slept under the tent set up nearby.

Above: One of the eight M4A3s—here a 105-mm—sold to Denmark. (*Private Collection*)

Right: A macabre sight for this M3 half-track's occupants. The smoking M4A3 bears witness to the recent confrontation. On the turret, the body of the tank commander is stuck in the hatch.

This crew is putting the finishing touches to the tank's concrete armor with great care. The shoring has been done with salvaged material and the tank commander is working the concrete mixer. An unbreakable M4 105.

4th Squadron

Platoon 1: *Tourane, Nha-Trang, Hué, Vinh.*
Platoon 2: Bien-*Hoa, Mékong, Pnon-Penh, Toule-Sap.*
Platoon 3: *Chaudoc, Angkor, Saigon.*

Each platoon was organized into two tank destroyer groups and a protection group. The squadron had two M20 armored cars, 12 M10 tank destroyers, two scout cars, two jeeps, two GMC trucks, two motorbikes, and

Below: Mission almost over for this M31 B2: the M4A1 is almost out of trouble.

a recovery tank (T2/M31). The regiment was equipped with M20 armored cars, M8 armored cars, 36 M10 tank destroyers, jeeps (12 armed), WLA 42 motorbikes, GMC and Dodge trucks, a recovery truck, and three recovery tanks.

The Régiments Blindés de Fusiliers Marins (RBFM) were equipped with the M10 Wolverine tank destroyer armed with a 76.2-mm cannon. These regiments comprised four combat squadrons, each consisting of three platoons of four tanks. This regiment was made up in a particular way, visible on the TED plate, because the composition of the 1st Squadron had changed after the liberation of Paris. Another particularity of the RBFM was that it included the Marinettes, the women ambulance drivers who landed in Normandy on August 2, 1944 with elements of the 2e DB. These nine women were assigned from the 2d Company of the 13th Medical Battalion to the RBFM.

The RBFM's unit number being 49878, the possessions and vehicles belonging to the Marinettes had a POM code: 49 was the number assigned to the 2e DB, so all the unit numbers began with 49. The number 49878 generated a POM code—brown, red, brown. The Marinettes were SFF (Service Féminins de la Flotte—Women's Service of the Fleet) and they wore the sailor's cap without a pompom or chinstrap; the unit commander, Lieutenant de Vaisseau Jacqueline Carsignol, wore a forage cap. The SFF wore the embroidered insignia of the Fusiliers Marins (crossed anchors) on the left sleeve, but the Marinettes' insignia consisted of two blue embroidered anchors (in place of the red for the men). The 13th Medical Battalion was disbanded in January 1945, but some women ambulance drivers served until Dien Bien Phu.

When it was formed in Morocco, the 1er Régiment de Marche des Spahis Marocains (RMSM) comprised five squadrons. In September 1944, a sixth squadron was created, then a seventh in October and finally an eighth in November. These three new squadrons were formed in exactly the same way, i.e. three platoons equipped with five HTs.

The 7th Squadron included a fourth platoon equipped with six 75-mm M3 howitzers, better known as the "lance-patates" (the spud throwers). In each platoon, one of the five half-tracks towed a 57-mm anti-tank gun.

The regiment was made up of a squadron of light tanks with three platoons of five tanks each and four squadrons of armored cars with three platoons of five armored cars; it had a strength of more than 1,100 men, split up among three Combat Commands.

12 The Success of the Sherman

An M4A2, *Bayard*, which according to its markings could have served in the 1er Régiment de Cuirassiers. The three-part front and the small hatches indicate an "Early" version. The tank is equipped with a "Low bustle" turret and the cannon is mounted on an M34A1 gun carriage.

The Importance of Shermans in WWII Landings

Although they were not the first time that M4 Medium Tanks were deployed, the importance of their role in the success of the landing operations in Europe cannot be underestimated. Most Europeans are familiar with one landing operation—that in Normandy, but there were many others, and in most of them the Sherman played an important role.

First landing operation: Operation *Torch*, November 8, 1942.

The Sherman tanks were engaged for the first time during the second battle of El Alamein, and this turned out to be important for the following stages of World War II. The second battle of El Alamein ended at the beginning of November 1942, and the Americans and British landed in French North Africa only a few days

later. The Tunisian campaign started on November 17, during which the French, Americans and British opposed the German and Italian alliance.

Second landing operation: Operation *Husky*, July 10, 1943.

Husky was the idea of Winston Churchill, a specialist in this sort of operation (Dardanelles in 1915 and Narvik, 1940). The plan was approved by "Ike" Eisenhower, the C-in-C. The Allies, under the command of General Alexander, landed in Sicily with 14,000 vehicles, 4,000 aircraft, 2,500 ships, 1,800 cannon, and 600 tanks. The American armored forces were under the command of George Patton.

Third landing operation: Operation *Baytown*, September 3, 1943.

This operation in southern Italy was launched by the British Eighth Army, which got a foothold in Calabria at Reggio di Calabria. Most of the troops were made

up of Canadian units; the British landed at Gallica and Catona. This maneuver was backed by Operation *Slapstick*. Both operations were so-called diversions, in preparation for *Avalanche*.

Fourth landing operation: Operation *Avalanche*, September 8, 1943.

Italy, the great forgotten one

(Under the command of General Alexander) The Corps Expéditionnaire Français comprised five divisions, which General Clark praised abundantly such was the price the French paid in making the operation successful, distinguishing themselves under General Juin.

The Shermans took part, served by American, British, South African, or New Zealand crews.

Fifth landing operation: Operation *Shingle*, January 22, 1944.

Following one of Churchill's ideas, the Allies landed at Anzio. Because the attackers knew very well they were going to be confronted with German armor—in particular the Panzer Division Hermann Göring and the 3d Panzer-Grenadier Division—the Shermans were there too.

Sixth landing operation: Operation *Tiger*, April 22, 1944.

This was for training Allied troops with a view to the landings in France.

The beach at Slapton Sands, in southern England, was chosen because it resembled the Utah and Omaha beaches. The Allies trained to land Shermans from LSTs. During one of the rehearsals, two LSTs were sunk by German E-boats, the famous Schnellboot. The American equivalents of these German boats were the PT boats. It was on one of them, PT 109, that Lieutenant Junior Grade John F. Kennedy fought for the first time (and earned his reputation) as its CO in the Pacific.

The *Bayard* seen from the front. All the items on the frontal glacis are what the crew would have piled up. The smoke mortar opening is operational. The transmission armor is in three parts and the extra episcopes are on the bulges of the driver's and co-driver's hatches.

A very good reconstruction of a typical World War II scene; the infantry have climbed aboard the rear deck of this M4A2. The infantryman on the right is holding a basic version of the US M1 carbine. The markings are those of the 1st Cuirassier Regiment. The unit number normally begins with the letters MF and consist of five digits— this unit number is not accurate.

The *Douaumont* is in theory a Sherman M4A2 of the 501e RCC of the 2e DB. (slc)

Eighth landing operation: Operation *Brassard*, June 17, 1944.

The aim of the operation was to neutralize the German troops on the island of Elba. It was a combined operation in which French troops took part: the 9e DIC, the Commandos d'Afrique, Commandos de choc, the Régiment d'Artillerie Coloniale du Maroc (RACM), and the 2e Groupe de Tabors Marocains, with a few British Commandos; the latter suffered heavy losses.

Ninth landing operation: Operation *Anvil-Dragoon*, August 15, 1944.

Dragoon—the name finally chosen for the operation—was not a mini-*Overlord*, neither was it a secondary operation to liberate France.

The French participated more in Operation *Dragoon* than they did in *Overlord*. The French 2e DB landed on August 2 on Utah Beach, followed on the 15th of the same month by the 1e and 5e DBs landing in Provence with a lot more Shermans. The landings in Provence involved 2,120 Allied ships, 10 aircraft-carriers, 25 cruisers, and 109 torpedo boats, escorted by over 1,900 bomber and fighter aircraft. The Allied landing forces comprised an Army Corps with three American infantry divisions and one airborne division, backed by five armored divisions and five divisions of French infantry.

In view of all these Allied operations, it could be said that the Sherman was without any doubt—and

Seventh landing operation: Operation *Overlord*, June 6, 1944.

This important operation was preceded by Operations *Fortitude*, *Bodyguard*, *Quicksilver*, *Skye*, *Zeppelin*, *Ironside*, *Vendetta*, and *Ferdinand*, whose aims were to trick the German command as to where exactly the Allied landings would take place. The Shermans were there of course, and their fight against German armor became the substance of legends on both sides.

A very beautiful "Early" M4A1. The black camouflage does correspond to the period, as does the low-visibility white star. This A1 is equipped with the Cullin Hedgerow Device, specific to the units landing in Normandy. The gun cradle is a World War II type. The turret does not have a pistol port and so was built during the first six months of 1943. The 75-mm cannon is mounted on the M34 A1 gun carriage, and the opening of the smoke mortar has been welded over.

Opposite, from top to bottom:

M7 Priest howitzer with 105-mm cannon. The emplacement for the 12.7-mm machine gun resembles a pulpit, hence the name given to the tank: Priest. In the two chests fixed to the front right-hand side of the tank were stowed the track grousers; in the two boxes on the left-hand side were the spare track links and the wooden chocks.

TD M10 with cast turret counterweight bolted to the rear, so it's a "Mid" version. The gun transport cradle is on the rear deck, so the barrel was at six o'clock when the tank was being moved outside the combat sector.

TD M36, the American response to the German 88-mm cannon. Equipped with a 90-mm cannon, later fitted with a muzzle brake. On this tank, the 12.7-mm machine gun has been placed on its travel lock and, on the rear glacis, note the road cradle. The exhaust deflectors are from the M4A3, since the TD M36 was equipped with the V8 Ford GAA engine. This tank is equipped with entirely metal, type T56 tracks.

will no doubt remain so—the symbol of the landings, an instrument of victory, a cause of Germany's capitulation. The reason for its success was not just the tank itself. If the Sherman itself was emblematic, it was the men who served it that forged its reputation, battle after battle.

The crews of all nations fought well beyond the European theater: in the cold of the Atlantic or the humidity of the Pacific. The Sherman, carried to the pinnacle by the self-sacrifice of its crews, was also hauled by prestigious leaders. One thinks at once of course of George Patton, but what would he have become without Abrams or Bradley? Leclerc is often mentioned, but what could he have done without de Lattre de Tassigny, Montsabert, or Vernejoul?

The rebirth of the M4 Sherman

The Sherman, although quickly replaced—by the Americans—after the war, pursued a long career on all continents, as it did in the French Army. As a standard medium tank it was replaced by the M47 Patton in 1950, just as it was in Belgium and Germany. It is still in service in the mobilization reserves or again in certain units of the Gendarmerie Mobile. A lot of the examples remaining in France after the conflict were used as targets on the gunnery ranges in several training camps.

Others served for a long time in anti-tank close-combat training. A number of them were salvaged or cannibalized during the fighting, and well after the war, when the lack of spare parts started to be cruelly felt. But the Sherman found other ways of surviving, helped in this by all those who had served it, those who had used it, those who had seen it fight, those who had towed, recovered, or repaired it. Grateful municipalities have wanted to immortalize and to pay tribute to

the fallen. The museums and the monuments on the sites where the fighting raged have elevated it to the rank of hero. Associations and collectors respected this need to remember by recovering all the wrecks and getting them to work again, with much perseverance and elbow grease.

Above: 2010 at Carentan, France. Posing in front of an M4 105 is a GI of the 5th Rangers Battalion. On the frontal glacis on the left is the famous EE8 campaign telephone (with call handle on the side).

Above, right: Olivier Vivas in 2014 at Sainte-Mère-Eglise. This time it's the photographer who is photographed in front of an M4A1. On the left, an M16 MGMG half-track and its quadruple gun carriage nicknamed the "Meat Chopper." It'll take some beating.

The Sherman cannot be forgotten. The tank has seen a second youth at all the gatherings in France, Germany, Britain, and Belgium; gatherings that bring together people from all walks of life but history enthusiasts, amateur renovators, and guardians of all these traditions that unite men. And all this is taking place in the 21st century, and the Shermans are still there, standing straight in their tracks. During parades in front of enthusiastic groups of people, the Shermans drive past, backfiring, under the both fearful and admiring gaze of kids held in their parents' arms.

The Sherman remains the star even today. It is not alone of course: it is often accompanied by the jeep, the GMC "Jimmy," or the DUKW. Seventy-seven years after the prototype was first presented at the Aberdeen Proving Ground in the USA, the Sherman still holds its own, a veteran with the weight of its years, but with the eternal vigor of legend.

The Sherman lives on

Due credit must be given to all the enthusiasts who give so much to the survival of the Sherman—the associations, collectors, and history and Sherman buffs get really involved in these activities and meetings, not to mention the times when they volunteer. Often—almost always—they pay from their own pockets to go there; what might appear inconceivable for a lot of people suddenly becomes very much simpler when you have attended one of these meetings or when you know the people, friends, or contacts who take part in them all over France.

Today, these non-profit-making organizations flourish, such as Touraine mémoire 44, Provence 44, Aisne Club 44, France MVCG, Véhicules Militaires d'Artois, and France44. The list, and I insist on this, is far from exhaustive. All those who do not appear on this particular one, please forgive me. For example, Duty First in Belgium or again Market Garden in the United Kingdom never hesitate to take part in these meetings in France.

Who do you gather, what do you see, what do you do when you go to these meetings? You meet "madmen"; well, that's what you might be led to believe. They come with their vehicles, vehicles that have been carefully prepared or even coddled. These vehicles keep up the memory, revive a memory, or honor a sacrifice. The markings conform to those in use in 1944; the uniforms are those of the period, as are the insignia and the rank markings. Here, it may be the 101st and 82d Airborne standing along side the 5th Rangers, whereas the sailors from the RBFM gather round the Marinettes' WC 54. There it is the tanks of the 6e RCA alongside the RMSM's spud-thrower. All these people talk, discuss, eat in a tent, and cook according to the standards of the times. Some sleep in their vehicle, others under a tent. And when morning comes, they go and wash in cold-water tubs.

You see Shermans of course, but also M3 howitzers and M5 light tanks; here and there a M3 half-track, parked next to a Ward la France truck. An M26 Dragon Wagon trundles two Stuarts around on its semi-trailer; as for the WLA 42 Harley Davidsons, they go into action when the convoy is formed up getting ready for the parade, ridden by larger-than-life MPs.

Weapons (demilitarized and quite safe, you can be sure) are not to be forgotten either, and the panoply is as cared for as it is complete (thanks also to some marvelous reproductions): the US M1 Garand, US M1 Carbine, Colt 1911.42 ACP, the legendary Thompson, and not forgetting, when fitted on the vehicles with the right mountings, the .50 caliber M2HB and the .30 caliber M1919 A1, A4, or even A6.

Sometimes, reconstituting a first-aid post will bring together a stretcher-bearing jeep and nurses that make you want to pretend you're wounded!

Repairs are carried out on a vehicle—a marvelous example of mutual aid and cooperation. All sorts of stands are all over the place: Mr So-and-so will find the exhaust pipe he's been looking for; another will at last dig out the tripod he'd been looking for at a reasonable price. That guy just bought a Beanie for five euros, but of course, it's a reproduction, at that price!

There is also trading—a caliber.50 belt ammunition box support exchanged for an EE8, or a frying pan or SCR 625 for a BC 603. Everything is debatable, exchangeable, and negotiable.

Sometimes these assemblies are real camps lasting several days and attract a particular type of crowd,

gently cradled by these vehicles' past, vehicles which for them are priceless, but which have a price. The mission of the moment is invested with all the respect due to their elders who fell for their country. Exchanges don't worry about borders. As far as frontiers are concerned, they only have one in common: souvenir and memory. These collectors are not mad, just impassioned, and as everybody knows, passion has no reasonable limits.

Neuvic, 2016. The members of the Resistance, FFI or FTP, were also honoured. Here they are talking beside an M4A2. The man on the right is wearing the black leather cartridge belt of the Wehrmacht. The one on the left has a P 08 Lüger holster with its extra clip.

The park in the Sainte-Mère-Eglise museum, with a patrol of paratroopers from the 101st Airborne going past an M4 105 howitzer.

13   The Sherman Since 1945

Below: The M50 Super Sherman used by Tsahal. (*Private collection*)

Bottom: The M51 was an upgraded M4A1 with a Cummings diesel engine, HVSS suspension, and the French FN CN 75-L50 F1 cannon.

Although many more effective and better-equipped tanks have been developed since 1945, the Sherman has continued in widespread use. It reappeared in other theaters of operations: Korea, the Marshall Islands, Okinawa, and the Philippines. A few years later, the Middle East cauldron heated up and Israel mastered the art of adapting the Sherman chassis. Then conflict spread with the start the Indo-Pakistan War; here again the Sherman took part. On the other side of the Atlantic, the fascist fever took hold of the South American continent. Panama, Columbia, Chile, and Argentina all "offered" themselves some Shermans, with the blessing of the USA, via the CIA.

The M4 as seen by Tsahal (Israel Defense Forces; non-exhaustive list)

Among the many versions put into service by the Israeli Army, there were bridge layers, a breakdown version of the tank equipped with a hydraulic crane and a 72-ton winch, and a large-sized Medivac version whose diesel engine was installed in the front of the tank.

One of the first modifications undertaken by the Israeli Army was to bring unarmed Shermans back up to scratch after the war: 75-mm Krupps guns replaced destroyed cannons. These same tanks were later equipped with 105-mm howitzers.

Super Shermans

The **M50** was an M4A3 or A4 equipped with an FN CN 75-L50 75-mm cannon taken from the AMX 13 and adapted to the Sherman turret. This model was equipped with HVSS. In total, 3,410 Sherman M50s were equipped with the Cummings diesel engine.

The **M51** was an M4A1 upgraded with a Cummings diesel engine, HVSS suspension, and the FN CN 75-L50 F1 cannon. The T23 turret of these tanks was modified to take a shortened version of the French cannon, equipped with a large muzzle brake. This cannon was referenced CN 105 D1

The **MAR-290** was a ground-to-ground missile launcher equipped with four missiles with a range of 22 km. It was a multiple rocket launcher (the Calliope type).

Instead of the turret, the **MAR-240** had a 36x240-mm rocket launcher—the Israeli version of the Russian BM24 Katyusha.

The **M50 155** was a self-propelled gun with an open structure equipped with the French M50 155-mm cannon.

Makmat 160 was a 160-mm mortar mounted on an M4 chassis.

During its first conflicts, Israel used 200 Super Shermans and 150 AMX 13s as well as 250 Centurion Mk Vs and Mk VIs, and 200 M48 Pattons.

Above, from left to right: The MAR-290 is a missile launcher with four ground-to-ground rockets.

The Makmat 160 has a 160-mm mortar mounted on an M4 chassis.

Opposite: The M50/155 was a self-propelled gun with an open-top structure equipped with the French 155-mm M50 cannon.

Bottom: The Egyptian Sherman had an FL10 turret—the AMX 13's—mounted on an M4A4 chassis.

The M4, Egyptian style

The Egyptian Army chose a simpler, but nonetheless interesting, solution consisting of adapting an FL10 turret—that of the AMX 13—on an M4A4 chassis, powered by the General Motors 6-71 diesel engine of the M4A2.[1]

The advantage of this adaptation was the quality of the 75-mm cannon with semi-automatic loading (by little side barrels), automatic ejection of the spent shells through the turret bustle slot, and armor-piercing ammunition with high muzzle velocity. It had hydraulic controls for elevation and traverse.

During the Israeli-Arab conflict, Egypt had 90 Shermans equipped by France with FL 10 turrets and also used 20 AMX 13s. To all that were added 450 T34/85s, 300 T-54s, 200 T-55s, and 46 JS-3s.

The Soviet M4: the M4M

Some M4A2s with diesel engines were sent to the USSR as part of the Lend-Lease. The Soviets received the CN75 and CN76 versions, and a few HVSS were also delivered before the end of the war with Germany.

---

1. These tanks were modified and equipped in France. This turret could also take a ramp and a launching system for four SS11 missiles.

The Israeli MAR-240 was a launcher for 36 240-mm rockets.

A Soviet M476 M1 A2 and its 76.2 mm cannon. *(Private collection)*

The Soviet Army equipped some M4A2s with the F34 76.2-mm cannon taken from the T34/85. Given that there was never any break in the flow of American 75-mm ammunition, these modifications were limited to only a few units.

The Argentinean M4

This was called Repotenciado and was a British hybrid Sherman transformed by installing a 105-mm cannon, the FTR L44/57, the local copy of the AMX 13 cannon. The coaxial machine gun was a MAG 58 and an M2HB machine gun was incorporated into the tank commander's cupola. In total, 120 tanks were modified in this way in 1979. They were powered a V8 diesel by the Frenchman Poyaud, rated at 450 bhp at 2,600 rpm.

The Chilean M4s

Chile bought 78 M4A1 E9 tanks. The Chileans subsequently acquired 70 Israeli M50/51s equipped with an IMIOTO cannon, using high velocity armor-piercing ammunition. It remained in service until 1989. Some examples remained the same until 2002, before being replaced by the Leopard IV and the AMX30 B2.

The Mexican M4s

Mexico received 25 M4 tanks, of which some were M32 B1s; it was called the Chenca and was powered by a V8 diesel engine: the Detroit 92T.

The Indian M4

M4A1 E4s equipped with the British 76-mm cannon and M4A3/76s made up the majority of the 200 tanks in service in the Indian Army. Two regiments of Indian Shermans were later equipped with the French 75-mm cannon.

The M4 in Greece

After the war, Greece equipped itself mainly with M4A1s, M32s, and M74s.

Turkey and the M4

Between 1943 and 1957, Turkey used M4s, TD36s, M7 Priests, and M74s.

The M4 in Holland

After World War II, the Netherlands bought 250 tanks off Britain and the Commonwealth. These were M4s, M4A1s, and M4A3 HVSSs.

Belgian M4s

In all 200 Shermans equipped the Belgian Army, among which were: **from 1949 to 1952,** M4A1 76 Ws and 76 HVSSs, M4s and M4A3 105s, and M32s; **from 1949 to 1953,** 36 TD M10s and TD M36s; and **from 1951 to 1964,** M7 Priests and M74s.

Canadian M4s

Apart from locally produced M4A5 Grizzlies and RAMs, the Canadians equipped themselves with 300 Shermans M4A2 76W E8s (HVSS suspension and T80 tracks), of which some were transformed into Kangaroos.

The medical version of the Sherman in the Israeli army: the Medivac. The diesel powerplant was installed in the front of the tank. A medical team and four wounded could be transported in the rear compartment.

Cuban Shermans

Following the Rio Treaty in 1947, Cuba received seven M4 A3 76W HVSSs (during the Batista period). These tanks were captured by the revolutionaries under Che Guevara at the battle of Santa Clara.

The M4 in Norway

In 1960, 26 M7 Priest howitzers were retrofitted in the armored arm workshops in France and dispatched to Norway.

The M4 in Pakistan

Pakistan was equipped with M7 Priests, TD M36s, and TD M36 B2s

Danish M4s

Denmark received eight M4A3 E4 CN 76s in 1949.

Portugal and the M4

In 1952, the USA shipped one M4A1 76W HVSS and eight M4A3 105 HVSSs to Portugal. In 1954, the Portuguese Army turned to Canada and ordered 50 Grizzlies and 40 Kangaroos, which were never used except in the driving school. Portugal later bought some M74s off Spain.

The M4s and Syria

In 1956, Syria equipped itself with 51 M4A1s (used especially as troop transports).

Yugoslavia

The Yugoslavia of Tito—his real name was Josip Broz—broke definitively with Stalin in 1948 and did not join the Warsaw Pact, which was created in 1955. As a result, the country was able to equip itself with American materiel and the Yugoslavs bought some M47 Pattons and TD M36s.

This Egyptian Sherman has had a rough time in one of the battles in the Sinai during the 1956 Suez crisis. *(Private Collection)*

Left: Ernesto Che Guevara talking with a Cuban rebel in front of one of the M4A3 E8s which the Americans had ceded to the Cuban dictator Ruben Fulgencio Batista.

Below: Has the crew of this Indian M4A4 "Late" Sherman called out a local breakdown garage? Yes and no, but it's highly unlikely that this recovery method featured in the American documentation!

Bottom: A group of Chinese M4A2. A tiger's head is painted on the front of the turret: common practice in Chinese battalions. The driver of the first tank has raised his windshield.

Appendix 1
Military Operations—ETO

Year	Operation	Action
1940	*Alphabet*	Evacuating troops from Norway
1940	*Dynamo*	French and British evacuation from Dunkirk
1941	*Skorpion*	Axis attack on Tobruk
1941	*Barbarossa*	German invasion of the USSR
1942	*Torch*	Anglo-American landings in North Africa
1942	*Aïda*	Afrikakorps in Egypt
1942	*Anton*	German occupation of the southern zone of France
1942	*Donnerschlag*	Evacuating the Sixth Army at Stalingrad
1943	*Baytown*	Allied landings in Calabria
1943	*Avalanche*	Allied landings in Italy
1943	*Polyanaya Zvezda*	Siege of Leningrad
1943	*Roumiantsev*	Operation against the Germans in Kharkov
1943	*Slapstick*	Allied landings in Tarento
1943	*Eiche*	Mussolini freed by the Skorzeny commando
1943	*Fortitude*	Disinformation operation against the Germans
1944	*Albany*	101st Airborne dropped into Normandy
1944	*Bergen*	Vercors maquis attacked
1944	*Boston*	82d Airborne dropped into Normandy
1944	*Bulbasket*	French Resistance sabotages communications
1944	*Cadillac*	Arms and materiel parachuted into the Vercors
1944	*Cooney*	4th SAS French dropped into Brittany
1944	*Deadstick*	Commando attacks on Pegasus bridge and the Orne bridges
1944	*Detroit*	82d Airborne lands by gliders
1944	*Dingson*	168 paras of 4th SAS (French) dropped on Vannes
1944	*Dragoon*	Allied landings in Provence
1944	*Dove*	Aerial part of Operation Dragoon

The five members of a tank crew, washing in the clear waters of a river in the Philippines. On the far left, two locals are doing their washing, quite unconcerned.

Breakfast for this crew, who have spent the night near their tank after escaping from it. At any rate they don't seem too worried, waiting for the recovery vehicle.

Year	Operation	Action
1944	*Market Garden*	Combined operation to take Rhine bridges
1944	*Morgenrot*	German operation to retake Anzio
1944	*Neptune*	Naval operation of *Overlord*
1944	*Nexton*	SAS (3e RCP) Champagne-Bourgogne raid
1944	*Overlord*	Allied landings in Normandy
1944	*Perch*	British assault on Caen
1944	*Samwest*	4th SAS French dropped into Brittany
1944	*Shingle*	Allied landings at Anzio
1944	*Span*	Diversion for Operation *Dragoon*
1944	*Spencer*	Raid by French SAS, with US armed protection
1944	*Spring*	Canadian raid on Caen
1944	*Stösser*	German paratroops drop into in the Ardennes
1944	*Switchback*	3rd Canadian ID, battle of l'Escaut
1944	*Tonga*	3rd British Airborne Division in *Overlord*
1944	*Totalize*	Allied offensive in Normandy
1944	*Zebra*	Parachuting supplies to Resistance in the Ain, Vercors, and Jura
1944	*Wacht am Rhein*	German offensive in the Ardennes
1945	*Alpenfestung*	Nazi redoubt in the Ebensee-Alps region
1945	*Amherst*	700 British and French SAS dropped into Holland
1945	*Sonnenwende*	German operation in Pomerania
1945	*Regenbogen*	Scuttling of the German fleet
1945	*Nordwind*	German offensive in Alsace
1945	*Paper clip*	Rush to recover German scientists
1945	*Plunder*	Rhine crossing by the Allies

Glossary and Abbreviations

A

ARV — Armored Recovery Vehicle.

Assembly, sub-assembly — Major part of the vehicle e.g. engine, gearbox, transmission, slip joint.

Azimuth repeater — Apparatus enabling the bearing to be known after the turret has swiveled.

B

BMG — Browning machine gun.

Bearing — Angle (on a horizontal plane) between a cannon and its initial position

Bearing pointing — Aligning the cannon along a horizontal plane.

Bogeys — An assembly of two wheels mounted on their own suspension and support.

Bore sighting — Adjustments made to an optical sight, to align the barrel of a firearm with the sights.

Breech block — System for closing the cannon (insertion side).

Bridge-layer — A tank, or another vehicle, used for deploying a bridging element.

Buckling — Twisting of (usually) a connecting rod as a result of hydrostatic locking.

Bustle — The rear part of the tank turret.

C

CEFEO — Corps Expéditionnaire Français en Extrême Orient.

CN — Abbreviation for cannon.

Combat Command — A tactical group assembling several units: armor, infantry, and engineers.

Cupola — A heightened hatch fitted with episcopes which could be fixed, mobile and sometimes fitted out for weapons.

D

DFL — Division de la France Libre.

DIC — Division d'Infanterie Coloniale.

D-Day — The usual term to designate June 6, 1944, the landings in Normandy.

Double declutching — Activating the clutch pedal which goes to neutral and giving a push on the accelerator (changing down).

Double pedaling — Activating the clutch pedal which goes to neutral (changing up).

Dragoon — Codename for the landings in Provence.

Drift — Correction made when firing at a moving target.

Dry — Method of stowing shells.

Duckbill — Extension on the track fixed to the connector and designed to reduce ground pressure.

E

EE8 — Line telephone used on the battlefield.

ETO — European Theater of Operations.

Early — Term meaning the beginning of production.

Elevation Pointing — Aligning the cannon along a vertical plane.

Emergency rack — The shell rack within easy reach of the cannoneer.

Episcope — Viewing equipment based on the principle of the periscope.

EVASAN — Abbreviation for EVAcuation SANitaire: the French equivalent of MEDEVAC.

F

Field manual — Document for use by the users (crews).

Firewall — Metal partition between the combat and engine compartments.

FlaK — Flieger Abwehr Kanonne—anti-aircraft gun.

H

HB — Heavy Barrel—large-caliber barrel.

HVSS — Horizontal Volute Suspension Spring.

Half-track — A vehicle driven by front steering wheels and rear tracks.

Hatch — An access flap for entering the tank fitted with a locking system and an episcope.

Howitzer — A cannon able to fire from a hidden position (artillery).

L

Late — Term meaning a model from the end of production.

Lubrication order — A table giving the order, periods, and vehicle parts for greasing.

M

Magneto — Apparatus supplying the spark necessary for the engine spark plugs.

Manhole	The opening used to evacuate the tank in an emergency.	**Rammer shaft**	Shafts which screw together to enable the rammer to be attached for cleaning the barrel.
Matériel	A department and then an Arm of the French *Armée de Terre* responsible for repairing and preparing vehicles.	**Rear deck**	The flat space behind the turret including the inspection hatches and various mountings.
Mid	Term meaning a model from the middle of a production run.	**Reduction gear**	Series of pinions between the gearbox and the sprocket wheel.
Mid-day	Bearing terminology: Mid-day : 0°, 3 h: 90° right 6 h: 180° 9 h: 90° left.	**Roller**	Full or spoked metal wheel over which the tracks pass.
		Running gear	All the elements which enable the tank to move around.
Muffling	A system of pulleys enabling crew to increase the initial power of a winch.		

S

Multibanks	An engine with several banks—one bank = one engine, in this case five.	**SMG**	Submachine gun.
Muzzle cover	Canvas or leather cover attached to the end of the barrel of a cannon.	**SNL**	Serial Number listing: spare parts catalogue.
		Silent block	Rubber shock absorber to absorb vibrations.

O

On-board gear	All the tools and equipment aboard the tank.	**Slip joint**	Joint System enabling the turret to be supplied with 24-volt current no matter what its position was.
Ordnance	American organization defining the implementation of armament and vehicle programs.	**Slot**	An opening fitted with a shutter enabling the driver to see out even with the hatch closed.
Overlord	Codename for the landings in Normandy.	**Sponson**	Space inside the tank located above the tracks.

P

PaK	Panzer Abwehr Kanone—anti-tank gun.	**Sprocket**	Wheel with toothed crown for engaging and driving the tracks.
Parking brake	A system to immobilize the tank when stopped.	**Squadron**	A part of a tank regiment.
Parking socket	Plug for 24-volt current.	**Squelch**	System for reducing the background noise (radio interference on a frequency).
Pioneer's gear	The kit of tools attached on outside of the tank, including spade, pick, axe, crowbar, and a sledgehammer.	**Strainer**	A system for filtering large particles, fitted to the opening of the fuel tanks.
Platoon	Subdivision of a company.	**Strap**	A metal attachment with a bolt, held shut by a spring.

R

RBFM	Régiment Blindé de Fusiliers-Marins.	**Steering levers**	The two levers (right and left) used to steer the tank; using both of them simultaneously braked the vehicle.
RC	Régiment de Cuirassiers.		
RCA	Régiment de Chasseurs d'Afrique.		
RCC	Régiment de Chars de Combat.		

T

RCCC	Régiment Colonial de Chasseurs de Chars.	**TEDG/P**	Tableau d'équipement et dotation guerre/paix— War/peace equipment distribution tables.
REC	Régiment Etranger de Cavalerie.		
RICM	Régiment d'Infanterie de Chars de Marine.	**TQM**	Transport Quarter Master.
RSAR	Régiment de Spahis Algériens de Reconnaissance.	**Technical manual**	Document for the use of the repair units.
RSM	Régiment de Spahis Marocains.	**Tensing clamp plate**	A system with teeth which enables a pulley to be held in position.
Radio sheath	A soft sheath (or quiver) with a belt and compartments for stowing radio accessories.	**Tightening system**	A system enabling the tracks to be tautened or loosened.
Rammer	A hard cylindrical brush used to clean the barrels of the cannon (nylon or brass bristles).	*Torch*	Codename for the Anglo-American landings in French North Africa.

Torque	Force producing the rotation of the engine crankshaft.	**Turret well**	The circular cut-out in the hull around which the turret swivels.
Torsion bar	Suspension system replacing the bogeys.	**U**	
Towing rail	Support welded to the chassis where the towing shackle is attached.	**USAD**	United States Armored Division.
Track idler (wheel)	The wheel where the track starts to return.	**V**	
Track return roller	Little wheel which supports and guides the track back along the top.	**VVSS**	Vertical Volute Suspension Spring.
Transmission	The assembly including the elements between the clutch and the reduction gear.	**W**	
(Travel) brace	A support on which the barrel of the cannon rests when the turret hydraulics are not working and the tank moving.	**Warhead fuse**	System enabling the charge of the warhead to be activated.
		Water bag	Canvas bag for carrying water.
Turret default	The place where the turret meets the hull or chassis.	**Wet**	Method for stowing shells inside the tank.
		WWII	World War II.

The Shermans of the 752d Tank Battalion occupying the whole of the Plaza Emanuele in Bologna in the spring of 1944. The wide variety of Sherman types in the same unit is clearly visible. (NARA)

Sources and Bibliography

Books

Halbertstadt, Hans. *Inside the Great Tanks* (The Crowood Press, 1998).

Vigneras, Marcel. *Rearming the French: United Statses Army in World War II* (University Press of the Pacific, 2003).

Books by Hano Spoelstra, Steven Zaloga, Joe De Marco, and Kurt Laughlin.

Technical Documentation

AR 850-5 Army Regulations US Equipment Military Markings 1942.

FM 1 730 Armored Force Field Manual Tank Platoon 1942.

FM 1 733 Tank Battalion 1943.

MAT 1 028 *Guide technique de la mitrailleuse américaine Browning de calibre 50. (12.7 mm) M2 HB.*

SNL G 104 Ordnance Supply Catalog.

TM 9-238 Deep Water Fording of Ordnance Materiel.

TM 9-731B Technical manual Medium Tank M4A2.

TM 9-731G Technical Manual 3-Inch Gun Motor Carriage M10 A1.

TM 9-754 Fr Char Moyen M4A4 (Medium tank).

TM 9-759 Tank Medium M4A3.

TM 9-767 U.S 40 Ton Tank Transporter Truck-Trailer M25.

TM 9-2 800 Standard Motor Vehicles 1943.

TM 30-502 French Military Dictionary.

Photo credits

ECPAD
Michel Estève
IWM
NARA
Private collections
Signal Corps
Tank Museum, Bovington
Alain Toméï

Websites

99percentinvisible.org
AFV Database (AMs in France)
chars-français.net
commons.wikimedia.org
dday-overlord.com
easy39th.com
focus.stockstar.com
forum.worldoftanks.com
histomil.com
HMVF Historic Military Vehicles Forum
imgur.com
mailer.fsu.eduImage
modelforum.upce.cz
modelhobby.eu
rbfm-Leclerc.com
Rhin-et-Danube.fr.
the.shadock.free.fr
TheShermantank.com
vmartois.forumactif.fr
warriorsaga.com
www.2iemeguerre.com
www.gettyimages.com
www.histomil.com
www.historylink101.com
www.reddit.com
www.warhistoryonline.com
World War II vehicles
ASHPM: Pierre Olivier Buan